Craig MacFarlane
Hasn't Heard of *YOU* Either!

I was landing recently at yet another impersonal, faceless airport. Let's face it, they all look the same to me. I was there to speak at yet another large corporate event when it struck me. Except for the possibility of some obscure reference made by the manager who hired me to speak at this event, I doubt if anybody coming to hear me has ever heard of me or has any idea of my story. They really had no reason, other than being ordered, to listen to my speech. It was humbling. Why should these people listen to me? Why should they care what I have to say? Why should I expect them to come away from listening to me feeling inspired?

There is never enough time at a single speaking engagement to explain all the reasons why. There is never enough time to meet everyone at every event and become someone they have not only heard from, but feel they know. I was challenged once again, in that moment, to summon up the resolve to ensure that I give my absolute best, not just that day, but every time anyone hears me speak.

This book, in many ways, is my effort to help you to get to know me. I hope to fill in the answers to the questions why and, help you find a boost of passion and inspiration in your own life.

Thus the title, Craig MacFarlane Hasn't Heard of you Either.

"Craig MacFarlane is a good friend of mine. I admire his strength, his courage and his enthusiasm. Nobody knows better than Craig what Pride in America is all about. For Craig it means having the desire, the energy and the perseverance to accomplish worthwhile goals which inspire and encourage all Americans. As you listen to Craig you will understand much better what the word PRIDE means."

GEORGE H.W. BUSH
41st President of the United States

"Just watching Craig's desire to excel and do anything everyone else does – and better – is totally uplifting to me."

MARIO ANDRETTI
Andretti Autosport

"Since 1982, when Craig came to live with my wife and I, I have seen him take his extraordinary talents and parlay them into an awesome career. Today, Craig has become a tower of inspiration in the lives of so many people, including myself."

GORDIE HOWE
"Mr. Hockey"

"I stand here with my friend Craig MacFarlane, who through hard work, dedication, and a lot of spirit has proven that being blind has nothing to do with your accomplishments."

WAYNE GRETZKY
All time NHL scoring leader

"A lot of things that people do in their lives can make a difference for others. Craig's story is an example of this."

TIM ALLEN
Actor

"I met Craig in the early 80s and what a positive vibe he let off. He was and is an inspiration to us all."

PAUL COFFEY
Hall of Fame NHL
Defenseman

"I believe that if professional hockey players or professional baseball players, football players, whatever, if they ever went out and approached their games and played their games with the heart that this guy goes at his sports and everything he does, the way he goes at it, I don't think there would ever be any empty seats in any building in any league. He's a very, very strong, super guy."

BOBBY ORR
Hall of Fame NHL Defenseman

"Craig is an inspiration to anyone who has dealt with adversity. His dedication and positive attitude have made a big difference in the lives of others."

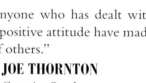

JOE THORNTON
Captain, San Jose
Sharks, NHL

"I marvel at a young man who has accomplished so much under such adverse conditions, but to see the fortitude and strength that this young man has exemplified, I think it should be a lesson not only to all of Canada or all the people here tonight, but to anyone who can touch the life of such a fine young man. He's an inspiration and a credit to a sport that probably doesn't receive the recognition, that say hockey or football or baseball does, but yet he continues to persevere because it's a self-lit flame that drives him. To me he's a true champion."

JOE THEISMANN
Super Bowl winning NFL Quarterback

"As I've come to know Craig MacFarlane, I'm deeply impressed with his intensity. I know he, too, is a true champion."

EVANDER HOLYFIELD
Heavyweight Champion

"I met Craig when he was 15 and I was an aspiring sports broadcaster in Sault Ste. Marie, Ontario. Craig's confidence and his ability to dominate any challenge defied his age and his handicap. A loss of vision has never prevented Craig from seeing life's big picture and 3 decades later he is still an inspiration to me!"

PAUL HENDRICK
Toronto Maple Leaf Television Host

"I can't tell you what a privilege it is to know this fella. He stands as an inspiration to everybody, to all the kids out there."

PAUL NEWMAN
Actor

"It's been my privilege to call Craig MacFarlane my best friend for nearly thirty years. We've watched our children grow, been there for each other during life's highs and lows, travelled our native Canada and to 45 states in the USA as well as many parts of Europe. We have been on two oceans, wondered at the Majestic Rockies, stood atop the World Trade Center and had a private conversation with Pope Benedict XVI at the Vatican in Rome. In my career I've witnessed many, many speakers but none have made me laugh harder or brought me to tears or left me with a burning desire to become a better man, one who works everyday to employ Craig's powerful yet simple message, "nothing and no one stands in the way of my success except me"! Craig's "Inner Vision" is his true gift, which he has shared with audiences around the globe, with some of the most powerful and recognizable corporations at conventions and in boardrooms. Seek him out, listen and act on his inspiring message, it's his gift to you!"

MICHAEL THEISEN
The MKT Consulting Group

"Craig MacFarlane is an inspiration to me. When I am feeling low I just think of Craig and how he battles and keeps going. I guarantee you will also be inspired by Craig's book."

DON CHERRY
Hockey Night In Canada

"Craig MacFarlane is the perfect combination of an extraordinary person who experienced adversity, celebrated abundance, and showed gratitude throughout the journey. His speeches are inspiring, his writings are thought-provoking, and his audiences are always appreciative."

DR. NIDO R. QUBEIN
President, High Point University
Chairman, Great Harvest Bread Co

"Working with Craig has been a wonderful, eye opening experience. Craig may lack eyesight, but he makes up for it with vision. His unique ability to connect with others, on their terms, in a meaningful way is truly inspirational. In addition to our business dealings, Craig and I have become personal friends."

RICK PARKER
Chief Operating Officer
Thurston Springer, Indianapolis, IN

"Craig's story is one of motivation and perseverance. He has an impressive ability to capture an audience in a way that touches lives on a personal level. It is an honor to see Craig inspire others to achieve their dreams beyond their limitations."

SCOTT LEONARD
Financial Professional,
Dallas, TX

"Craig is astounding! Craig was the opening keynote at our national conference and everyone loved him. He was funny, engaging, and provided an uplifting message that was the perfect kickoff to our show. He was also fantastic to work with. I can't recommend Craig highly enough – he's just the speaker every conference needs to set the tone for a great event!"

TOM ERB
National Conference Speaker Chair
National Association of Personnel Services

"Craig MacFarlane's life's story is an extraordinary example of integrity, discipline, passion and an unrelenting commitment to excellence. Craig's message is a powerful one that inspires me and, no doubt, everyone who has the privilege to hear him. We are honored to be able to provide Craig a home as he spreads his inspirational message around the world."

ARNE SORENSON
President and Chief Executive Officer of
Marriott International

"I've covered the sports beat for nearly 40 years of my life. Worked with the great ones at close hand - Jackie Roosevelt Robinson, Muhammad Ali, John Unitas, Johnny McEnroe, you name them. But I must tell you the most remarkable athlete I have EVER seen, ever known, is Craig MacFarlane."

HOWARD COSELL (1986)
Legendary Sports Broadcaster

"Blind in sight, visionary in life, Craig is a passionate and engaging speaker who uses his personal triumphs – overcoming extraordinary challenges – to motivate and inspire audiences around the world."

JIM JESSEE
President
MFS Fund Distributors, Inc.

"Craig MacFarlane is a rare and impressive man. His accomplishments themselves are noteworthy but it is the spirit and attitude with which he lives his life that most command your attention and respect."

BOB COSTAS
NBC Sports

"Craig's story is one of persistence, personal strength and triumph. His athletic achievements demonstrate how much can be accomplished by anyone who aspires to be the <u>best</u> at what he or she does. Craig's story is an inspiration for athletes as well as non-athletes young and old. He is a truly remarkable individual!"

JIM WEDDLE
Managing Partner, Edward Jones

"Craig captures his audience with an uplifting message of courage and determination through his positive attitude and zest for life."

DAVID GLASS
Former President and CEO Wal-Mart Stores, Inc.
Owner, Kansas City Royals

"Craig MacFarlane is real life honest to goodness proof that there is no life challenge that cannot be overcome. Further, Craig is proof in life there are no problems, but only opportunities. I am so very honored and proud to call Craig my friend. Congratulations Craig on your latest achievement!"

DON S. COHN
Miami-Dade County Florida County Court Judge

"Craig's story is one that we can all learn from. His approach to life has been to focus on what he can do, not what he can't do, and to turn adversity into opportunity. In doing so, he has achieved extraordinary things. A simple but powerful formula for success."

KEVIN P. DOUGHERTY
President, Sun Life Financial Canada

"Unequivocally, Craig is one of the best speakers I have ever heard. I have hired him dozens of times and without exception, his speech ends with a heartfelt and enthusiastic standing ovation. This is due to Craig's ability to remove the blindness that we may have as we attempt to understand certain issues of our life. With humor and humility, Craig provides a remarkable inner vision that makes him memorable and so much more than a motivational speaker."

SALVATORE CAPIZZI
Executive Vice President/CSMO
Dunham & Associates

"Craig MacFarlane and I have been great friends for over 20 years. I really enjoy his sense of humor which has led to so many laughs. *Craig also has a delightfully developed power of persuasion.* I've listened to Craig speak on so many occasions and I always walk away with a different perspective on life. *You will too when you read his story."*

JEFF CRAUSE
Edward Jones
Ann Arbor, MI

"I have watched the facial reactions of audiences to Craig's speaking engagements, and I have seen the wonder and respect, combined with amazement at ones man's story and journey through life. The wide eyes and the astonishment that accompanies the beginning of his talks, changes and gives way to a sense in the listeners of "what now can I do with my life?" and that for me is the genius of Craig and his willingness to share his story with others."

JAMES T SWANSON
Chief Investment Strategist and Portfolio Manager
MFS Investment Management

Craig's life and his journey has been remarkable and impressive. He is a special person who gives so much to others yet asks for little in return. Craig's life's story is truly a remarkable one.

BRAD STEVENS
Boston Celtics Head Coach

Craig MacFarlane
Hasn't Heard
of *YOU* Either!

ARCHWAY
PUBLISHING

Archway Publishing books may be ordered through booksellers or by contacting:

Archway Publishing
1663 Liberty Drive
Bloomington, IN 47403
www.archwaypublishing.com
1-(888)-242-5904

ISBN: 978-1-4808-0371-8 (e)
ISBN: 978-1-4808-0386-2 (hc)

Library of Congress Control Number: 2013919527

Printed in the United States of America

Archway Publishing rev. date: 11/08/2013

Contents

Winner

I met him only briefly
but still I felt I knew
This young man was very special
and so I listened to
All the kidding and laughing and joking
that hid the person inside.
He was more than what he displayed
and so again I tried
To see if I could see
what pushed him so very hard.

He had fulfilled so many dreams
and come so very far
But there was still a hunger
a constant, burning drive,
Like a lion on the hunt
...it made him come alive.

There was an energy all around him
that came from deep inside
This was the key to Craig MacFarlane
...the word he used was Pride.

Perseverance and respect,
individualism and desire.
These were the fuel that gave him the chance,
...enthusiasm lit the fire.

Nature isn't always fair
She made this young boy blind
Yet in doing so, she made him better
...She forced him to use his mind.

It's not our faults that make us fail
or our talents that mean success
it's what we do with what we've got
that separates one from the rest.

Somewhere along life's highway
some winds will have to blow
Some will dwell in the mud and slosh
...A winner sees fresh fallen snow.

One man is angry if he doesn't have
what other men have got
A winner develops just what he has
...A loser complains he has not.

And Craig MacFarlane has always been a winner
in the biggest event of them all...
This young man sees life as it is
and simply refuses to fall.

Craig sees all of his problems as raindrops
instead of storms.
He just smiles and smells the roses...ignoring all the thorns.

And so to himself he has proven
success is all in the mind
Craig sees life as a marvelous challenge
I wonder...which of us is blind?

James Bruce Joseph Sievers

Acknowledgements

When you have lived a life like mine, it is hard to know where to begin when it comes time to acknowledge everyone who has contributed, in so many ways, to my amazing journey.

Some go without saying.

My mother Joyce, my father Earl and my brother Ian. The most amazing people you could ever hope to meet. I am blessed to have them as my family and give thanks in my prayers everyday for the wonderful course they set me on and how they have supported and encouraged me every step of the way. Thank you so much, Mom and Dad. Bro, you know I love you, too.

My awesome wife, Patti, and our four fabulous kids, Dalton, Derek, Ashley and Morgan. They give a never ending series of surprises, adventures and memories, all delivered with unbridled love and boundless enthusiasm. They give my life meaning. They give me a reason to get up every day. They energize my world. They are why I fight the battle and they are the beneficiaries of everything I accomplish. I love you all, more than words can say.

I can't write a page like this without mentioning my two dearest friends. Michael and Roberta Theisen, who I have known just longer than forever, and my business partner and best bud, Mark Harris. Michael, I appreciate you always being at the other end of the phone when I need you. Mark, the memories of our exploits together will always put a smile on my face, let's keep it going. I can't end a paragraph on friends without reference to one of my closest confidents too, Jeff Crause of Ann Arbor, Michigan. Jeff is in a special friend category, buddy, pal and a top financial advisor who has taken excellent care of me for many years.

I would also be remiss if I didn't thank Mr. Jim Croson here, as well. Jim, you are the most wonderful, compassionate, generous man I have ever met. Your support for me, and my foundation, are unparalleled. The world could use more people like you.

Don Cohn, my long time dear friend and my lawyer for many years has also always been an invaluable resource to me. Don, our legal system needs more judges like you. You set a standard others should aspire to.

Sam Mishelow is Executive Vice President and Partner with Meyer Najem Construction in Fishers, Indiana. A very successful and well connected businessman, Sam helped me tremendously when I first arrived in the Hoosier state. Sam helped me develop the connections I needed and gain profile within the Indiana business community that has proved invaluable ever since. We remain friends to this day.

On the subject of Indianapolis, I want to mention Thurston, Springer, Miller, Herd & Titak and, specifically Rick Parker and Jim Titak. I truly admire the company, its culture and philosophy. The work we do together has been meaningful and I am grateful for your friendship and continued belief in me.

There are two other entities that must be mentioned here. The family of Marriott Hotels where I sleep more than one hundred nights a year and Delta Airlines, who I fly with more than 100,000 air miles a year.

Glenn Miller of Fort Myers, I can't forget you either. Your service and input as editor of this effort was much appreciated. Tom Casalini of Zionsville, your photography and advice provided fabulous input that I very much needed. Kyle and Kelsey Martin, your photo contributions are much appreciated as well. Eric George of Roberts Camera, your help with the rest of my photos was tremendous. Lastly, I must mention Rob Chinn who takes care of the rest of my media and, as he has so often before, made great contributions to this project .

While I'm talking about photography, I can't say enough about the "heavy lifting", both figuratively and literally, that was done by my dear wife Patti as we sorted through the boxes, and files, and drawers and Cd's searching for the best pictures for this book. It was primarily through her efforts, with a little support from our friends, that we were able to find so many of the special pictures that I am so pleased to be able to share with you in the following pages.

As for the rest of you. There are not enough pages in the Library of Congress for me to list you all. You know who you are. I want to tell you that you all live in my heart. Some of you showed me a small kindness as our paths crossed somewhere in the course of my journey. Some of you showed belief in me and gave me support that changed my life. I don't know how to compose words here that would even come close to expressing my gratitude. I truly have been blessed and I remember each and every one of you with fondness, appreciation and love.

Foreword
By George H.W. Bush

It is my pleasure to tell you about a truly remarkable person, Craig MacFarlane. I first met Craig in 1984 when President Reagan invited him to carry the Olympic torch through Washington D.C., on its way to the Los Angeles Games. Craig is a man whose own inner flame of determination, boundless energy and courage served as a point of light in countless lives. That is why we asked Craig to join our Reagan-Bush All Star Team during the 1984 Republican National Convention. Each time, Craig carried with dignity and clarity, his inspirational message that through hard work, dedication, strength of character and purpose, we can all achieve our goals. Despite being blinded at the age of 2, Craig's accomplishments in a wide variety of sports are incredible. He exemplifies the kind of indomitable spirit that makes America great. Craig's career has continued beyond athletics. Craig MacFarlane has taken his message of P.R.I.D.E. - Perseverance, Respect, Individuality, Desire and Enthusiasm - to almost 3,000 high schools and countless businesses. Barbara and I are proud to call Craig a friend. I invite you to meet him yourself through the pages of this book and discover the fire within that can touch and inspire us all.

GEORGE BUSH
41st President of the United States of America

Introduction

How do you introduce Craig MacFarlane? I have had the pleasure of calling Craig my friend and business partner for many years and yet every time someone asks me about Craig I still find it difficult to know where to start. This is such a multi-faceted man. There are the athletic accomplishments yes. There's the business success. There's the personal success. Then there's the man. Over the years my introduction has shifted from a discussion of Craig's stories and Craig's successes to simply a discussion of Craig.

When I was asked to write the introduction for this book I was excited. There were so many stories that jumped to mind, both Craig's accomplishments and our adventures together, but when I sat down to write I struggled with how I would tell people all of this. I spent time writing the standard prose about his accomplishments but I knew I would not be doing Craig justice unless I introduced you to his character.

The simple reality of Craig MacFarlane is that this man has more integrity than anyone I have ever had the pleasure to know. He has, over the past decade not only become my business partner but my best friend, there is nobody else I would rather have covering my back. He'll support me when I deserve it but he is just as capable of telling you the truth when you need it, even if it leaves you bloodied and hurting on the board room table. Of course, he is always there to pick you up again too. The bottom line is that this man truly WALKS HIS TALK!

Let me tell you what I mean.

I first heard about Craig MacFarlane many years ago. A member of my youth and business committee at the Brampton, Ontario, Board of Trade suggested we pursue Craig as the keynote speaker for our up-and-coming youth and business luncheon. I listened as my associate described Craig's accomplishments and circumstances. I was impressed with how taken my friend was with his experience of communicating with Craig. In fact, as I listened, I realized that I had read about this man, many years before. I couldn't remember the details but I knew I had read about him. I asked Craig and he confirmed it. He was featured in Reader's Digest in 1986. The article was titled "The Abiding Vision of Craig MacFarlane." He reminded me too that he had been interviewed on the Canadian edition of "Wide World of Sports" several times. Not surprising then that I had some awareness.

Of course, when you're selecting a speaker, you also have to do your own due diligence and, as most would, I went to Craig's website. The website is impressive. Right there on the first page are quotes from the likes of Howard Cosell and Wayne Gretzky and Gordie Howe and Mario Andretti and George H. W. Bush. Impressive company to say the least and the story that is told by the website is equally as compelling.

You start learning about a young man beset by a horrible tragedy at the age of two, about how his unique upbringing led him to take on the world rather than shy away from it. Briefly you learn about his long list of accomplishments. You learn that since moving to the business world that his successes continued and that his message has been received with such resonance that even the Pope requested an audience with this unique and special man. You will see how this man stepped up and established his own foundation when he saw a need. You will ultimately learn how this man will make sacrifices to stand up for his ideals.

That unique and special person is the one I want to introduce you to here. Craig will tell you his stories better than anyone else ever could, but if you know the character of the man behind the stories, I promise you will be infinitely more impressed.

Hearing Craig speak for the first time was a treat. In fact, that was the first time I ever introduced him. Craig took command of the room from the second he stepped to the podium. He was engaging and funny, he was thought-provoking, he was insightful. What he was not was boastful. I have to admit that I was expecting to be regaled with a number of stories about his successes in wrestling and track and field and golf and skiing and water ski jumping, but he didn't tell us about that. He told us the lessons that he learned in the process of taking on his challenges to accomplish those feats, but he didn't brag that he was any better than anybody else. In fact, if anything, he was modest and self-deprecating. By the end, his message was clear. "Strength doesn't come from what YOU CAN DO, it comes from OVERCOMING the things that you once thought YOU COULDN'T."

Unfortunately, that is where most people's connection to Craig ends. They leave the event inspired and energized, but with no idea of how this man makes his message reality every day. He doesn't rest on his laurels. He can't! Life would eat him alive if he did. But by walking his talk, truly personifying the words he says in his speeches, he has built a life most of us would envy, and yet most people miss that point. It is not the events of his life that make Craig special, it is the application of the lessons, and not in big ways but in all the little ways the rest of us take for granted. That is what we hope the readers of this book will take away.

Craig has always said that his life is not extraordinary. That he is just an ordinary man dealing with his circumstances as best he can. It is how well he has learned and applied the lessons from his experiences (more valuable than the classroom in his opinion) that make Craig extraordinary, and when you watch him day to day you begin to understand that this man really walks his talk, that his everyday life truly resembles the message he gives at the podium.

LET ME MAKE ONE THING VERY CLEAR AT THIS POINT!!!!! When it comes to Craig I am not talking about learning tricks and techniques to deal with a disability. Yes, Craig MacFarlane is totally blind, but as he has often said, that is just a minor inconvenience in his life. Many, many people have learned to live with

blindness, and impressively at that, but when you look at Craig's life you realize that he has earned success, on an enviable scale, despite the added challenge of blindness. In fact, if you spend a weekend with Craig, you start to forget that he has an alleged handicap. Craig does not wear dark glasses, does not carry a white cane, does not use a guide dog, and yet he travels more than 100,000 air miles a year, without a companion most of the time. Does this man sound handicapped to you? I think not. There is a bigger message here, so get ready.

My memories of Craig are dotted with day to day remembrances of how this man does things most people assume he could never do with surprising ease. Think about it this way:

- Can you imagine a man who cannot see taking you sight-seeing? I've had that experience and the first time it is a little unnerving but at the same time, inspiring. On my first visit to Craig's adopted home town of Zionsville, Indiana, Craig guided my daughter and I on a tour of neighboring Indianapolis, from the elite shopping districts of Carmel (where he had actually taken the time to locate my daughter's favorite store) to Monument Circle, Lucas Oil Stadium, Victory Field, the then named Conseco Field House and even Indianapolis Motor Speedway. Craig sat in the back seat of my car and without benefit of even a GPS guided us through the city. The first time he said "coming up on your right should be..." or "you'll need to turn left just ahead..." or "can you still see..." I wanted to look back and ask "Are you for real?" or "How did you do that?" but soon I found we were just in a normal conversation, asking Craig questions, having forgotten once again about his "handicap" until he would respond with "I don't know, can you describe it for me?"
- I mentioned my daughter's favorite store above. It is just another little thing but it impressed me nonetheless. Being from Canada my daughter, a teenager at the time, did not have access to the Hollister chain and had a strong desire to visit one of its stores. I honestly didn't even remember mentioning this to Craig as we were making arrangements for a working

weekend in Indy, but he did. He had encouraged me to bring one of my children along, for company on the drive and apparently he remembered all the details of every conversation we had. So when we found ourselves with a half day free, he incorporated a trip to her favorite store into his sightseeing tour. Not only that, but he slipped her some shopping money to buy gifts for her brothers and sister. As I said, a little thing, but a class act.

- Then there was the time, sitting in Craig's kitchen discussing an upcoming conference, that he just started unloading the dishwasher. My colleague and I watched this in the beginning with disbelief, tempted immediately to get up and help, only to quickly realize that we would just be getting in the way. Then, without interruption to the conversation, we watched him put everything exactly where it belongs without any hesitation and you find yourself thinking "This man isn't handicapped at all." Especially when you consider that he was home alone with his 2 and 1/2 year old daughter Morgan at the time.

- Craig, and his wife Patti, are very well connected to their children, not just Morgan but Derek, Ashley and Dalton as well. I have shown up at Craig's house numerous times to find him pitching batting practice to Derek in their backyard which begs the question who is braver, Craig or Derek? Other times I've found him waist deep in the bushes with Ashley, looking for specimens to add to her insect collection (I think Craig was braver in that case.) Of course there is always the Craig and Morgan show. I can't tell you how often I have arrived with pizza, only to find Morgan riding Craig around their living room as her own personal sheep.

- As for Dalton, you just have to say that the apple really didn't fall far from the tree. An aspiring MMA fighter with an undefeated record, Dalton often calls his dad for advice and inspiration. I have listened to Craig's end of a few of those calls and was inspired myself by the time they hung up. Like father, like son.

- Speaking of Patti, she is the light of his life and his commitment to her speaks volumes about Craig's unwillingness to compromise. You have to admire a man who makes such an effort to bring a smile to the face of the woman he adores, in ways beyond the mundane and routine. I know, I've been on the other end of the phone, researching the answers to Craig's creative questions on ideas to surprise his wife, particularly when it comes to the family's frequent getaways and vacations. Of course he isn't all about surprises, but he does insist that everything for Patti is first class.
- Patti's character, too, is beyond reproach. She has been my white knight on more than one occasion, at times when I'm sure it wasn't convenient, or necessarily easy, to be a friend, but she was there. She makes my best friend better, he knows it and it shows - in everything he says, and does.
- My cell phone rang at 7:00 a.m. one day and it was Craig. When I asked him what he was doing working so early in the morning, he told me he always got up early to reach the important people he needed to speak with before their days got too busy. Ok, lots of people claim to do that but as we put a wrap our conversation that morning, Craig ended with the comment that he had to go because he was speaking at a breakfast in San Francisco and didn't want to be late. As I hung up the phone it struck me that on that particular day it wasn't 7:00 a.m. for him, it was 4:00 a.m. How is that for walking his talk?

There are so many more stories, like the detour through rural Indiana in an ice storm or breakfast in Terra Haute or dropping Craig at the airport or grocery shopping or our workshops with 20/20 Inner Vision Foundation or negotiating with Senators and Congressmen and Governors.

Professionally, I've travelled with Craig to countless speaking appearances throughout the United States and Canada. It seems that we would move from standing ovation to standing ovation. I've watched Craig provoke laughter and tears as he holds the audience captive, leaving them excited, inspired and always wanting more. Every speech just generates more demand for Craig's message.

Meeting that demand has, on occasion, resulted in some truly frantic, exhausting schedules, especially when you put his business commitments together with his charitable speaking engagements. On tour I saw Craig speak twenty-six times in nineteen different states, all within the same calendar month, which, being March, fortunately had 31 days. It is yet just another example of his passion and commitment.

Craig may choose to tell some of these stories later in this book. They are all great examples of how this man has accomplished so much by learning the important lessons throughout his life and applying them in a consistent and persistent manner. I expect, though, that Craig is going to tell you the sensational stories about setting world records and winning gold medals and thrilling crowds doing the seemingly impossible. I also expect that he is going to tell you the stories about doing the work, the preparation, the need for passion in order to succeed.

I promise you this, the stories you are about to read will enthrall you. They are about and being told by a man with the unique ability to inspire both individuals and entire stadiums. They will challenge you to take action. Most importantly, they will make you ask yourself "What are you willing to do to Succeed?"

MARK HARRIS
April, 2013

Why Now?

I have to admit, right up front, that I was persuaded once before to write a book about my life. I went along and we produced a rather ordinary, run of the mill autobiography that never made it into distribution because the publisher went bankrupt before the book ever saw a shelf.

I did come away with the rights to my book and for years many of my friends and colleagues have encouraged me to find a new publisher and release my book. I have resisted because I just didn't consider the story compelling enough to deserve a spot next to so many more worthy biographies on the shelves of Barnes & Noble.

Most autobiographies are boring, mine among them. I haven't led a nation through a crisis. I haven't built a great company. I haven't written a brilliant piece of software that affected a generation. I never performed a heroic act that saved countless lives. I have simply spent my life working hard to provide for my family and build a strong relationship with my wife, Patti.

Maybe I have been given a unique hand to deal with, but as I have always said, life is just about playing the hand you were dealt to the best of your abilities. It's about developing your God-given gifts the best you can and using them as effectively as possible without losing time and energy lamenting over what you don't have. That is all I had been doing, or so I thought.

There has been one constant stream of conversation, however, that I was too dense to recognize, but that finally struck me recently when a couple of my closest friends, Michael Theisen and Mark Harris, bought me lunch and had a little intervention with me.

That stream of conversation I referred to went something like this. After every appearance, every interview, every workshop, every meeting, someone would invariably ask me "Where did you learn that?" I thought my answer was always different, but I learned through the brutal honesty of my two friends, that it was actually always the same and that is where, in their words, I had so much to offer and needed to tell my story.

Actually, that is wrong. What they said is that I needed to tell "my stories." You see, my answer would always be something to the effect of:

- When I was pursuing the Blind National Skiing Championship I learned...

or

- Mario Andretti always reminded me...

or

- When I was preparing to jump at Cypress Gardens...

or

- Gordie Howe always told me...

or

- When I was wrestling I realized...

or

- When my father used to take me hunting with him I discovered...

That was when their message hit home. I may be leading what I consider an everyday life. I learned my lessons of success in some unique, sometimes dramatic, ways that profoundly impacted me and gave me the foundation to live this life that so many others find re-markable. The principles of success are always the same, but the way we learn to apply them can be so totally different from one person to the next.

This is not a "self help" book. Only you can help yourself, but I do know that we learn in different ways and at different times. A message we failed to grasp in one form may totally inspire us in another. If even one of my stories can impact or inspire or just "help" one person find greater success, happiness or simply contentment, then telling my stories will be worthwhile.

A lot has happened in my life since I was first approached about writing a book so many years ago. I am much happier with the idea of sharing my stories and the lessons I've learned today. The unbridled ambition and perpetual motion of my youth has been tempered by time and reflection. I have gained a maturity that has brought clarity and meaning to the values and principles I hold so dear. I believe as well that a modicum of wisdom has crept into my understanding of the world, making me better able to communicate the lessons and benefits of my life's experience.

I also like to think I have gained, may I say, a unique perspective on what it takes to be successful and happy. I'll share that perspective with you throughout the book.

And YES, I am going to tell you my stories, successes, struggles and failures.

Please let your mind wander as you read. Take a break from the serious world, from the political and business issues that stress so many of us day to day. Just sit back, experience the stories in your mind, and let the feelings sink in. Don't study this book, enjoy it.

I will also share with you what the experiences meant to my future, how they are reflected in my life today and I intend to challenge you to find similar meaning and results in your own life. No matter what your circumstances or situation, I believe that over time, you can make the changes in your world, as I did in mine.

Some of what follows may sound like it was written for a Disney movie, but I assure you every word is true, no exaggeration. I will tell you what I did to pursue my goals, what I was thinking along the way, what I learned from the pursuit and how I used it to do better next time.

I do hope you enjoy my stories.

Imagine my World

George Bernard Shaw once said, "The problem with communication is the illusion that it occurred."

Recognizing that this is too often reality, there is one thing that it is critical we both understand on the same terms. If we can establish that starting point, it will punctuate everything else this book has to offer, in the most dramatic way.

In a moment I am going to ask you to try an experiment, but first, please let me establish some ground rules.

I am going to ask you to close your eyes. NOT YET! You need to read this first, but in a moment I will ask.

Once you have closed them, there are a few more things I would like you to do. First, eliminate any sense of light or shadow that may be filtering through your eyelids. No grey, no light or dark, no motion whatsoever. In fact, try to eliminate the blackness too. I honestly see absolutely nothing. I have no knowledge of color. I don't know what blackness is, or redness or blueness either. I have absolutely no vision. Can you create the equivalent of that in your mind, just for a moment? GREAT, but not yet.

Once you do, imagine that you have no memory bank of any images at all. You know what absolutely nothing looks like. All of the mental images your imagination is about to create on the inside of your eyelids to compensate for your lack of vision do not count. They do not exist. You have never seen a toothbrush, or a bar of soap, or a shower (or a toilet for that matter.) You don't know what a cereal bowl looks like, or a spoon. You have no reference for your imagination to create any images to help you with the tasks you must do, or learn. Even if you have read, or have a verbal description to draw on, the chances of your imagination, working without reference creating the right picture are slim. Can you have faith in the picture?

Let's start out, first thing in the morning. You have just awoken and need to start your day. How are you going to get ready? How will you tell the shampoo bottle from the conditioner, or, if your partner is like mine, the other 14 bottles and cans and tubes and bars in your shower? How will you set the water temperature? How will you shave, be it your legs or your chin? How will you be sure you are putting toothpaste, not hemorrhoid cream on your brush? How will you be sure it's your brush? How will you comb your hair?

Once your shower is finished, how will you dress yourself? How do you make sure your clothes coordinate? Remember, you've never seen a dress or a suit. You have no idea what red or yellow or black are. How will you tie your tie? Is it the right tie? Can you find your shoes? Are they the right ones for this outfit? Will you be confident when you're done? Will you be ready to face the world?

Assuming that you are, imagine preparing your breakfast. How do you know you're pouring Raisin Bran and not Fruity Pebbles or elbow macaroni? Are you sure that cereal bowl was clean? What about the milk? All gallon milk jugs feel the same. Is that white or chocolate milk you are about to pour?

And where is your phone? Where did the kids leave it?

Now you are out in the world. You would like to try your hand at golfing. Problem is you have never seen a golf club, let alone somebody swing one. What would you do if you were handed one now? How would you learn the swing? How would you learn to model something you've never seen (a person) doing?

Not interested in golf? How about skiing? You've never seen skis or a skier. What is your starting reference? What does a crouch look like, feel like? Can you translate this experience to water skiing, or wrestling, or throwing a javelin, or changing a diaper?

This is the one thing I hope you can understand about me. I am not visually impaired. I am totally blind, with no visual memory bank for my memory to access.

Now, please close your eyes and try to imagine learning and doing in a complete vacuum, void of any light, shadow, color or motion. Try to imagine getting out of your house in the morning, or out of your hotel room. Try to imagine learning to golf, or ski, or throw a javelin, or run in a straight line, or water ski jump and do it at a highly competitive level. Just try.

I hope you can read my stories from that frame of reference and really listen to the thoughts that come.

That's all I ask. Now, if you are ready, Let's Go!

3
Over Fifty Miles per Hour

What am I doing here?

- Standing in the vast silent emptiness at the top of this mountain, the voice in my head saying "you can do it, you can do it" while the mountain seemed to be answering "No you can't Craig, No you can't!"
- The pain in my knee... The one that was so badly torn up by yesterday's injury that I wasn't supposed to be standing, let alone skiing. Now it was screaming as the agony seemed to shoot all the way up between my shoulder blades.
- My skis pointing into nothingness as the world seemed to totally fall away, wanting to suck me into an abyss.
- My stomach churning. I struggled to control the butterflies, trying to harness the nervous energy.

I was about to make my final run at the 1983 Blind National Snow Skiing Championships in Alta, Utah. I wasn't even supposed to be here let alone be in contention. If I could push the envelope, take it to yet another level, throw myself into the unknown ahead, using all the skill and focus I could muster, and somehow let myself fly with all the reckless abandon that maximum speed required, I still had a chance to win this thing.

That is when the adrenaline kicked in. Suddenly I didn't care that my knee was swollen like a balloon, that the pain was knifing up my back, almost cutting me in two, I didn't care if I left my leg on the mountain that day. I was electrified in an instant, ready for the challenge, ready to launch myself, to take the maximum risk. I was going to leave it all on the mountain, it was the only way I knew.

This was "the moment." The final confrontation, me against the mountain. Two minutes, toe-to-toe. The gauntlet had been tossed and all I could think was "OK, Alta, it's just you and me. You gave me your best shot, now get ready, here comes mine!"

New Pursuits

For most blind athletes, regardless of the level of success you achieve, your career usually ends when you graduate from high school. The vast majority of blind athletes compete in individual sports. Unfortunately, the majority of competitive opportunities for adults and professionals are in team sports. Because of obvious limitations, this is rarely an option for a blind athlete.

In the fall of 1982, I was trying to resign myself to this reality, but without much success.

I was making what most people considered a successful transition to the business world. In fact, on September 19, 1982, I moved to the United States on a permanent basis in order to accept a position in the Community Relations Department of the Hartford Whalers of the National Hockey League. To make this an even more exciting beginning in the business world, I was actually living with Gordie and Colleen Howe.

Can you imagine how exciting that must've been for a Canadian kid of my generation? It's well-known the Canadians consider themselves to be the world's greatest hockey fans and for the most part that's true. When you talk about the kids of my generation, those of us born in the late 50's and early 60's, as the first generation to grow up with hockey on television, it is absolute reality. It's almost as if an entire generation of Canadian boys were born with skates on. Our first words were "he shoots, he scores!" Most of us even knew how to throw our stick over our head in celebration of the goal by the time we could walk. So imagine, not only was I employed by a professional sports organization, a National Hockey League club no less, in a very fulfilling job, but I was living with an absolute hockey legend.

Of course, we Canadians think that the world revolves around hockey, but I know that isn't reality, so please let me put this in perspective for you. Imagine an inner city kid in America, growing up playing basketball on hot, outdoor, asphalt courts all the time dreaming of using basketball to create an opportunity for a better life and then having the chance to move in with, and be mentored by, Michael Jordan. That is how big this was for me, that's what Gordie Howe means to the world of hockey.

Gordie, better known as Mr. Hockey, dominated the National Hockey League throughout an amazing career. Believe it or not, he actually played 32 seasons of professional hockey, at the highest level. He was competitive right until that final NHL season, scoring 15 goals and posting 41 points while playing in all 80 games, at the age of 51. When he retired he was the all-time scoring leader in National Hockey League history and to this day remains second on the all-time list, behind only Wayne Gretzky.

Despite all these great things that were happening for me, I was struggling to come to grips with the end of my competitive athletic career. That doesn't mean I wasn't active. I had the opportunity on most days to skate with the hockey club, usually toward the end of practice. I would sit in the dressing room, lacing up my skates, putting on my equipment, all the while getting the tutelage from Mr. Hockey. When we went on the ice, Gordie would teach me how to take a wrist shot and a slap shot. He would get the players to engage me in a little bit of activity. I even got to take shots on the goaltender and on one occasion I actually scored. Gordie roared with laughter, shouting "you're so bad, even a blind guy can beat you." It was great fun.

The challenge, for me at least, was that this active part of my life was too pedestrian. It was too passive. I wasn't competing at anything and I felt too much like a spectator even though I was living a dream existence.

Truth is, I was still feeling the burn to compete. It wasn't that I wanted to win anything else, or so I thought, but I still craved the opportunity to push my body to its limit. To perform, in whatever sport, to the best of my ability and still strive to improve. Athletics had been my vehicle to prove I could lead a regular life in the normal world. It had always been my springboard to move forward, whether it was acceptance in mainstream school, enrollment at Carleton University in Ottawa, Canada's Capital City, or coming to America. I had pushed myself very hard for many years and in the process I had developed an addiction to the adrenaline rush that comes from striving to get better and achieving new levels every day.

It's not that I was unhappy either. I had the perfect job for the highly social athletic type that I am. I was out in the community representing the team by meeting people and giving speeches. Perfect. Not to mention being able to just hang out with and soak up the wisdom of a Gordie Howe was tremendous. Colleen had a lot of wisdom to offer too.

It really was a great place to be, especially considering I had just achieved the ripe old age of twenty. I kept telling myself that, but I was restless. I couldn't shake the need, the itch, the burn. There was a void and if I didn't fill it I was going to drive myself crazy.

I never actually went searching for a pursuit, but I did keep my ear to the ground, hoping inspiration would find me. I spent most of my free time thinking about alternatives. It wasn't long before the idea of skiing popped into my mind.

Once I let my mind start to run with it, the idea really started to appeal to me. It was fresh and new. I had never been on skis, but I would remember the sound of skis crunching on the snow as my dad watched "Wide World of Sports" every Saturday. Listening to that, you just knew there was a rush that came with creating that sound. It was physical, challenging, competitive (in more ways than I realized) and dangerous, all of which got my juices flowing.

Danger? Was that what I was looking for? Maybe. I wasn't reckless, at least not totally, but I was restless big time. I wanted something that would push my physical limits and that always came with an element of risk, calculated as it may be. I liked that, I craved it.

The more I thought about it, the more I wanted it. I had made up my mind, I was going skiing.

I didn't know much when I started looking around for opportunities, but soon found out that there was a large, well respected, blind skiing program in Kirkwood, California, near Lake Tahoe, and another in Winter Park, Colorado. I also learned about the Blind National Snow-Skiing Championship that would be held the following April in Alta, Utah and that really set my imagination on overload. These all sounded fabulous, but I was young kid, in a new job, in Connecticut. There was no way I could afford the money, let alone the time, for either of these options. I settled for an option closer to home, and contacted the best blind skiing program on the east coast, hosted at Smugglers' Notch, in Vermont.

Smugglers' was a great place for my skiing adventure to begin, mostly because I was introduced to a wonderful man, George Spangler. I was told that George was a particularly good instructor, but he turned out to be much more. Without him I suspect that my skiing story could be very short, and possibly tragic.

I remember my first conversation with George. I liked his style right from the beginning. He was obviously patient. He took the time to listen and made the effort to understand. I told him about what I had done, how I did it, some of my accomplishments, how I approached athletics and my expectations from skiing. I was very emphatic that I was not interested in any leisurely, casual, recreational experience, No! I told George that I was coming to Smugglers' Notch to learn how to race.

Racing, yeah right. Here I was, a totally blind person, who'd never been on skis in his life, telling an instructor he hasn't even met yet, that he wants to race. But the idea of racing brought excitement to my mind. There are numerous ways to race in skiing and as much as I craved physical competition the idea of competing against myself, against the clock and against the mountain brought back that sense of exhilaration that I was seeking.

At any rate, when we finally met, several weeks later, everything I sensed about George was confirmed. He grabbed me by the shoulders, gave me a friendly shake, like a father would grab his son, stood me up straight and said, "My, God, you're built just like a bulldog, this is going to be a piece of cake."

I knew exactly what he meant, and it excited me that he recognized it. I was still in really good shape at that time, residual benefit of my wrestling career, and I am built kind of low to the ground with a broad sense of balance. I was solid, could take a spill and get up from it without losing my spirit or desire. Heck, I almost looked forward to it. George knew right away that he could push me a little harder, that I wouldn't break, wasn't about to fold my tent from a few bumps and bruises, that I wouldn't get discouraged. That was important. Just because I was an adrenaline junkie looking for a fix didn't mean I wouldn't need a little encouragement and the occasional kick in the pants. George gave me just the right amount of both. We were a great pair.

Of course, not everyone was as supportive as George.

Gordie, who respected my need for competitiveness (Gordie was easily the most competitive person I had ever met in my life) said, "I'm not sure about this, Bat. I'm sure the last thing they need is a blind skier racing all over the Hill." Gordie always called me Bat, as in "blind as a..." But I respected where he was coming from. Colleen, who had always been like a mother to me, had a slightly different thought. Colleen thought I should take a scholarship at Yale and study prelaw. "You have a secure job here and a chance to start building a future. How many more championships do you need to win? You've proven yourself already, you don't need to do this."

I understood the sentiment of my friends and colleagues who made a good case for playing it safe and just trying to nurture the secure job. I just couldn't do it. The newness of skiing, the excitement of it and the semi-impossibility of it all beckoned me.

I had made up my mind. I wanted to ski and I wanted to ski fast.

Now I had to make it happen. Fortunately, I had some time. It was early December and I wasn't going to Smugglers' until January. That was a long wait for someone like me. The anticipation was going to be as torturous as it was exciting. My imagination painted continual pictures for me of the race down the hill, despite the fact that I had no idea what skiing looked like. The imagination is so critical for a blind athlete. If you can't see it in your mind, you probably can't do it. I can imagine myself doing almost anything but this was new, the pictures were developing, but I needed more information for a clear vision. I also needed some skis.

I have been blessed many times with a great deal of help from supportive people who got excited for me as I pursued my goals. I have never been interested in charity, no hand outs for me, but a hand up, that was different. I would never have achieved so much without the support, encouragement and involvement of my friends, both new and lifelong. It never failed that the more committed I was to a goal, the more support that would come my way.

My pursuit of skiing proved no different. I had begun telling everyone who would listen about my upcoming adventure on the ski slopes. I was just so excited that I couldn't help it. The interest and encouragement energized me and then the unexpected happened, yet again.

Preparing for my trip meant finding skis at a price I could afford. So I went shopping. I was in a sporting goods store one day, trying boots and skis and the rest, and, as usual, telling my story with unabashed enthusiasm. I must have been very convincing because by the time I was leaving the store, the owner had generously offered to donate my skis and other needs to the cause. I remember his name was Tim and wish I could thank him here properly because, unfortunately, his store is no longer in business. I trust he is enjoying a successful retirement, reaping the benefits of his generosity. Thank you so much.

By the time I left for Smugglers' Notch, skis and boots stowed on the bus, I was like a kid on Christmas Eve who couldn't wait to play with his new toys. My anticipation was reaching a fever pitch. I was an anxious and excited ball of energy. I could barely sit still on the bus ride. This was really happening.

Unfortunately, it was evening by the time I arrived at Smugglers' Notch. I still had to wait, how was I ever going to sleep, I was so keyed up.

By the way, you might wonder if blind people can tell day from night. The answer is yes, and in obvious ways, when you think about it.

It's not light or dark. I am totally blind. I can see no shadow or color or image, or any kind of subtle way of explaining vision. I notice night by the density of the air. The air gets thicker and more dense at night, heavier too. It's damper. The noises of the night, be it cicadas or the eerie droning of semi's on the highway, are all different than in the day. The smell of the air is different, I can smell the night. I can almost taste the dampness, or the dew.

And of course, I know the night by its stillness, not everywhere, but especially in the country, and there on the mountain.

Anyway, being evening, George and I went to the lodge at the foot of the mountain to grab a bite. Entering the lodge, I knew that skiing, or at least the skiing environment, was something I was going to like. I could tell the lodge was large by the distance my voice travelled and listening to the chatter of so many other skiers who were there. This place was warm and inviting. I could feel the heat of the fireplace and hear the crackle as the fire burned. I could smell the aroma of steaks on the grill and other delicious dishes being prepared in the kitchen. There was the clinking of glasses and the lively chatter of other skiers who were enjoying a social evening together after a day on the slopes. This was a fraternity, a social network attached to an athletic pursuit. Earning my way into this circle added another layer of excitement. It was an individual sport but I sensed now that I might not have to pursue it alone.

During dinner, George went to work. He seemed to understand my needs perfectly. As we enjoyed our dinner, he painted pictures for me with his words. He filled in the blanks and helped me create those clear visuals in my mind that I was going to need if I had any hope of being successful as a skier. Having George as my instructor that first time out really was a godsend. Did I mention that he was donating his services for my four days at Smuggler's? Like I said, a hand up.

Morning came early for me. I was awake hours before anyone else had even rolled over for the last time, and that was probably good. It gave me quiet, uninterrupted time to focus on the pictures George had painted for me the night before. Any success would be completely dependent on focus and mental preparation and I fully intended to succeed. Even so, we were about to embark on a two-day comedy of errors as my trial by fire on the slopes of Smuggler's Notch was about to begin.

Everything started out positive enough. As morning slowly came to the rest of the resort, George greeted me with a big smile in his voice as he said "Well, this is it! Let's go have some fun." I really liked that, and it became somewhat of a motto, if not a rallying cry for the next four days, "Let's have some fun." Of course, that was a little challenging in the beginning, and there were still a couple more reality checks to endure first.

I had given very little thought to just how naive I really was when it came to skiing. After all, my vision was of me racing down the hill, going for broke, succeeding every time, performing perfectly in my imagination and expecting to transfer that to the slopes. It had never occurred to me that I had no idea how to put on those skis that I was going to use to race down that hill, or any of the other equipment either.

I had absolutely no clue. I had to be painstakingly walked through every step of getting into my gear. I was a rookie on display, revealing my weaknesses, right out in the open where everyone could see, or so I thought. I could hear the other skiers gliding past. That wonderful sound skis make when you stop, occasionally even feeling the spray when someone was close. The busy, happy sounds of people having a good time were all around us. I felt I was in the middle, being taught at age 20 the basics most of these people learned at age 6. Blind people tend to be more insecure about looking foolish and the last thing we ever want to be is a novelty, but my feeling of naiveté made me feel I was just that. The feeling didn't last long but for a moment it was terribly disturbing.

George didn't leave me anytime to dwell on my insecurities. His approach to the next couple of hours relieved all my tension and brought my focus clearly back to my goal.

It was time for the visualization to become real, not on the slopes, too soon for that, but between my mind and my body. George continued to paint his word pictures but now he was physically moving me at the same time. He was giving me a physical sensation, a movement, a position that I could attach to each image in my mind, making the sense that I could really do this very believable. It was a great way to teach a blind person and after just a couple hours I was ready.

It was finally time for the games to begin but the fun was still some time off.

I was ready to break huddle, bubbling with energy, ready to start measuring myself. Honestly, I was ready for a little adrenaline injection. Then I heard something that totally bummed me out. As I'm standing there, skis sliding back and forth, anxious to push towards the hills, listening to skiers all around me, thinking how great it is that I am about to become one of them, George announces "here, we need to put these on." I knew exactly what he meant. I'd heard it before but I still asked, "What?"

"We need to wear these vests. Yours says Blind Skier and mine says Sighted Guide."

"OK," I replied, "but let's switch." At least George laughed.

I know I may sound a little hyper-sensitive about this but, damn, I'm here to strive for success and now I'm wearing a label encouraging others to handle me with kid gloves. To me it was no different than dark glasses or a white cane or a guide dog. They were essentially labels, too. I never used them and didn't want this one either. Why did they have to draw attention me this way, before I was ready?

That attitude changed very quickly. It wasn't long before I realized that other skiers were coming down the hill like missiles. The vest wasn't a label to attract attention. It was a heads up that could save my life. I came to appreciate the vest in short order.

Of course, I grumbled as George put this thing on me, even though he kept telling me, "You can't see it but people are falling and wiping out all over place." "You aren't unique here, you blend right in, Let's go have some fun!" I appreciated his attitude and his efforts but it didn't make me feel any better, yet.

Finally, we headed for the slopes. Well, the bunny slope at least.

The next 2 days were an adventure, to put it mildly. A learning experience, yes, some lessons encouraging, others painful, literally. A sensorial experience too, as I finally was able to appreciate the majesty and scope of this mountain which brought me tremendous inspiration. Let me give you the headlines.

- I didn't even make it to the top of a hill before I had my first wipeout. We had to use the rope tow to get to the top of the Bunny Slope and I must have made it a good, oh, 10 feet before I crossed the tips of my skis and wiped out, right there, where the waiting line could still see me. I felt so hopeless, so embarrassed, not 10 feet into my first try, not even into a run yet, and I was down. To make matters worse, and the fact that everyone could still see me made it pretty bad, now I was not only failing but my failure was affecting everyone else. They rushed over and helped me up, reassuring me all the time but I hated it.

- If the Rope Tow was embarrassing, the chair lift was comical. The Bunny Slope had been a reasonable success. I only wiped out once in 3 runs, so we decided it was time to try a bigger challenge. Of course, that meant we had to take the chair lift. George had a system for the chair lift and he walked me through it a few times. Essentially, I assumed a crouch position, waited for the chair

to approach and when it got close, George would count down, 3-2-1, and I would sit. When we did it for real, that part worked great. Problem was, George was so focused on me that he missed the chair himself.

I felt the immediate lift as the chair started to rise but those things swing back and forth and I wasn't ready for that. I tried to sit perfectly still and called out to George as I reached over in his direction, looking for a little stability. Imagine how my heart dropped when I felt nothing. I called his name again and then I heard him, coming from behind, and below. He was on the next chair! He kept calling to me, telling me it was all right, we'd be fine, and slowly I felt my heartbeat return to normal.

Normal in that case was still beating faster than usual. Even for a blind person that first ride up a chair lift is a thrill. As the chair climbed I got a greater and greater sense of just how vast and how tall this mountain was. The echo was growing, the distance to the next slope getting greater and greater. The same with the sound of the skiers down below. I didn't know exactly how high I was, but I knew I didn't want to slip off my seat. This was a "trip." Wow!

It wasn't long before we reached the top. George was still calling out to me. Now he was going to start his reverse countdown. He would count 3-2-1 and I was supposed to slide off and wait for him, so I listened. THREE -TWO-ONE, I stepped off. Maybe I was anxious, I can't imagine George misjudged so badly, but I stepped off into. ...nothing and dropped, what seemed like 10 feet. I thanked the Lord for snow at that moment as I landed in a snowdrift, which did wonders to break my fall. Of course my skis went flying off, who knows where, and I was definitely shaken, but I'm sure it looked worse than it really was. George was there in seconds, and so were several other skiers, all helping me, worried if I was OK. (To be honest, this was one of the most reassuring things about the skiing experience, the realization that I was not alone.) Once I was back on my feet and reintroduced to my equipment, I reassured everyone that I was all right, and thanked them for their concern. They were so encouraging. I remember one of them in particular, who must have noticed the vest. He said to me, "Man, you must have some guts, you just tumbled out of a chair lift and you're still going to tackle this mountain. I admire that." What could I say?

- My first "real" run was OK. It was nothing special because George was keeping a tight leash. Basically, his instructions were simple. George would call out "go, go, go" as we traversed across the slope, then, "turning left, turn, turn, turn... go, go, go." Sometimes it would be a HARD left turn, or EASY turn but you get the idea. We would ski 10, maybe 20 feet then he would call out turn, turn, turn and I would switch direction. He wanted me to keep the turns tight so that I wouldn't build up any speed, so that I didn't find myself headed too directly down the hill. The big fear, big risk actually, especially for a blind skier, is a collision with an inanimate object. If that happens going slow, not so bad, but at speed, not good. Once I didn't make my turn tight enough and all of sudden felt myself starting to race. George's voice started to fade in the background, but I could hear him yelling, screaming really, SIT, SIT, SIT! I did as I was told and came to a rather quick stop. I knew I had gone off the main run because the snow had become deeper and echoes had changed. George rushed to me, yelling all the way, "Craig, are you OK, are you OK?" Then, when he got to me, he went silent for a second. "Craig, reach out your left hand." As I did George also told me to reach out my right hand. Each hand came almost immediately in contact with a huge tree. I had landed right between two huge pine trees. George slapped my shoulder and said, "Man, this is your lucky day, you should go buy a lottery ticket or something." Years later, when Sonny Bono was killed by colliding with a tree on a skiing vacation, I couldn't help but think how lucky I was.

- By the way, echoes were a big tool that I had to use to know my place on the hill. Those first two days were stressful. It took total concentration to not kill myself, to have any awareness at all, to ensure that my turns stayed tight so I didn't meet more trees, and to always be aware of George who was constantly calling instructions to me from behind as he watched my course and form. This was actually awkward, I was constantly going forward, into an unknown that could bring devastating consequences, while relying on sounds from behind, but George assured me this is how it was done. I trusted him, but it was totally exhausting.

- The chair lift experience did improve. In fact, the next ride was awesome. We did the 3-2-1 program again and this time George and I made it on the same chair. No fear, no worries, no doubts about the ride. Instead there was George, sitting beside me, painting a brilliant word picture of the scene that unfolded below us. He described the forests that dominated the mountainside and the ski runs that snaked their way through the trees, covered with fresh snow that had just fallen the night before. He told me how the mountain rose and the peaks and valleys that he could see beyond as we approached the top. He talked about the other skiers and the brightly colored outfits, and even gave a little "play-by play" as other skiers wiped out below us (to keep my confidence up no

It's amazing how far you can hear from this altitude.

doubt.) He helped me create a wonderful vision of this majestic setting, which I could relate back to my snowy Canadian roots. I took comfort in that.

- We talked to a lot of people over those first two days but the most insightful comment came from another instructor who asked how my first day went. I told him "Great, I didn't fall much." His reply opened my eyes and really set the tone for day two. He said "Sounds like a lousy day. If you're not falling, you're not pushing yourself enough." When I heard that it was like my subconscious beating me upside my head. "See," it said, "you're an all or nothing kind of guy and today was nothing, tomorrow give it your all."

- I did get aggressive on my second day and the spills happened, some collisions too. Over the course of day two my entire focus was on pushing the envelope. I wasn't a kamikaze, but I was aggressive. In the course of testing my limits I managed to collide with the icy snow bank that separated the slopes from the parking lot, jumped that and actually hit a car, hipped checked a nice girl named Beth during one of many turns, spilled numerous times up and down the hill (but never missed the chair lift) and worst of all, collided head on with a snow hydrant. That really was the worst.

- I hit the snow hydrant head on and fortunately, head up. It caught me full in the chest and totally knocked the wind out of me. I realize now that if I had been head down, going for it, I'd probably be dead. It was still very painful, I got up and back on my skis but I knew I'd done some damage.

- When Day 2 was over it was obvious that I needed a trip to the hospital, not that I was dying, but I was feeling some distinct pain, especially when I took a deep breath. The hospital confirmed what I already suspected. The collision with the snow hydrant had resulted in a cracked rib. In my wrestler's mentality, it was par for the course, all in the game as they say, but it did hurt like crazy.

• I never thought about giving up, or quitting, but I did think a lot. When we were back at Smugglers', in the lodge for dinner as usual, I told George I wanted to make some changes if we were going to continue.

Plunging into the unknown...
pine trees ahead!

This is what I had figured out. The traditional method of teaching blind skiers was fine for the passive, casual, past-time approach. I didn't see skiing as a past-time. I wanted to race, but how could you cut loose and go for broke when you are constantly skiing with an element of fear that a calamitous collision may be right in front of you. The snow hydrant made my point rather emphatically. If I was going to ski fast, race, go for broke down the mountain I needed to know that I wasn't going to kill myself running into something I couldn't see, or anticipate!!!!!

I told George I wanted to make a change. This just wasn't working for me and I wasn't prepared to go back up on the mountain and take the same risks. After all, if you had collided with an icy snow bank and a car and other skiers and a snow hydrant, not to mention almost meeting two pine trees head on, and all you had to show for it was a bunch of bumps, bruises and a cracked rib, would you keep doing things the same way? I wanted George to ski in front of me. He resisted at first. His rationale was that he couldn't train me if he couldn't see me and how could he warn me if he wasn't watching me? Valid concerns for a sighted person but I saw things differently, literally. We had to take advantage of that, if this was going to work. I explained to George my rationale, specifically my experience in high school when I competed in track. There, my coach would always be in front of me on the track and I would be constantly running to his voice. Running individually in races like the 100-meter dash, my coach would stand at the finish line and call out five, five, five, as long as I stayed in a straight line. If I veered left he would call four, four,

four, until I came back to straight. If I veered right he would call six, six, six. It took some practice to perfect our lefts and rights, considering that my right was his left, during the race at least, but it worked. It is the ultimate form of trust, but when it works, it's magic. With nothing on the track between the two of us I could go for broke and just focus on sprinting in his direction. On the slopes it just made sense in my mind that I could follow George easier than I could navigate on my own. Not only could I follow his voice but I could follow the sound of his skis as well. I was used to navigating by sound and this way I wouldn't have to worry about any more collisions. After all, if there was something to run in to, George was going to hit it first, my way.

George agreed we needed a change and so we tried my idea the next day. The results were instant. I immediately felt more comfortable. I felt like I could physically relax and just focus on the act of skiing. It was like being able to jump into a pool instead of trying to walk across it by stepping on stones. Full immersion, just what I wanted. George noticed too that my form improved, I was deeper in my crouch, focused straight ahead, not stiff, awkward and apprehensive like the previous days.

Ultimate trust

From the first run it was night and day. We actually skied almost three quarters of the way down before we had to stop, and that was more for George to catch his breath. I remember him saying "I'm going to have to start carrying oxygen if I have to keep yelling like this." Maybe so, but we both realized that this one change had made all the difference.

We were no longer wiping out all over the mountain. We were, in fact, making one full run after another. We weren't setting any speed records, yet. After all, we may have been crazy but we were not nuts, but with each run we were getting smoother, fewer and fewer of the "tight turns" that had been the order of the day when we began two days earlier. We were starting to have some fun.

The third day was actually quite uneventful, which was good, in the way that saying a flight from New York to Los Angeles was uneventful, considering the alternatives. I felt really good by the time we got to the lodge that evening, thoroughly exhausted and my ribs aching, but still really good. I had been skiing that day, not stumbling and struggling, but actually skiing. I was beginning to feel like I could really do this.

I was expecting another night of talk about our experiences of the day but as we entered the lodge that night George caught me with a surprise question, "don't you play the piano?" I admitted that I did and, with a little prodding by George, agreed to play a couple of tunes.

Playing the piano at Smugglers' Notch was great fun, I just wish they had the lit the fireplace earlier.

I played a couple songs by Elton John and the Beatles and even got brave enough to play a couple I had written myself. People actually started to gather around the piano and joined in on some of the songs. Between songs people were introducing themselves and commenting "Nice to see you here." "Loved your piano playing." "You were looking good out there today." Even the girl who had been one of my collisions on the second day came by and told me how she and her friends had seen me go past that afternoon and that we looked great.

There was starting to be a lot of chatter by others on the mountain and in the Lodge about what a tremendous progression we made after only three days. In that short period of time, I had created a new way of teaching blind people to ski. Other instructors were talking about the change. "Your spirit to move forward was something they had never seen even out of a sighted skier," George said.

This was all affirmation. Welcome to our club. Welcome to our world. You have arrived. I was now a part of their fraternity of skiers, and that was important to me.

By day four, I ached all over. I could've ripped through 10 matches in a row on a mat and not felt this bad. I hurt in places I didn't even know I had, plus my quads and hamstrings were especially sore. My feet were aching from being cramped in those boots. My shoulders ached from all the spills.

But when we got up on the mountain, those aches evaporated. I felt much better. I was invigorated by the idea of improving and George observed how much more relaxed I was skiing. Physically relaxed I mean. Maybe the word would be comfortable. I was hearing subtle sounds, like the birds in the trees, and feeling the warmth of the sun on my face. I was in the environment now, not just the action. I even got playful enough to throw a snowball at George during a run, which took the toque off his head.

There was no opportunity to relax mentally. I knew what the consequences were of letting down my mental focus and I wouldn't let that happen, but once I relaxed my body, skiing was so much easier.

We skied hard and we skied a lot that last day. We skied more smoothly, without some of the previous excitement. It was one of the great confidence building days for me snow skiing. It was such a quantum leap forward. I came into the lodge that night and said to myself, "I am a skier."

That was also the day the light bulb went off over my head.

"George," I said. "I'm going to go for it, I'm going to ski at the Blind Nationals."

George didn't exactly leap out of his chair when I told him this. He was actually kind of lukewarm. "Oh man, let's leave that for next year. You wouldn't be ready for this year."

My time with George was coming to an end. He had to return home and go back to work. He was never negative about my chances. He was just trying to dial in some reality.

I didn't let go of it. I was so excited by the progress we'd made. I wasn't prepared to just pack my bags and say, "this was a fun experience, see you." I wanted to take it to the next level.

Reality was, by the end of that fourth day, we were going through tougher and tougher runs without incident and even skiing blacks, those really steep runs. Admittedly too, neither of us knew how good or how fast the competition would be at the Blind Nationals.

One thing George was certain of was that my skills were good and with continued training, especially with the intensity I was feeling now, I could compete with the best. That was all the encouragement I needed. My unbridled ambition would take care of the rest.

The following afternoon I walked into the kitchen back home in Connecticut, still riding on high from my decision to ski the Blind Nationals. I couldn't wait to tell Gordie and Colleen. I had the vision all worked out in my mind now. I was going to find some sponsors and dedicate the next couple months to training.

Considering my success at Smuggler's Notch, Gordie was pretty supportive of the entire idea. Of course I didn't tell him or Colleen about the cracked rib or running into the snow bank, or the car, or the girl. I left out a few minor details and just gave them the highlights. They both knew me well and knew I was ready to breathe fire about skiing. They weren't about to try and tame the dragon.

I was committed now. I didn't know how I was going to do it, but I knew that when I threw myself at my goals 100 percent, things had a way of coming together. This time was no different.

I was the beneficiary of yet another Godsend. A week later, I was on a plane, flying back to Hartford from New York, where I had given a speech. As usual, I was sharing my plan and my vision with anyone who would listen and was lucky enough to be sitting next to a guy who took an interest in me. Noticing I was blind, he struck up a conversation and before long I was excitedly telling him about my ambition to ski competitively. He asked me my goal and I told him, "The Blind Nationals."

At that point he said he would love to help and handed me his business card.

That guy, Arnold Kleinfeld, paid for much of my next phase of training. He was making it possible, now it was up to me.

I had three months, that's all, and I was determined to be the fastest blind skier in the world, or at least in the United States. This had become the most important thing in my mind and my world. The only way I knew to succeed at that point in my life was to get totally immersed in my projects and this was no different. That meant I was going to California.

Sadly, it meant leaving The Hartford Whalers. Unfortunately, and more regrettably, it meant saying goodbye to Gordie and Colleen, at least temporarily. I thanked them for putting me up and putting up with me, then packed my bags and left for California.

I had spoken with a man named Bob Weber in Kirkwood, California. Kirkwood was a Mecca for blind skiing and Bob was the focal point. I talked to him about my experiences at Smugglers' Notch with George, how we had accomplished so much in four days and how that had inspired me to pursue my ultimate capability. I told him that I was looking for the most aggressive, no holds barred, damn the torpedoes, full speed ahead instructor I could find.

Bob introduced me to an instructor named Cliff May. Cliff had the reputation of being a total "go for it" skier. He had raced competitively and Bob thought his personality was very much like mine.

Bob was right. Our personalities totally meshed so much so that after just a week at the resort I moved out of the Lodge and into Cliff's guest bedroom, where I stayed for the next three months. This was unreal. Cliff and his wife Christine were the most amazing hosts and, if that wasn't enough, they lived right at the foot of the mountain. Every morning we simply walked out the front door, put on our skis and we were there. It was great!

As for Cliff, he was a total trip. He was funny, he was kind, he was passionate, he was patient. Trust me, when you're teaching a blind skier patience is more than a virtue. He totally immersed himself in my goals with a can-do attitude that virtually matched my own. He really was as determined to succeed as I was. What a great team we turned out to be.

Right from the beginning, Cliff understood that this wasn't just another instructor's job. He understood what I meant by "racing mode" and he was in that mindset right from the beginning. His focus wasn't simply on technique and helping me stay on my feet and make it down the hill. He was focused on developing rhythm, on helping me get in sync with him, on developing the connection we needed to focus on speed.

Cliff's passion led us to try many new techniques. We often skied down the hill in tandem, connected to each other using a pair of 10-foot bamboo poles. With Cliff in front and me behind I was able to feel his rhythm and how he shifted his weight. Some days we wouldn't even use the polls. We simply skied with me holding his hips, my skis between his.

We developed so many techniques like this. All focused on the tactile experience of syncing me with Cliff and it proved to be a great method of accelerating my development. After all, you can explain skiing to a blind person all you want, but Cliff's techniques took the message out of my imagination and made it tangible and real in a way that I could translate into more and more speed.

That, of course, was the objective. This wasn't about tight turns and bleeding off speed in the name of safety. This was about going for broke, about seeing how fast we could get down that mountain and it worked. In no time at all I was able to gain Cliff's groove, his tempo and as a result, more speed.

Of course not every run was brilliant. You can't go for speed without an element of risk. With risk comes collisions, and we had more than our share. I ran into Cliff from behind, I flipped over his back, got my skis tangled with his, so many wipeouts. Cliff had the patience of Job. He never complained about any of the trouble I caused him or any of the help that I needed. He simply stayed focused on the goal and kept reminding me of what we were about to accomplish.

We really became a team. Yes he was still the instructor, he was still teaching me the techniques and refining my physical skill, but he was a mentor as well. He persisted when I didn't want to push through the pain, he was patient when I lost my rhythm, he toler-ated me when I was going too fast or too slow to match his pace. It didn't matter to Cliff. He just continually came up with new and creative ways for us to go faster, for us to communicate better and to inspire my confidence to try harder.

We lived and breathed skiing, 24/7. We spent every possible minute we could on the mountain. When we weren't skiing, we were talking about skis or poles or boots or bindings or wax or snow conditions. When that conversation slowed down Cliff would read me articles about skiing. It was like being in military boot camp. We were totally locked and loaded, possessed with my wacky idea of winning the Blind National championship, and as a result I'm sure I learned more about skiing in a few weeks than most learn over many years. We were totally invested. If I didn't win, we were certainly going to make sure that it wasn't from lack of effort. We left everything on the mountain, every day.

Winning was our obsession, but I don't want to lose sight of the fact that Cliff and Christine made this a dream like existence. Cliff had a way of making the hard work fun. Christine made coming home from the mountain just as inspiring. She cooked buckets of food, she made seafood, pasta, steak, whatever we wanted. They gave me a great room, run of the house and every morning I stepped out onto the bottom of the mountain. It was just an incredible experience.

Of course when you're pushing yourself that hard, when you have such an unrelenting focus and a complete and utter refusal to surrender, even to the weather, you are going to have some exhilarating experiences, but sometimes you can push too hard and Cliff and I were guilty of that on more than occasion as well.

As I said earlier, we were determined to leave everything on the mountain every day. With that in mind, there was always the question of what is enough, should we make one more run? The answer was almost always yes, but it wasn't always the right answer.

Let me explain. I remember one day when we felt like we had been making great progress. Even though the weather was not pleasant, we decided to go back up to the top and make one more run. As we rode up the chair lift we started to doubt this decision. The wind was howling, snow was blowing and it was becoming bitterly cold.

We actually discussed just doing a safe run, simply making it back down the mountain and calling it a day. Then we realized there was nobody else on the mountain. This was a rare pleasure as it meant that there was nobody else for us to run into. Cliff suggested making the run without even using the bamboo poles, a trial race, if you will. This kind of free skiing was something we treated as a reward at the end of a good day but now it was an opportunity to actually test ourselves, or so we thought.

Our philosophy worked for the first third of the run. Then, all of a sudden, I lost Cliff's voice and in an instant collided with a tree. It doesn't take long at that speed for things to happen and in this case it was almost instantaneous. In that instant I went off course, into the deep powder that had been accumulating throughout the day, and the tip of my ski caught a tree. My shoulder slammed in hard, sending me into a spin and corkscrewing me down into the deep, powdery snow. I, of course, lost my skis and my helmet.

I was buried literally up to my neck. Cliff couldn't even see me from the run and told me that when he finally caught sight of me, he thought I was dead. If not for the powdery conditions, I might well have been. There, but for the grace of God...

Cliff dug me out and we crept down the mountain, laughing with disbelief and relief at our good fortune, and maybe at our foolishness. My body hurt more than usual that night, but I think it was my spirit that was really hurting. That crash felt like failure and I hated that.

Christine, of course, reminded us that we were insane to be on the mountain in those conditions, but, of course, we already knew that. The question that night was just how insane.

That evening was spent in reflection, asking ourselves why this happened. What we concluded was that Christine was right. We had to be insane to be up on the mountain in those conditions, but we also took comfort in the fact that no matter how we dissected the crash, we found no fault in our technique or our method, just that it was sheer stupidity to have been there at all. We had no realistic hope of coping with those conditions and I should have realized how hard it would be to track Cliff's voice in such a windstorm.

We recognized that we needed a stabilizer, a rational, objective voice to temper our gung ho enthusiasm. At this point we had been going hard for three or four weeks and were really starting to crank the speed. We were also of the belief that every minute not spent on the mountain was a minute of opportunity lost that we could have spent gaining an advantage over everybody else who wasn't training. We realized now that wasn't necessarily true.

We started working more with Bob Weber as our stabilizer. Bob would often join us, skiing behind us, observing our efforts and providing suggestions. It was invaluable to have another set of expert eyes critiquing our efforts as we worked to fine tune our skill to generate even more speed. It was also great to have Bob's experience helping balance our time on and off the mountain.

By now I was getting anxious for some competition. I felt like I was making great progress, a sentiment Cliff and Bob echoed wholeheartedly, but we still wanted to know how my speed matched up with the "competition." Fortunately, an opportunity to find out just where I stood was coming up in the form of Kirkwood Invitational. It was scheduled to take place about six weeks after my arrival in California and now we focused our preparation on the race. What was really nice about this event was that many of the skiers from the nationals, including several past national champions, also trained occasionally at Kirkwood and most were entered in this competition.

Of course, none of them were training at Kirkwood for three months straight but most didn't need to. Many of them had been skiing for years, and some had actually learned to ski before losing their sight. Still, it was in this event that I was going to find out just how far I had come and where I stood in the big competitive picture. I was ready for that but I wasn't ready for the other lesson, learning just how ostracized I was from the blind skiing community.

I couldn't really blame anybody, but I really didn't feel that I was part of the blind skiing fraternity. I was the new kid on the block and an interloper of sorts, coming from nowhere and challenging to compete against them on an equal footing. Who did I think I was?

In reality, I was an intruder. I was too busy in my own little world with Cliff, trying to absorb everything I could possibly learn.

We didn't hang out at the lodge or try to suck up to the status quo, we didn't need to. The food was tremendous at home and Christine was all the company we needed. This wasn't social fun and games for me, it was a mission and so I was an outsider, maybe I was even a threat.

In any event, the Invitational was going to be a good measuring stick. Was I ready to play in the majors or was I still a minor leaguer? Cliff and I were both anxious for an answer and by the end of that event we would have it.

Needless to say, I was pumped, eager to go. It was a one day competition with the giant slalom in the morning and the downhill in the afternoon. When it was over, I had come in third in the giant slalom and won the downhill, quite handily in fact. I don't remember the exact times, but I do recall that I won by more than six seconds in a field of twenty-three skiers.

Now we knew.

I think we were both a little disappointed at the third place finish in the Giant Slalom, but it was really downhill that excited me. That is where all the speed and adrenaline resided and now I knew I could compete. That didn't mean that Cliff and I rested on our laurels, or even let ourselves begin to think we had arrived. It just reassured us that we were on the right track. We still had six weeks before Alta and I was determined to keep training just as hard. I had to stay sharp. I had to get better. Maybe I had won this little dance but we didn't know how the competition would be training. They had experience to rely on, they had instincts to call upon that I was still developing. I didn't know if they could catch up to my time, all I could do was focus on getting better, if I was to feel confident.

For those first four months of 1983 I just shut off the world. When I wasn't on the mountain I was, for all intents and purposes, in school. Cliff and I would spend our evenings sitting by the fire. Cliff read me articles from "Skiing Magazine" and then we discussed, studied really, the intricacies of skiing. I may have been all about power and speed but I knew it was mastering the fine points that would give me my ultimate advantage and we never lost our focus.

To paraphrase Yogi Berra, "Blind skiing is 90% mental, the other half is physical." All the time on the slopes was invaluable because I had to not only develop the physical skills of skiing, but also the muscle memory which I would have to rely on to fully surrender to the speed I desired, especially during the excitement of the actual competition. After all, repetition is the mother of skill, and so we repeated the work every day. I also needed to develop the physical stamina required for skiing. It was essential that I be able to rely on my body without doubt, but that was just the beginning. The physicality was important, but there was a more important element.

The truly exhausting element of skiing for a blind person is mental. Reaching full speed, and surviving, would be totally dependent on my state of mind, my ability to not only hear Cliff but instantly translate that into the physical action that would keep my vision of the perfect run real. All of that happens in the mind first, and too fast for conscious thought. I firmly believe, the skull sessions with Cliff were more than just entertaining, they were invaluable. They made it possible for my mind to sync with my body, and that was the core, the foundation of all my success.

All the study allowed me to go to sleep every night with a clarity that renewed my faith, on a continual basis, in surrendering to my subconscious and letting my instincts play a greater and greater role. The components of the "Grey Zone" were being assembled and it showed in my daily progress.

Focused as we were, there was still time for a little diversion now and again. A couple of nights a month we used to slide over to Tahoe for dinner and a show. Sometimes we'd even pull the handles on a few slot machines just for fun. I saw Frank Sinatra one night, which was a super experience, and another night Cliff and I decided try our hand at blackjack. I actually came away with about $1,800. Not bad considering I had only about $50 in my pocket when we started.

Having $1,800 of my own felt like I had turned Pro. Up until then I only had the generosity of Mr. Kleinfeld to rely on, but I couldn't use that for pleasure or personal purchases, that would not have been fair. Now I could treat myself just a little and Cliff too. I was able to buy him new ski boots and some other accessories, and that made me feel really good.

Another adventure I'll never forget took place one night driving home from Tahoe. We were almost buried in an avalanche. It literally happened just seconds in front of us. Cliff caught a glimpse of the snow falling and was able to stop just in time, so close in fact that some of the after-fall sort of skiffed onto the hood of the car.

When Cliff slammed on the brakes we skidded into a bit of the snow that had landed on the road. We both jumped out and when we did we could hear the snow rumbling and groaning in the distance.

"That's tons of snow moving" Cliff said. "Let's get out of here!" We turned the car around and went back to Tahoe for the night, stopping several others cars along the way to warn the drivers what was happening.

That was the closest we came to an avalanche, but it wasn't the only time I heard that sound. Occasionally while we were skiing I would hear the rumbling groan in the distance, especially on warmer days.

I was always concerned about the risk but I loved skiing on those warmer days. Some days the temperature got as high as 60 degrees and we skied in shorts and T-shirts. There seemed to be more birds and an entire new array of senses that came to life when the weather warmed up. I could hear the snow melting and would listen to the water dripping off the trees. It reminded me of the spring thaw back home in Canada and made me a little homesick, but I loved it nonetheless.

I also loved it because you can take more time on the mountain to talk to each other. After all, your teeth aren't chattering.

The warmer weather came with other benefits as well. It meant it was time for the Blind Nationals.

Among my other blessings during this adventure was the blessing of time. With the support of Mr. Kleinfeld and having spent only a minimal amount thanks to Cliff and Christine's generosity, plus my $1,800 windfall from the casino, I could afford to take us to Alta a full week before the competition.

What an amazing place. As we drove to the resort from Salt Lake City I remember thinking, "How much farther can we climb?" but we just keep going up. When we finally got there, Cliff reminded me that we still had a chair lift ride to the top. It was just an awesome place to be taking such a big step.

Overwhelming as Alta may have been, I still would not let anything take away our focus. The finish line was close now and I was determined to be the most prepared skier here. That meant training continued.

I'd been in California for three months at that point and skied seven days a week, every week. I had lived and breathed and studied skiing incessantly. I had gone from neophyte to novice to capable to competent to victory and now stood in contention, or so I believed, to win a National championship. You would think I'd have gained a little wisdom by now but I still had one more brain cramp to survive before the ultimate event.

I was energized, Cliff and I both, and I couldn't wait to get on my skis every day. I wanted to learn the mountain, to absorb the environment, to hear Cliff's voice and study how the sound echoed and reverberated off the trees. Alta just felt different, smelled different, sounded different from Kirkwood. I needed to internalize the scope of the space and develop the trust needed to surrender to my desire for speed. Equally important, I needed to maintain that same level of trust in my physical skills and stay as fine tuned and instinctive as possible.

The only way I knew to do that was to ski!

We had four days to practice at Alta, and just like at Kirkwood, we were on the mountain for six, seven or (foolishly) sometimes eight hours a day. Our first two days were sweet, we skied run after run without incident, we traversed all over the mountain, I heard all the sounds, all the echoes, felt the ebb and flow of the mountain and was getting a great sense of the subtleties I would be contending with on Saturday.

Thursday morning the course for the race was set. Determined to raise our focus one more level, we now set out in race mode to master this course, to go on auto pilot, if you will, and install victory in our subconscious minds, to become undefeatable.

In theory, and practice, it was a fabulous approach, until that last, involuntary, brain cramp.

It was Friday afternoon, late afternoon, but still early by our standards. There was still time for another run. The weather, however, was turning a little unfriendly. We were still in the mindset that to be fully actuated, we still had to leave it "all on the mountain, every day" and felt we had no choice. We could cope with the conditions one more time, and got back on the chair lift.

Maybe it was stupid male machismo. I prefer the term unbridled ambition, but there we were, back on top of the mountain. We had been in this position every day for the past three months. We had made run after run, invested hour after muscle aching hour refining and fine-tuning our technique, communication, rhythm and skills. Did we really need one more run? Was this going to make all the difference between winning and losing? It very nearly did, but not in the way we expected.

We didn't even go overly fast on that last run. The wind had become very bitter and was blowing right in our faces. We had to do it right, technique, communication and focus, all of which still meant speed, but we didn't push it. Unfortunately, when you tempt fate once too often, well...

We were coming to the end of the run and moving well. As we entered the last turn I could hear Cliff yelling "tuck, tuck, tuck" and then all of a sudden - nothing. Some guy had started up a snow groomer (probably somebody who couldn't believe a couple of yahoos were still skiing in that weather) and the noise instantly drowned out Cliff's voice, and all other audible references.

We were seconds from the finish line, which in competition was marked by two clusters of bamboo poles sunk into the ground on either side end of the line. I didn't have a reference to follow between the poles and my left ski slammed right into the middle of one of the clusters. I twisted severely, slammed my forehead into the bamboo, lost my skis and went down in a tumble.

My head hurt but I knew right away that something much more serious had happened. The pain exploding out of my left knee was excruciating, nauseating. It was bad, there was no question about that. My greatest challenge had just arrived.

Cliff was livid. He was screaming at the driver of the Snow Groomer. "How could you be so stupid? Can't you see these vests? There have been blind skiers out here all week, they need to be able to hear, they need silence, you..." I finally got Cliff's attention.

I was angry too, but I wanted Cliff to cut the guy a break. Yes, what he did was wrong, but Cliff and I were really to blame, we shouldn't have been out there. I was so mad at myself, at the weather, at the world probably, but now I wanted answers. How bad was this? What was I contending with? I never considered not skiing the next day, but I am a realist. I needed to know so I could strategize in my mind how I would fight through this.

Fortunately, the snow groomer guy had a radio. He had already called for the paramedics and I was making my way down the rest of the mountain in a matter minutes. When we were back at the lodge the paramedics cut away my ski pants and gasped. I sensed immediate, frantic activity around me. Apparently my knee was turning shades of black and blue they had never seen, and was already swollen like a balloon, and growing. They didn't want to touch me. They wanted me en route to the hospital, right then and there, no time to wait, not even for an ambulance. They found a pickup truck, and loaded me into the back.

It seemed a side trip to Salt Lake City was in order.

The news wasn't good. It was a badly torn medial collateral ligament. I might be able to avoid surgery if I stayed off it for six to eight weeks. Not just take it easy but completely off it. This was hard to hear, not because it made me consider quitting, that thought never entered my mind, but in that environment, it was hard to summon up the resolve to struggle on. Remember, my memories of hospitals weren't full of success. I lost my final glimpses of the world in a hospital, not long after my second birthday. Went through so many trials and surgeries and treatments in hospitals but I never got those glimpses back. Yes, truth is that I don't remember those glimpses. They came well before any conscious memories that I have, but the sounds and smells of that place, of any hospital, always brought back that spirit breaking sense of futility. Fortunately, I had learned one big lesson in my life.

Everything I had achieved up to that point, and since, was the direct result of a decision, and I was always in control of the decision. At that moment I decided I was going to ski tomorrow, and I was going to win. I had all summer to recover, but only one chance to race and that was tomorrow.

When the doctors left us alone, I told Cliff to find Bill, it was his pickup truck, and get me out of there. Whatever they had to do, do it. The events of that departure seem like a comedy of errors in a light-hearted spy movie when I think back now, but they did it. Two hours later I was back at the lodge.

That was a long and difficult night. Of course, the pain was off the charts. There was no doubt left about how serious this injury was. My knee was hot to the touch and I continually felt sick to my stomach, but eventually even agony becomes just a state of mind. The challenge that evening was mental, with gusts to spiritual.

I have never been demonstratively religious but I am a Christian man. I rely greatly on my relationship with God. I had several long conversations with him that night. I had to understand why this happened and talking to him was how I found my answers. I also needed his guidance, but even with his guiding hand on my shoulder, he couldn't put on my skis and race for me. The challenge of succeeding in this quest was still up to me.

If 90% of blind skiing was mental, I decided the time had come for me to get my mental game face on. It really is a decision. You can take control of your state, regardless of your situation, and be just as happy, positive and confident as you want to be. It is that simple, but that doesn't mean it's easy.

I was never unclear about my purpose. I was there to win, I was there to succeed, not only on the slopes but in the "real" world. Now I had something to prove to myself as well.

I really wanted to win, that is where the juice was for me, to be the best, but more important than the juice was the effort. I knew there would be challenges in my life that I could not overcome, and maybe this was one of them, but the one unbending thing I could never accept, even against these odds, was quitting. If I had learned anything about myself (and trust me, knowing yourself is paramount, more on that later) it was that losing is OK but quitting, giving up, giving any less than everything I had, was not acceptable. It just absolutely wasn't.

So, I spent the night envisioning myself winning. I knew the course, I had physical memory to call upon, so during that long night, when I wasn't lucky enough to be enjoying a few minutes sleep, I watched myself winning this race, over and over and over on the cinematic screens inside my eyelids. I saw my knee performing perfectly, I felt my left leg pushing off when it needed to, again perfectly, I saw myself crossing the finish line and even Cliff and Bob hugging me and jumping up and down in celebration.

When morning finally arrived, I was ready. I won't lie and say I wasn't in pain. Heck, every morning started with pain. We had skied so much and so hard that my body ached every morning. I ached in places I didn't know I had before this began, but this morning was different. It was still agony, but I had reduced it to a dull roar in the background that you could tolerate, if not ignore.

I could tell Cliff was making an effort not to talk about my knee. He helped me with my boots and skis and told me about the conditions without even asking how my knee was, which didn't offend me at all. I knew he wanted to keep me as positive as possible. Still, once I had my skis on, I tested my knee. I almost blacked out the first time I tried to bend it, I had trouble reaching a full crouch the first time, but I was finally able to crouch although I am sure there were tears in my eyes. I pushed the pain to the background again. I was doing this.

The slope was icy and that buoyed my spirits. Icy meant speed and I always liked that, but it also meant the best sound, it would be easy to follow Cliff. Bob Weber knew this too and he had waxed my skis special for the occasion. The stage was set, icy slopes, 10 degrees Fahrenheit and very little breeze. I couldn't ask for more. Now the show was all mine.

I wasn't talking much that morning and everyone respected my silence, until we reached the approach to the chair lift. Then Cliff put his hand on my chest and stopped me. "Do me a favor" he said. "Slide your skis back and forth." We were on a gradual slope that led down to the chairlift. It was icy, just like the hill and Cliff wanted to see how I reacted. Then he asked me to ski down to the lift, not coast on my skis, but get in an actual crouch and "ski" the 50 feet. It hurt but it was also tolerable. I was going to be able to do this. What an amazing boost to my spirits. I never was able to thank Cliff enough, at any time, but this day, he deserved so much.

We didn't say much as the chair ride began. Cliff asked, "How are you doing, buddy?" I quietly mumbled something like, "I'm almost ready," and I was. All of my mental rehearsal, my visualization, my focus was coming to its apex. There is a point in mental preparation that I call the Grey Zone. It's that place where you consciously surrender to your instincts, where you let your sub conscious take over and trust your ability without hesitation. It's:

- what allows Michael Jordan to play better than the rest of the NBA even when suffering from a devastating case of the flu
- what gives Kirk Gibson, despite a pair of knees both probably worse than mine, the capacity to hit his bottom of the ninth game winning home run in the first game of the 1988 World Series
- what makes it possible for Bobby Baun to overcome the pain of an ankle, broken by a Gordie Howe (yes the same one) slap shot in the third period, to score the overtime winner in game six of the 1964 Stanley Cup playoffs
- what would allow me to plunge down that mountain in total darkness without hesitation or pause and take my speed from a cautious 35 mph to a potential 50 or 55mph

I had been there before. I was often in the Grey Zone by the championship match of wrestling tournaments, relying more on instinct and preparation to battle through injuries and exhaustion to win most of my gold medals. It was my ultimate advantage.

It came to me about halfway up the lift. The worry of the moment just left me. At that moment I was ready to totally give in to my inner vision and preparation, ready to go for broke.

Now don't get me wrong. I'm not saying that there is some supernatural, Zen like voodoo mind magic that takes over and if you just show up you win. Not at all. Focus and awareness and concentration were still the key, but the willingness to believe your body to be able to perform whatever was demanded of it, and trust in your subconscious to process all the data that comes in too fast for you to think about was critical. Then it is just damn the torpedoes, full speed ahead.

By the top of the mountain Cliff and I were laughing and joking and totally loose. The tension was gone. We were here and we were going for it.

There were sounds too at the top of the mountain that day. There was a public address announcer, the chatter of other skiers, the murmur of the crowd. I thought "What a wonderful venue for this. This is what it's all about."

I could also hear some of the comments of the competitors. Comments like "Hey, there's MacFarlane. I thought he wasn't supposed to be here." or "He's done, we don't have to worry about him." If I wasn't ready enough, those words put me over the top. Now I had something to prove to more than just myself.

Finally, our turn came. Cliff and I entered the starting gate (well I entered it, Cliff was about 10 feet down the mountain like all other guides). The last variable to our success would come as soon as we heard the starter's pistol. It was imperative that we find our pocket, that spacing, about 4 to 8 feet apart, where our rhythm and communication were at its best.

I don't know why but we were in the pocket almost instantly. Cliff was yelling commands in perfect clarity and the chatter of his skis seemed connected directly to my ears.

My ears were my cameras on the world, in this run more than ever. That was where the winning and losing would be decided and that is where I stayed focused. Every turn was sheer agony, every push had me wanting to drop my head, or vomit, but I wouldn't let it happen. I kept snapping my head higher, again and again, pointing my ears forward, staying focused on Cliff. I refused to go where the pain wanted to take me. After all the endless hours, days and months of training, two minutes of sheer living hell and agony was not going to keep me from my goal. I would have all summer to heal.

It was all working, we were hitting the turns like never before, but then a third of the way down the hill my knee bobbled. That meant I had to straighten up for a second. I slowed just a little but it was enough to lose the pocket. Cliff's voice evaporated. I managed to regain my crouch but by then Cliff was bleeding off speed to get back to me. I raced up and bumped him from behind. (Fortunately we had practiced this hundreds of times, now the preparation paid off again.) We stayed on our feet, I pushed off and were back in the pocket, racing to the bottom of the hill.

It was a minor mishap in the big picture. So many other skiers wiped out completely so finishing the race on our feet was admirable but I was furious with myself. Furious that my body gave out on me, even for an instant. That instant pushed us back to fifth place. Cliff and Bob were ecstatic and it seemed everyone was congratulating us on a great finish. I barely heard any of it. I was so upset. I didn't come here to finish fifth!

Somehow I had to be better in the next run, no bobble, no wobbles, no slips. I needed a perfect run now if I was going to take home the gold.

I barely remember getting into the starting gate again. I was totally in the Grey Zone now. Once again we found the pocket instantly, and from that moment to the bottom of the hill, I was locked onto Cliff's voice, following his skis like freight cars on rails. Cliff's voice was inside my head, guiding me like a heat seeking missile, taking this most intense moment to an even higher level. We sliced down that hill, cutting some gates so close they whacked my shoulder. Jumping headwalls in perfect form. It was like riding the wildest roller coaster, dropping almost in free fall but landing without missing a beat. The exhilaration was off the charts. The sensation of the wind stinging my face keeping me locked in despite our almost unbelievable speed. I didn't feel the pain in my knee at all. I was in total unison with the mountain. If I didn't win I would owe no apologies to anyone, including myself. We left everything up there this time.

I knew I had it by the time I was two-thirds of the way down. I could tell from the chatter of my skis that I had never gone faster in my life yet by that point it almost seemed like a practice run. This fast, furious, some said death-defying race down this huge mountain was now playing in my mind like a dream. We cruised to the finish line, at breakneck speed.

Then we finished in spectacular fashion, almost apropos, and anticlimatic, but appropriate considering the events of this adventure.

I knew we were reaching the finish line when I heard Cliff yelling, "tuck, tuck, tuck!" Cliff crossed the finish line and began to slow down but in all his excitement he forgot to tell me. I crossed the finish line at light speed, ran into Cliff once again but this time did a double-binding release and started sliding backwards down the mountain. Before I could stop I had taken the legs out from under a camerawoman. I actually became her "human toboggan" for a few seconds before we came to rest.

Fortunately, this time, nobody was hurt and we were laughing out loud and joking as we untangled limbs and equipment and regained our feet. I even remember saying "this gives a new meaning to the term "close up."

Cliff was more animated than ever, "Whoa man," he was shouting, "we pushed the envelope this time, and you stayed right with me. That was incredible." I turned to him and said, "well, you know my motto. If you're not living on the edge, you're taking up too much space!"

Then I heard my time. I was still shaking the snow out of my hair and thought it must be in my ears as well. Could that be right? They were saying I had skied 11 seconds faster than the leader of the race. We were still marveling in disbelief when this guy came running over to me and said, "Hey, I run the speed gun. I was on the steepest part of the course, and when you came through the gun you were in excess of 50 miles per hour."

We didn't know exactly what that meant. No official speed records are kept by the United States Association for Blind Skiing.

It really didn't matter to me at that moment. With God's hand on my shoulder, I had gone more than 50 miles per hour, lived to

talk about it, and won the competition. With a quick, and well deserved prayer of thanks, I had all I needed to know. I did it!

All of the usual pomp and circumstance of a national championship took place right there at the bottom of the mountain. I was a
very different man in that moment than I had been at the beginning
of the day. I wasn't hobbling or leaning on Cliff for support. I was
no doubt riding the residual effects of the adrenaline overdose, like
a double espresso with extra sugar. I was still energized, standing tall
and loving it all. They pulled out the podiums, called our names on
the loud speaker, and placed the medals over our heads while the
media swarmed, taking pictures and asking questions. I have always
regretted that Cliff did not receive a medal too, but there were no
awards for guide skiers. Cliff deserved a medal that day, even more
than me.

By the time the ceremonies were over we began to realize that
we were famished, starving. We had eaten very little, since the night
before when you think about it. We had been so consumed coping
with the injury. The trip to Salt Lake City, bouncing around in the
back of that truck in the cold, being examined, and X-rayed, and
escaping the hospital and a night of sheer agony had kept our minds
off eating. Now, it was all we wanted and we headed back to the
lodge to clean up and chow down.

That is when my adrenaline pump turned off. It was as if all
my energy just left me as I passed through the door into my room.
I wanted to drop to the floor, and I did slump back against the wall.
The agony of my knee was returning and, for a moment, I didn't
want to test it any more, not even to take a shower. I did eventually
pull myself together, took a quick shower, and hobbled to the restaurant for a very late lunch.

Cliff and Bob were still pumped and their energy brought my
spirits back quickly. I spent most of that meal thanking Cliff. I was
sorry that he had not been recognized with me and I wanted him
to know how much credit he deserved, how important he was to
this victory, and how important he had become to me. Humble as
he was, he shrugged everything off saying "my reward, and yours
really comes tonight, when they announce the national team for

Switzerland. We're going to Switzerland, buddy, how much more could I ask for?" Indeed.

Tonight meant the awards banquet. As banquets go, it was pleasant enough. We ate, they made a few speeches, gave out a few awards and then, suddenly it seemed, they were announcing the members of the national team.

I honestly do not remember the names of the team members announced that evening. All I know is that I wasn't one of them!

Cliff, totally incensed, jumped from his seat and ran over the organizers. I could hear his voice rising in volume with every word as he all but screamed, "What the h... is going on here?" I loved that guy, he still had my back, even now.

The reason they gave was lame, politically spin doctored propaganda, offered to cover up that membership on the national team was earned not on merit but, as so often happens in life, determined by who you knew and how much influence they could wield.

It turned out that the selection committee included a couple of guide skiers for other competitors and the rest comprised a close knit old boy's network. Membership on the national team had been predetermined, even before the races had been run. My acceptance into the blind skiing fraternity had essentially begun and ended during the medal ceremonies at the bottom of the mountain.

I lost a great deal that evening. Not only did I lose a chance to ski for my country at the world championships, something I would have died to do, and almost did trying, but I completely lost my zeal and enthusiasm for competitive skiing. I suppose you could say that the selection committee did to me what my injured knee and the mountain were unable to do.

They whipped me. I could have returned the following year and earned my place on the National Team. I could have continued to improve until my place on the team was undeniable, but they had totally broken my resolve. I did everything in my power to win this National Championship. I was clearly head and shoulders above all my competition, the best skier on the mountain that day. I still believe I deserved a place on the National team. I have no doubt that I could have earned that place for years to come. On merit, I was the best blind downhill skier in America, but in reality, I wasn't even considered good enough to represent my country at the World Championships. The selection committee chose an entire team that they evidently considered better than me. This just served to show me that there are battles I can't win, regardless of what I accomplish.

In my mind, it was a matter of principle. I didn't want to play political games. If I couldn't earn it on merit, I didn't want it. I never snow skied competitively again.

Happiness is a Choice

The successes of my life have all been the result of the choices I have made. I'm not referring to choices like becoming a wrestler or a skier or an inspirational keynote speaker. I'm talking about much more important decisions, like the decision to work hard and the decision to live my life enthusiastically, like the decision to be proud and independent, like the decision to be self-reliant.

The most important decision I have made, and continue to make every day, is to be happy. Yes, being happy is a choice. Don't get me wrong. I am a realist. I'm not here to give you the goody, goody Pollyanna message that you can just smile and act like everything is great in your world all the time. That is a very false happiness.

No, happiness, once again, is about knowing yourself and making the conscious decision that you are going to cultivate and maintain a happy attitude in your life, regardless of the circumstances, conditions or people you are dealing with. I believe we all have more good times than bad, more happiness than sadness, but there will be times when you have to deal with unpleasant, frustrating, aggravating realities. Control your state and deal with them from an attitude of happiness. It will be easier and the return to pleasant times will be effortless.

Happiness is, in my opinion and experience, the very essence of who you are. It is nourishment that is critical to your soul, critical to your psyche and your spirit. Without it, not only will you never truly appreciate the good times and good things in your life but you will never be able to sustain yourself through the challenging moments and harsh experiences, and they will happen.

So why not take charge of your happy attitude. Happiness, your happiness, is completely under your control. Just be aware that it takes some work, especially in the beginning. Like with so many other factors in your life, a successful decision to live happy is dependent on a true understanding of yourself. You have to learn what triggers happiness in you. You have to learn what behaviors you demonstrate when you're happy and what messages you are listening to in your own head.

You also have to develop the discipline to take charge of this knowledge and create these circumstances within yourself and take the actions necessary to sustain them.

Think about a time when you were truly happy, a year, a day, an evening, an event that brought that feeling. Spend a few minutes now in that memory. Visualize it, really feel it.

What made it that way? What triggered the emotion at that moment? Were you doubtful or optimistic? Were you in action or sitting passively? How did you behave? How did you stand? What was your posture? What expression was on your face? How did you talk to yourself? How did you move? What were you saying to yourself? What were you thinking about?

Why don't you choose to do those things that way all the time? Why don't you decide to stand that way right now? Why not adopt that posture as a matter of course? Why not make that expression the permanent look you present to the world?

Don't worry, be happy.

You can choose to do that!

The next time you feel your mood slipping, be aware of it. Stop. Take stock of your posture, your stance, your facial expression. Get up, or at least move, make a change in the moment. Take charge.

When something negative happens to you, don't let it ruin

your day. That's a perfect time to take charge. We all have challenging moments, bad times, but we don't ever need to have bad days. Learn how to put yourself back on track and make everyday a good one. Remember, it's not what happens to you, it is how you deal with it that matters.

If you know the circumstances that are present when you are happy, you can bring them about instantly, at any time:

- If you are slouching, pull your shoulders back and stand or sit up straight.
- If you are frowning, then smile. (Even an insincere smile will make you feel happier than a sincere frown.)
- If you are looking at your feet, lift your eyes.
- If you feel tired, get in motion.
- If you are sitting passively, get up and move, do something.
- Are you putting something off, then go do it. (Interestingly, most people are happier actually doing a task, even an unpleasant one, than when they are avoiding it.)

My point is, once you know the circumstances, your circumstances, in your mind and your body, that are present when you are happy, you can create them, and recreate them at a second's notice. Eventually, it will become a habit to demonstrate these circumstances, this behavior, this physiology as a matter of course and the resulting happiness will become an ever-present attitude that you present all the time.

Insanity is so often defined as "doing the same thing over and over while expecting different results." That time tested definition applies here more than anywhere. I listen to my friends, colleagues, clients, continually complain about how miserable they are while they continue to deal with their circumstances in the same way, over and over. Six months may go by but they will still be unhappy about the same things. They perpetuate it and that is such a waste of life. If you are constantly unhappy, make a CHANGE.

Your happiness does not need to be an illusion, you have the power to make it your reality. The choice to be happy. The decision to sustain that attitude, regardless of the circumstances of your moment. This will make dealing with problems and difficult people easier and less stressful. It will also make the good times more enjoyable and special people and relationships positively awesome and inspiring. It will make your career more rewarding, your friendships more gratifying and your family life more satisfying and worthwhile.

I like being happy and choose to live my life that way. If I can, I know you can.

Why don't you start now?

Darkness

I wasn't exceptional when I was born. I came into the world with two arms, two legs, one mouth (which my mother says has been in motion since that day), one nose, two ears and two working eyes. I was the third healthy child born to Joyce and Earl MacFarlane. Despite all three of us being born healthy, in our early years my mother and father endured heartache no parents should have to go through.

My older sister, Bonnie, who I never met, had died when she was only 8 1/2 months old after being diagnosed with a rare form of tracheitis, a disease that caused the throat to swell completely shut. Ian, my older brother, had also given my parents a scare before I was born with a severe bout of intussusceptions, where the small intestine telescopes inside the large intestine and creates a complete blockage. The nurses at the local hospital had actually tried to send Ian home, claiming he wasn't that sick. My mom remembers telling them at the time: "I only had one other child and she died in this hospital. I don't intend to lose this one." She insisted they take another look which may have saved Ian's life.

As for me, I enjoyed a normal, happy childhood for two years, four months and 1 day in this world, all of 853 days. At least I'm told it was normal. I honestly remember almost nothing of that time in my life, certainly no visual images, not even my mother's, or father's, or brother's face.

Most of us do not have exceptionally clear memories from those early days of our lives. That's just normal, but for me, the chance to see the world, to see my family, to create that visual memory bank most of you rely on came to an end on Saturday, October 17th, 1964.

I remember very little about that day, as traumatic as it was, but I know every detail because my mother remembers it with vivid clarity. This is how she has told the story to me.

Mom and I were in the house where she was giving me a bite to eat, after which she cleaned me up, then took me outside to play with Ian. She left me for a minute, playing with Ian, who was four at the time, and his friends. Mom was extremely watchful of me, who could blame her? She only intended to hurry inside to get her cup of tea and she'd be back to keep an eye on all of us. She had told herself, "It's a nice day, he's with his older brother and the other kids, he'll be okay for a minute or two."

While she was in the house, one of Ian's friends reached up on my dad's peg board on the shed wall where he kept many of his tools

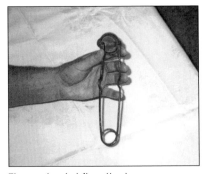

and grabbed a striker. A striker is a metal gadget that apparently looks something like a nut cracker with both ends closed off, but with a flint on it. When you squeeze it together it makes a spark. Dad used it for lighting welding torches and things like that. When you see the picture of it, you'll have to agree that it looks essentially harmless. Oh, and the spark function had nothing to do with my injury. It had an opening at one end, so you

The actual striker that caused my blindness!

could hang it up, but Ian's friend had his finger through that and was twirling it around. We've all done that. I do it with my keys sometimes when I'm bored and waiting to lock the house. It seems like a harmless, playful thing except this time the striker flew off Ian's friend's finger, directly at me. Before anybody knew what had happened, it struck me, directly in the center of my left eye.

I don't remember it hitting my eye, but I do remember screaming in pain, and then bumping my head on the door as I ran to the house. I remember Mom picking me up and trying to comfort me, but not much after that.

Mom had been talking to a neighbor, but, as she recalls, she suddenly wasn't listening any more. All she could see was a tiny, V-shaped cut in the center of my eye. What alarmed her more was that there was also fluid running down my cheek, not tears but just a clear fluid, and it had a tiny bit of blood in it.

Mom knew I needed immediate medical attention. She needed to get me to the hospital but my dad was away that weekend. He was moose hunting, as so many men from my home town of Desbarats did that time of year. He would be at least 85 miles away, by her estimate, up the Chapleau Highway. He had our car and he wouldn't be easy to find. My dad was a true outdoorsman and would be sleeping in a tent that night.

Then Mom remembered my dad's cousin, Clifford Phillips. He hadn't gone moose hunting with the other men, and he had a new truck. She called him. He was in the barn, milking the cows, but when Mom called he jumped right in his truck and raced over to get us.

Clifford wasted no time and the three of us took off for the nearest hospital, in Sault Ste. Marie, about thirty-two miles to the west of Desbarats. Mom says I didn't cry much on that ride, I just kind of whimpered as I lay in her arms as she held a cloth over my eye. Even at that point Mom tells me that she had a sense, deep down inside, that this was serious, very serious.

At Plummer Memorial Hospital in Sault Ste. Marie (we actually call it the Soo, everyone does), our family doctor examined my eye but said not much could be done at that facility. The ophthalmologist on staff at that hospital, the only eye specialist in the Soo as a matter of fact, was away at a medical convention and wouldn't be back for a couple days. When we look back now, we have come to regret just how unfortunate this bad timing turned out to be.

The best they were able to do that night was sedate me, and put some drops in my eye, maybe to numb it, we don't know. I am, when I hear Mom tell this story, glad I have no memories of it, because it must have been horrible. I know it was for her. They put me in a crib, and after giving me the medicine, they tied my hands to my sides so I would not be grabbing at or rubbing my eye. That must have been a torturous night, for both of us.

Mom claims she felt herself slipping in the direction of self pity a bit that evening. She was hurt and trying to understand why this was happening to me. Like I said, she had already known tragedy and she had been so watchful of me, while often seeing other parents who weren't caring for their kids half as well. Why was this happening?

I can't blame my mom for feeling like that, who could? Even so, my mother was, and still is, a resourceful woman. She didn't just sit idly by. She got on the phone and contacted a hospital in Sault Ste. Marie, Michigan. The doctor there didn't want to touch my case because he hadn't seen enough like it. Then she called the hospital in Sudbury, Ontario. Sudbury was a city about twice the size of the Soo, 180 miles to the east. There she found an eye specialist who would see me the next day.

While Mom was busy searching for a doctor to help me, good fortune did smile down on us in a small way. A family friend, Arthur Maitland, had driven up the Chapleau Highway hoping somehow to get a message to my dad. This would usually have been all but impossible but, for some reason, uncharacteristically, Dad had told a clerk at a general store where he was camped. Arthur, checking everywhere he could, visited that store and was able to find Dad. They raced back, down a treacherous river road to the hospital, arriving about five o'clock Sunday morning. Mom says they started praying for my sight that very night.

We spent the next three weeks in Sudbury. My eye was apparently getting better and I could still see with my other eye. Mom says that the time in Sudbury was encouraging and that I didn't suffer too much. In fact, the way she put it was, "Craig's natural live-wire personality was in full effect. He would chatter with anyone and everyone. Nurses would comment on how well he could talk in complete sentences and how he could already count." I guess I was making the best of it, even then.

The improving trend did not continue when we got home from Sudbury. I took a turn for the worse. It wasn't just my eye either. I was becoming irritable, cross, angry, lashing out, which Mom said wasn't my normal way at all. At the same time, the white of my eye started turning pink and I developed a head cold. A head cold in November in the wintery conditions of northern Ontario is nothing special, everybody gets one over the winter. Unfortunately, the symptoms of my cold fooled the doctors. They prescribed eye ointment and drops and said the redness was due to the cold.

Ten days later, my cold, like all colds (isn't that what they always say on the medicine bottles - take three times a day, drink plenty of fluids and rest for seven to 10 days), was gone, but my eye was getting worse.

By now Mom was seriously afraid that I was losing my sight. I was bumping into doors and walking into furniture. It was back to the Soo, with my mom's hopes fading with each passing hour, the fright growing.

What happened next must have matched, or exceeded the horror of my first night in the Soo. The ophthalmologist in Sault Ste. Marie, Dr. Shamess - the one who was at the convention on my first visit - put me in a sheet and then rolled me over and over until I was bound up completely, unable to move my arms or my legs. Then he pried my red eye open. He shone bright lights into my eye so he could examine it. Maybe if this had happened that first night, I'd be telling a different story. Mom says, "Craig screamed and screamed and those screams are indelibly etched in my mind!" A mother's pain, like I still can't imagine.

This time we got a diagnosis. Sympathetic Ophthalmia. That's a very rare and complex condition where one eye is injured and the trauma from that injury travels to the other eye. It works like an inflammation eating away at the back of the eye and doesn't quit until this part is destroyed. Simply put, it is where the good eye goes in sympathy with the badly injured one. In short, doctors offered little hope I would ever see again.

I mentioned above that we would come to regret the timing of my injury. This is where that came home to roost. The most unfortunate, or regrettable, thing about my condition is that when diagnosed right away, the injured eye can be removed and the other eye saved. Needless to say, my diagnosis didn't come in time.

Sympathetic Ophthalmia is so rare that few ophthalmologists ever see a case of it. We were advised to see Dr. Jack Crawford at Sick Children's Hospital in Toronto. Dr. Crawford, who was the premier ophthalmologist in Canada at the time, confirmed the diagnosis.

I stayed at "Sick Kid's" for four months, right through the winter of 1964, into 1965. I underwent an experimental treatment that

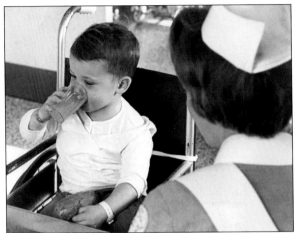

involved massive doses of Prednisone. Even the doctors admitted they were going out on a limb. They had never given a child such large amounts. This was done, in part, to control the pressure and potential hemorrhaging at the back of my eyes. Essentially, they were trying to protect my brain.

At my first "home away from home."

"I felt so terrible," as Mom tells it. "Here was this tiny little guy, my baby, so small, so helpless, lying there. We had no idea whether what they were trying would work."

Prednisone wasn't the only experimental treatment the doctors tried with me. At one point, for reasons that were never explained to me, it was determined that I should not be allowed to eat salt in any form for an extended period, several weeks at least. That didn't mean anything to me at that age except that I would be denied my most favorite passion, potato chips. This concerned my mother as she really didn't know how she was going to explain to me, or console me, that a favorite treat was being taken away, especially with all the other perceived hardships that we were dealing with. This hardship, fortunately, miraculously in fact, never came to pass. Somehow, word of this injured little boy being denied his favorite food, while battling blindness during an extended stay at "Sick Kids," reached an executive at Hostess Potato Chips. The story must have moved them because days later a huge box, at least four feet square, arrived for me at the hospital. Hostess had made a special production run of unsalted chips and sent them all to me. Mom was ecstatic, and so grateful. Apparently I was too. She often reminds me how I ate everyone of those chips and enjoyed them all. I am sure exceptional stories of corporate kindness like this still happen today. I only wish the media could give more time to such positive events.

Despite the expense and the hardship, my parents made the 400-mile trip to Toronto nineteen times in that first year after my injury. They would bring me home and administer the medicine but at the first sign of pinkness in my eye, they would rush me back.

My parents began selling things to cover the expenses while sliding deeper into debt. They even had to sell our home and rent a small house in Desbarats. Eventually, we would build a home of our own, several years later, but the sacrifices my parents made were considerable, yet they never hesitated, ever.

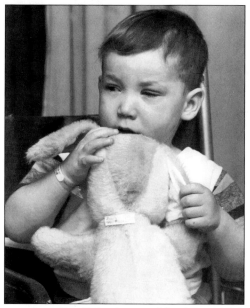

There were at least a few smiles along the way. Mom remembers how Dr. Crawford would spend so much time just playing with me and how Mrs. Hibbins, the ninth floor desk clerk became almost a second mother to me. I had the freedom to wander that ninth floor, but, being a highly social creature even then, would, occasionally, just get on the elevator, talking to new friends or families

Even the Eater Bunny visited me at the hospital.

I had met. I had become so known to the staff by then that nobody panicked, they just brought me back to the ninth floor. (Can you imagine the chaos that would happen if a little, visually impaired - boy wandered off his floor these days?)

The smiles helped everyone cope, but the day my mother dreaded did eventually come. We were back in Desbarats, out for a family walk, making our way back to our house along the gravel edge of the road. I walked right past our driveway.

"Craig, couldn't you see our house?" Mom asked.

"No Mom," was all I said.

It was official. I was totally blind.

Later that evening, when I was fast asleep, Mom and Dad sat together, consoling each other, trying to come to grips with what lay ahead for our family and, in particular, for me. They had so many fears, so many questions:

- How would Craig learn?
- How will we teach him?
- What will we teach him?
- Will he ever graduate high school?
- Will he be able to go to college?
- Will he ever get a decent job? Could he carve out a career?
- Will he ever get married? Ever have a family?

They talked about my future and prayed for me late into that evening, and on many others, so I'm told. It was in those moments that they slowly put their fears to rest as they asked for guidance in their prayers.

"It would all be in God's hands."

6
It's Not What Happens to You

Over the years, I've found that the happy and successful people in our world have some significant traits in common. One of the most significant is that they consistently take action, whether it is in pursuit of a goal, or dealing with a consequence. They don't wait to see what will happen to them. They take charge of their world.

I do want to make a point here. When I say happy and successful people, I don't just mean the super wealthy or famous. I've had the privilege of working with many people who fit that description but much more, most in fact, of my life has been spent around the proverbial common man, that man or woman who works for a living, who is raising a family, who is paying bills and saving for retirement and struggling, as I have, to carve out a little bit of happiness in this harsh world we live in.

The one most consistent trait I see in these people I consider happy is that they take control of their destiny. They are people of action, people with a plan. They are making their own decisions and following through with the actions those decisions require. They are not standing idly by and letting circumstance dictate the condition of their life. No, quite the opposite. They are choosing the actions that dictate their circumstances and result in a life that they can be proud of and enjoy. Of course, if you don't choose to take action, you have no one to blame but yourself.

That's the other thing that sets happy people apart. They take pride in their lives and make an effort to enjoy themselves every day. That doesn't mean that their worlds are perfect. Far from it.

It doesn't mean that they don't have big goals or ambitions. Many of them have far bigger plans than their unhappy colleagues. It doesn't mean they never suffer or feel heartache or anguish or worry. Every one of us faces those challenges every day.

What they are doing is taking action, every day, to advance closer to those goals, dreams and ambitions. They are also reacting to and dealing with their worries and stress and challenges. They are doing what has to be done, when it should be done, as it should be done without putting things off or feeling sorry for themselves. In fact, most of the time they have dealt with their problems and moved on to more pleasant tasks and circumstances while their unhappy friends are still wallowing in despair and worrying about "What is happening?" or worse, "What is going to happen next?"

That is, in fact, where the trait of action truly, with all due apologies to the many strong and competent women I have had the pleasure to meet, separates the "men from the boys."

Let's face it, life is about dealing with problems and for some of us the occasional catastrophe. No matter how much you have in this world, you can be confident that you will still have problems. I have often said, if you want to be more successful, you need a better class of problems but what is even more important to understand is this. Bad things, stressful things, demanding things happen to all of us all the time. The differentiator between a happy life and a sad life is not what happens to you, it's what you do about it. More to the point, be proactive, not reactive. It will give you control over your life and even your problems.

Do something, anything. Honestly, any action is better than no action. If you do nothing it will get worse and happiness will seem more impossible than ever.

My parents were a tremendous example of this behavior. Their lives provide me the best example of how the trait of action brought happiness despite extremely modest circumstances, with a tragedy, several actually, thrown in for variety.

I had a tremendously happy childhood but if you were to stand on the outside looking in at our life as a family while I was growing up you may well have felt sorry for us. Not only did my parents have to deal with my injury and me losing my sight, they had to deal with the consequences of the consequence. Then they had to deal with the day to day reality and the financial challenges in addition to the challenges I represented (as I said, the consequences of the consequence.)

It wasn't easy but it would have been far more difficult if they were not people of action, who figured out how to make the most of the hand they had been dealt, and then took the action to make the "most" reality.

Consider these examples:

Money - The economy, if you can call it that, in Desbarats was never great. Mom had a steady job but the income was modest. Teachers were not revered and rewarded in those days as they are, and deserve to be, now. Dad worked at Algoma Central Railway and as a carpenter when there was work available. What set my parents apart was that they did not sit around and wring their hands when things were tight or work was slow. Dad would hunt, and literally feed us with his catch some days. He would trap, as was common practice at that time, and sell the pelts to supplement the household income. Mom gardened, not to raise pretty flowers but to raise vegetables and fruit that she preserved so that we always ate well, even on cold dark days in February. They took action. Sometimes it was easy, sometimes it was hard, sometimes it was even unpleasant, but the benefits far outweighed any hardship, and we were happy.

Our home - My injury and the resulting cost of the treatment and travel took a huge toll on our family finances. The toll was so great that we did have to give up our family home and move to a small, very modest rental for a period of time. It was so modest that we had to deal with an outhouse because we had no inside toilet. My parents, and I respect them so much for this, recognized this could be a possible consequence of dealing with my needs and took action early to make the move tolerable and comfortable. They didn't wait for the expense of the medical costs to eat them alive. They took action, tough action, when it was necessary, and we were happy.

They also didn't settle. They may have accepted that modest little house when it was necessary, but they made a plan to work towards building a home of our own and, through action and discipline, made that happen too, sooner than later. When that came to fruition we were very happy.

My Childhood – Raising a handicapped child is never easy. I grew up as one and I give thanks to God everyday that my children are strong, healthy and "normal." My parents could have so easily thrown up their hands saying "Woe is me, what will we do, somebody help us," and let me get lost in the system, sitting on the sideline, as happens to so many handicapped children. The state, or the church, would wind up providing the care because the parents were so overwhelmed by "what happened to them" that they couldn't do anything about it." Fortunately, that was not my parents' style. As you'll read in the next chapter, they made a conscious decision to raise a normal, active, involved child. They included me in everything, regardless of the sacrifice it took or the grief I caused them, intentionally or otherwise. They believed it was the best way to give me a realistic shot at a happy life. They stuck to their decision and I am so glad they did. I have been able to lead and live a normal life. My life has been very happy, decently successful and I credit it all to their decision. They admit they didn't know how to raise a blind kid so they simply just raised a kid.

Those are just a few examples. Humble ones at that. My parents didn't change the way people live their lives, or make huge sums of money. They didn't seek fame or glory, or even credit. They just decided on the action necessary, with positive expectation, and then followed through. It was a simple formula that brought us a happy life.

If you have challenges in your life today, if you have dreams, desires, frustrations, heartaches or worries that you feel are denying you the happiness you want and deserve, I assure you that there are actions you can take that will move you progressively in the direction of that happiness you seek, and make the journey an enjoyable one as well.

Whether or not you take the action you know you should is your choice, but I assure you, if you do, the benefits will far outweigh the price you pay.

It's time to do something, now!

7

We Just Raised a Kid

I was blessed in many ways, starting with my parents, Joyce and Earl MacFarlane. As a couple they have incredible strength and character.

They were married in October of 1950, and as of the writing of this book, some sixty-three years later, are still going strong. Of the two, my greatest blessing was no doubt my mom. Dad was great but my mother was a teacher. I don't mean by nature, but by profession. She was trained in how kids learned. She also understood the issue of survival, especially in northern Ontario.

Desbarats, Ontario was, and still is, a small dot of a town in a rugged landscape of dense forests and granite-encrusted wilderness. A small blip on the Trans-Canada Highway. If I described it as an infinitesimal dot on the 100 degree windswept plains of Texas you would begin to get the idea, but that would not do Desbarats justice. Ontario is roughly twice the size of Texas(imagine the isolation and distance we coped with) and my tiny home town of 400 people not only experienced 80 degree plus summer days with black flies big enough to carry off small pets, but it also endured temperatures below zero Fahrenheit for as many as 57 days in a row in winter, with more than 200 inches of accumulated snowfall in an average year, at least in the 1960's. That is what we had to contend with when I was growing up. It is rugged country and produces tough, rugged, self-reliant people.

My mother understood that I needed to be one of those people, especially because she had to assume that was where I would live my life.

In Mom's words, "You had to be tough to live up here. I don't think of it as backward. When I see books written about how "remote" it is, I don't really think of it as remote. When I think of that, I think of a good 14 hour drive from here to the Manitoba border. James Bay. That's what I consider remote." (Are you getting a sense of how vast the region is?)

Remember too, this was 1964. Even in the socialistic democracy known as Canada, in 1964 there were no public health nurses dropping in three times a week. There were no government funded community youth centers offering special programs and "youth socialization." There were no social workers being assigned to guide parents in the tips, tricks and techniques of raising any handicapped child, let alone a totally blind one. There were no handbooks on how to raise a blind kid or radio talk shows full of advice or blogs or podcasts or even the internet. In fact, the nearest school for the blind was almost 500 miles away and I wouldn't qualify to go there until I was 6.

Ian and I, Grandma Jefferies, Grandpa Jefferies and our dog Blondie.

Facing this reality, my parents made one very simple, conscious decision about my future. It is, I am certain, the single most significant factor in the success of my life. Mom put it this way, "We didn't know how to raise a blind kid so we decided that we would just raise a kid."

Simple, sure. Brilliant, absolutely!

As much intuitive as it was rational this decision meant one thing to my parents. I was included in absolutely everything we did as a family. There may have been an extra watchful eye around whenever possible, but I cannot remember ever hearing the word "can't" spoken by my mom or dad. Wherever we went, whatever any of us were doing, I was included, certainly never excluded. I also had the freedom to explore and experiment. I was a kid, not a blind kid, and I lived that way.

When I say everything, I do mean EVERYTHING! Sometimes, an activity was modified slightly for my benefit, like Dad talking to me along the trap line so I could follow his voice when he might have just let Ian follow on sight, but it was rarely more than that. I learned by touch and experience, failure and success. Let me share a few of those stories:

Hunting: Hunting and trapping were not recreational activities to our family. They were part of the fabric of our lives, essential to our survival. Trapping may not be politically correct in some circles today but growing up in rural Canada in the early 1960's it was a natural part of life. It put food on our table, literally and figuratively, and provided sources of income that helped my dad provide for us.

It was a great part my childhood; very instructive, very much an example of how my life would work. Everything was hands-on and it was physically challenging too. I would get down and feel the traps, before they were set of course. Often Dad let me feel the otter or muskrat or mink or beaver while they were still in the trap. I would feel their muscles, faces, fur and tails, learning to tell one from the other.

Of course, trapping meant being out in the bush, following the trapline, often in snowshoes. I would follow Dad through the woods by listening to his voice and to the cracking of branches and the crunch of the snow underfoot. We would stop and Dad would have me feel the bark on the trees, the rough bark of the oak and maple trees, and the smooth bark of the poplar. I would feel the pine needles and the cedar trees. I learned where to set traps and what kind of animals we were likely to catch by knowing their behaviors and patterns. We would be out in the bush all day together. I got to know my dad really well on those days and by the time we came home we would be totally exhausted. I loved it.

One time Dad fell through the ice. We were making our way along the edge of Desbarats Lake, where the water was only two or three feet deep. Dad was checking the traps we had set along the shore. All of a sudden I heard a loud "CRRRR-ACK!"

I remember calling out, "Where you going Dad?"

"I guess to the bottom of the lake," was his reply.

Thankfully the water was shallow. When you trap, you are going to fall, you're going to get wet and it is going to be cold. We were often out there in temperatures of ten degrees below zero, or colder. You just knew this. Dad never complained, so neither did I.

We would hunt as well as trap. I mentioned that Dad went moose hunting farther north in the fall. Closer to home we would hunt partridge and deer. I used to love this, especially because on a quiet day I could often hear a deer coming before Dad would see it. He didn't believe the first few times I would whisper to him, "Dad, I hear one coming. It's that way." After I was right a couple times, Dad would always check out my tips.

The other thing I used to love was shooting the rifle. Dad never actually let me hold the gun, too much risk of accidents for that, but often he would aim his rifle and ask me if I wanted to pull the trigger. That was such a rush.

Fishing: As early as age five, I would fish with Dad off Desbarats Dock into Desbarats River. Dad showed me how to put the worm on the hook and how to cast. I felt the fish when we got 'em in. Dad usually took the fish off the hook, but sometimes I did. Again, the whole thing was very hands on.

House building: We built our own house. I was seven at the time. I hammered and nailed alongside the older men. In fact, my mother remembers seeing me up on the roof helping put down shingles. Yes, there were several watchful sets of eyes around, but I was still in the middle of the action.

Baking: I used to bake pies. I got so good at it and enjoyed it so much that I had my own special pie plate. Mom and I used to bake every Saturday morning and it was wonderful way to spend time together. Mom had a way of making me feel special, like this was my special time to bake, but of course she was also busy. It seems she always had a special project going on Saturday morning whether it was making jam or pickles, or whatever, and of course, she would bake pies, too.

For my part, I loved making epic pies. I would stuff my pies full to the limit with raspberries, blueberries (my personal favorite), raisins and whatever other fruit Mom had. It seems my pie was always the one to boil over because it was so loaded. I didn't care what the mixture was either. I always ate every bite. It was such fun and I looked forward to that time with my mom so much that I would never risk disappointing her by wasting even a single berry. I think Mom still has my pie plate, too. I think it is safe to say we both treasured Saturday morning back then and still treasure the memories now.

Making Maple Syrup: Mom was not the only one who participated in my contributing to our family's culinary experience. Dad loved to involve me every spring when we made maple syrup. I was involved in every step, from tapping the maple trees, to inserting the spiles and hanging the cans. Then there was the daily ritual of going tree to tree and collecting the sap. Sometimes I'd sneak a taste straight from the can. The sap was so sweet. There is nothing better than a fresh drink from a maple tree.

Dad would boil the sap in huge kettles over an open fire. It takes approximately forty gallons of sap to make one gallon of syrup. That's a lot of boiling. Throughout the day I would continually be carrying armfuls of wood to keep the fires stoked and blazing hot enough to boil the sap. Some years, when the spring thaw was a little late, just finding enough wood could become my biggest challenge because there was still three feet of snow on the ground in some places. On the final batch of syrup, Dad would often continue boiling until he produced maple sugar candy. Now that was awesome. Is there anything more delicious than a stack of pancakes drenched in homemade maple syrup?

Gardening: I helped my mom plant the garden too. Corn, beans, peas, radishes, onions and carrots. Mom would let me feel all the vegetables as they grew, in all their stages. What a great education. She taught me how to tell the difference between raspberries, blueberries and strawberries, how to tell when they were ripe and just ready for baking. I used to love to pick wild blueberries up on the rocks and bluff behind our house.

I helped pick the green and yellow beans and peas. I helped dig the carrots and pull the onions. I loved to pull a carrot right out of the garden, break the top off, wipe the dirt off a little bit and start chowing down. I never washed it. Now that's a real carrot. Yes, you might get the odd grain of sand and dirt, but the freshness made up for it. It was the same thing shelling the peas and eating them right in the garden. That was delicious.

One day I picked a green apple off the tree and started eating. I had it about three quarters gone when Ian looked over and said, "Craig, there's a worm crawling out of that!" God only knows how many worms I'd eaten to that point. I was always eating apples right off the tree.

Gathering eggs: Life at home was always busy with continuous tasks and chores to be attended to. Our home was actually a small farm, not so much a commercial operation but still a real farm. Mom's garden wasn't a postage size hobby garden but a large working garden that produced enough to feed us all year long. By the same token, our barn wasn't just an oversized tool shed. It was a full, two story working barn. Yes we had a shed and the tools, the snowmobile, Ian's dirt bike, Dad's hunting gear and the rest of our mechanized stuff was in there, but the barn was also full of animals and hay. There were the horses but we also raised rabbits and pigs and, of course, chickens. One of my chores became gathering the eggs from the chicken's nests every day. I thought this would be a really cool job when Mom first asked me to do it. That was before getting my hand pecked all the time by hens who didn't like me reaching in to snatch their eggs from underneath them. I didn't give up my chore, I hated quitting on anything, but I did have to develop my own techniques to do my job without coming back empty handed in need of a bandage or two. Eventually, I started carrying a small stick with me. I would gently feel around each nest with my stick and once the coast was clear, reach in and make my collection. I looked forward to this daily task. Sometimes the eggs were freshly laid and would still be warm. Doing that chore was another way I felt like I was part of the family and doing my share. It also left me with a nice sense of independence.

In addition to the rabbits in the barn, there was one more that we had a sort of special connection to. Fluffy, which is what I called him, didn't live in the barn. He was a wild rabbit who we only saw on really cold days in the winter time. He used to scratch at the back door of the house and one time, feeling sorry for him, Mom let him in. That started a routine that lasted a couple of winters. Fluffy would come for a visit, Mom would let him in, he would hop over to the treadle on Mom's sewing machine and sit over the heat vent for a while. I would pet him and maybe feed him a carrot or some lettuce and when he was warm, he would hop back to the door and we'd let him out.

I don't know what happened to him. He just stopped coming around after a while, but I always thought he was a cool visitor.

I was never shy around animals, ever. My parents wouldn't let me be. I was hands on with all our animals, of course, and Dad made everything about hunting and trapping hands on too, but it didn't end there. I remember sitting in my own backyard and feeding peanuts to the squirrels and chipmunks that lived all around our property. I don't mean tossing the peanuts out in the yard and letting the squirrels come and collect either. I mean holding the peanuts in my hand and the squirrels taking their treats directly out of my palm. Once they trust you that much, there is a gentleness in their touch that you have to experience to understand.

Baling hay: One day I was loading the hay wagon with Ian. Ian tossed a bale and clocked me right in the side of the head, knocking me off the hay wagon. I didn't really care. The job still was fun and made me believe I was capable of contributing to the family.

Baling hay was tough work but we loved it. In those days hay was baled in squares, not the huge round bales you see in fields today. We used to have to collect those square bales from the field and then put them in the hay mow, which was on the second floor of the barn. Two of us would work on the trailer, unloading the bales onto the elevator, a conveyer belt really, that took the bales to the mow. Up in the mow, somebody would be taking the bales and stacking them up to the rafters.

One time, Ian and I were unloading the last few bales from the trailer. I was usually up in the mow. When we were finished I was up near the roof inside, arranging the last few bales. I heard Ian yell that he was going to start putting things away and to meet him downstairs. No problem, I climbed down off the bales and walked back toward the elevator, as always. The elevator pushed inside a few feet and I would walk until I bumped it, turn left and come down the ladder. Problem that day was that Ian put the elevator away first. I didn't bump it, I simply walked straight out the open door, on the second floor. I fell about twelve feet, which is a shock when you don't expect it.

Thankfully Ian wasn't too efficient cleaning up. There were still several broken bales on the ground under the hay mow door. Without those, that could have been a painful trip.

Swimming: Mom got me into swimming lessons at the age of seven. She took me to learn swimming at Caribou Lake. My teacher, Nellie, was wonderful. She was an older lady with only one arm who was a dynamite swimmer herself.

They had two weeks of swimming lessons for kids every summer. It was great for me because Nellie may have had only one arm but she was a fabulous example, teaching me what can be accomplished if you put your mind to it.

She won my confidence and when you trust and believe in a teacher, you learn so much more. One thing I learned was simple: here was someone with a physical problem that could have stopped her, but in no way did she let it slow her down. She made it exciting and by the end of those first two weeks I could really swim quite well.

Skating: I like swimming, but I preferred the lake frozen. I was probably three when I started to skate. It wasn't a great achievement where I come from; this is just what everyone did. When I was a kid we used to shovel off a spot on the Desbarats River, right across from Bud Mill's gas station. The Desbarats River stretches out quite a ways before it reaches Lake Huron. We would clear an area 60 feet wide by maybe 150 feet long, about the size of a decent hockey rink. Now that was a workout before you even started to skate.

Hockey: Hockey was huge in my upbringing. Hey, I'm a Canadian. What else am I going to breathe, but hockey, eh? Oxygen ranks just below ice as a necessity to every Canadian and I was no exception.

Some of my best memories as a kid are listening to hockey games on the radio. I could listen to three radios at once, three games at a time. Mom and Dad were amazed I could follow it all. Ask me anything about those games, I could tell you every detail. Who scored the goals. Who got the assists. Who was winning. I would know all the answers.

I guess I was beginning to learn that other senses compensate when you lose the use of one of them.

Bike riding: I rode my bicycle all over town, constantly. "Actually, he wore out two bikes, riding all over the place," says Dad.

I'd cruise all over with Blake Marcel and Matthew Hunter, two friends of mine. We were like the Three Musketeers, never very far from each other. I could follow them all over town because all the roads in Desbarats were gravel in those days and it made it easy to listen to their tires.

One day Blake was riding double with me. I was doing the pedaling; Blake was supposed to be steering. We ran straight into a telephone pole beside Stella Moore's house and I was absolutely cold cocked.

Another day we hooked a rope between my bike and Blake's and went blasting down a hill where the road makes a hard right turn. Blake put on the brakes to turn right, but forgot to tell me. I kept right on going and when the rope jerked, I went flying and so did Blake. We both came out of the ditch, muddy and bloody from head to toe.

My refusal to back away from anything almost did do me in one day. I was out on the road riding along with Matthew and a dump truck came along, so we pulled over. I heard it go by, then pulled back into the road. I was not aware a second dump truck was following. Matt jumped off his bike and, in a flash, shoved me and my bike into the ditch. Thanks Matt, for saving my life.

Snowmobiling: What a ball of fun! At Christmas time, my dad's side of the family would get together for snowmobiling. We had these little plastic skis that were about 2 feet long. We used to get a rope and ski behind the snowmobile on those little skis. When the snow crust gets really hard, you could really get those things rocking. You'd be going 35 mph. These were the things we did as kids that you would never do as an adult. You look back now and think, wow, that was crazy but a great way to develop your sense of balance.

One time when no one was home, I jumped on the snowmobile myself, revved it up and started to take off across the field. I didn't

"Always a kid at heart"

get very far before running head-long into the side of the barn. It was an abrupt end to a very short ride.

Dirt biking: Full out was just my way. I don't know why, really. Maybe it's just my nature. Maybe it's partly because that's the way my parents made me feel. I could take anything I wanted to the limit. Nothing could stop me.

Occasionally, my dad paid the price for helping me to cultivate this healthy attitude. He had bought a dirt bike for Ian and that sounded like way too much fun for just my brother to enjoy. I jumped on it and got it around to where my dad was.

"Hop on, Dad. I'll take you for a ride," I said.

What was he going to say, after teaching me I can do anything? He climbed on board then I peeled out as hard as I could crank that thing. We were going like a blur when I just missed the big telephone pole by about three inches. "That was the end of my passenger days with Craig on the dirt bike," recalls Dad. C'mon, I didn't hit the pole, did I?

Poultry Plucking: Sometimes on his hunting trips Dad would shoot partridges. Occasionally he would aim his gun and then let me pull the trigger. That was a rush and a half. My brother, Ian, often had ducks and turkeys. They, of course, needed to be plucked. I sometimes helped. I actually got pretty good at it, Ian says. I didn't leave many feathers. My sense of touch came into play. You've got to pluck them right down to get all those little fine feathers, too.

Camping: In the summer time, the family would go camping on weekends and pitch a tent up the Chapleau Highway, known as Highway 129. We'd camp by a lake and fish and swim. I would help put up the tent. We'd have a big bonfire at night and roast marsh-mallows. One night we had a bonfire and I didn't realize Ian walked up beside me. I pulled my toasted marshmallow out of the fire and accidentally stuck it right on his face. He wasn't hurt but it didn't exactly tickle.

We would cook pork and beans, eat salami and crackers and just keep warm by that fire. We'd make hot chocolate too. These are fond memories of great times spent with my family. Until recently my father continued to enjoy the great outdoors that way. Cutting wood, hunting and fishing.

Outhouse: Long winters remind me that we didn't have an in-door toilet for a short while in my early childhood. It was the old outhouse routine. They were just part of the landscape in Desbarats. Let me tell you, when it's forty below zero Fahrenheit in the out-house in January, a person doesn't sit around and read the sports sec-tion or daydream about what he was going to do tomorrow.

Tree climbing: We loved to rip and run. We'd get up on the bluff in the back of our house and play cowboys and Indians. In the summertime, we'd play up there morning, noon and evening. Mom knew that was a pretty safe place for me.

Except one day.

"He was just over five," Mom says. "I looked out and I couldn't believe it. He was in this tree, about twenty-five feet high, and he was way up at the top."

Ian came out to see where I was and called up to me, "Do you know how to get down?" "NO." I said.

Together Mom and Ian guided me down, telling me where to put my feet and what branches to grab. Somehow I made it.

It scared my mom but she had a theory about raising me: "If you don't let a child develop normally, how does he develop?"

That was an extreme example but finding me up a tree was nothing special. I climbed trees all the time. In fact, Ian and I even had several tree forts that Dad helped us build. Maybe I was just scouting for a new location with a better view when I climbed so high.

Eventually, Dad built us a real cabin, just a small, one room thing, but for us it may as well have been a castle. It was two or three hundred yards from the house, at the base of the bluffs, really like having our own place. Ian and I and all our friends would play in and around the cabin for hours. It would be an army bunker one day, a wild west fort the next and on some days, for our purposes, it really did serve as a castle (The Three Musketeers, remember). When I was a little older, maybe ten, we would sleep out there at night, just us kids, no adults allowed. That might have been the best, except the night a bear came scratching on the side of the place. I will admit to being scared a few times in my life, but never more than that.

Kindergarten: One of the things that definitely made me better was going to kindergarten when I was five. I truly loved Mrs. Martens, who was my teacher. Mom told her not to show me any favoritism or undue attention and it worked. My classmates accepted me as an equal and I was able to be my friendly, outgoing self, even then.

Mrs. Martens describes my time in her class this way. "He was a leader, an idea person, always making suggestions. He preferred to be with people, to play with others rather than be alone. He quickly learned the other kid's voices and would call them by name. The other kids responded well to Craig."

"Craig had a sense of direction and a sense of humor. He played jokes and teased, but he was never hurtful. Craig had a sense of fun and others could laugh with him."

"He could put on winter clothing by himself and he could be helpful too. There was a challenged girl from Desbarats and Craig would always help her get ready. Another little boy had Down Syndrome and Craig always watched out for him when it came time to get on the bus. The children would line up and Craig would call out "Howard, where are you?" That sweet boy would answer "Craigie, here I am." Craig would take his hand and lead him to the bus."

Speaking of the bus, Mom made sure I didn't get any favoritism there either. I rode the regular school bus, all the way around the back roads, picking up all the kids from the rural routes eventually reaching school in Bruce Mines, a little town eight miles away.

I did love Howard, and that challenged little girl too. It was pretty easy to feel that way about others because so many people in Desbarats, and other places, have been so nice to and supportive of me.

Trial and Error: If Mrs. Martens makes me sound like a saint, I have to admit, I wasn't always an angel. I did have great freedom and wonderful experiences growing up, but when you learn that way you also have many frustrations as well. Sometimes my temper got the better of me.

One day Dad was having fun squirting me with a garden hose. I got so angry that I hauled off and threw my baseball glove at him, hitting him right in the face. Another time, a few years later, I was kicking a soccer ball in the back yard and I tripped over a wheelbarrow. In a flash of anger, I picked up the wheelbarrow and heaved it all the way on top of the garage roof. Experiences like these were the price I sometimes paid for all the freedom I enjoyed.

Along with my freedom came the need to learn how to get around on my own, to navigate the house, our property, and to find my own ways to keep up. I never wanted to be left out but there were no special circumstances provided for me. I had to learn, and I did.

One of the best tricks I developed to stop running into things was the use of echoes. As my hearing became more sensitive, I learned to make clicking sounds with my tongue, sharply clicking my tongue off the roof of my mouth, and listening for the echoes to bounce back. As I became better at this, I was able to avoid running into trees and telephone poles, and walls and doors. Wheelbarrows were still a problem though, too close to the ground for the echo. That was okay, I kept learning, and wouldn't trade the lessons for anything.

As I became better at getting around independently, I was even able to get to my Grandma MacFarlane's house. I'd go to the end of our driveway, turn right and follow the road from our house, feeling with my feet for the edge where the long grass met the gravel. In the summertime I could also hear the long grass on my right side, rustling in the wind, so it was easy to keep my bearings. I would walk to the first road, turn right and continue the same way until I reached the second driveway on the same side. After a right turn I would follow the side of the drive until I reached the corner of the house and I would have arrived. It was only a five minute walk but it brought such a feeling of independence and pride. I visited Grandma as often as I could.

Horseback riding: No doubt, the absolute highlight of my childhood was getting Rebel. When I was six years old, we'd go down to southern Ontario to visit a man named Jack Manders. He owned and raced horses. He had a sulky racer named Rebel. Rebel was an Ontario champion. He was an awesome sulky racer and Jack used to take me on sulky rides behind Rebel. I would always ask Jack how much he wanted for Rebel.

He'd always tell me, "$11."

I decided to save my money. Finally, I had saved $11.50, which was a pretty hefty fortune for a kid my age. We went back to Jack's and I told him I was ready to buy Rebel.

After a little haggling, I'm sure it was just teasing on Jack's part, he agreed to sell me Rebel for $11.50. I found out later that Jack gave my money back to my father and told them to put it in an account for my future. I'm kind of glad Dad didn't tell me at the time. I was proud of buying my own horse.

Rebel was my friend, as much as my human mates. To me, he was like a dog following me around. I spent hours brushing him, feeding him, cleaning his stall. I'd even feed him apples and sugar cubes right out of my hand. I'd stand on his back and jump off. I'd hang from a tree and jump on his back like I heard they did in the movies. Rebel let me do anything with him.

When I went to the fence he would come to see me. I spent hours with him. He was my celebration, my life, my tranquility, my peace of mind. So gentle, so quiet.

I discovered that if I tied a pole on a 20-foot rope and dragged it behind him, the instant he heard it, he took off. He thought it was a sulky. He'd tear off through the brush, up over the rocks, sometimes the pole would get caught on a tree, and send me flying.

Another time Rebel went under a low hanging branch. Needless to say, that was a quick exit for me. Then there was the time I didn't realize I was riding straight into a barb wire fence. Rebel stopped. I didn't. I sailed over his head into the fence and got 10 stitches for that lesson.

Despite a handful of incidents like those, Rebel and I had a special communication which worked almost without fail. I always rode him bareback. Usually I rode with no reins. He'd let me pat his neck to make any turn I wanted. If I carried a little grain in a can and rattled it, he knew to take me back to the barn.

Through all the years and changes, Desbarats has retained a strong spirit and sense of community. When I look back on those times, I'm grateful I was allowed to make my own mistakes. My parents gave me my wings and let me fly. The place I grew up in instilled independence, helped me gain confidence in myself and helped me develop self-esteem. Most importantly, let me be a normal kid. For other parents with children who have physical challenges, let this be a guide to raising them so they can live a rewarding life.

My wonderful pony, Rebel.

I really can't say enough about this. I had an experiential, tactile, sometimes trial and error upbringing that let me discover that I was capable, despite being "handicapped."

With only enough "modification" or "special attention" to keep me from suffering serious consequences, I was allowed to test my limits, discover my boundaries, and then revel within them, often, expanding them as a result.

I grew up willing to try. Nobody made me sit on the sidelines. Nobody made me hold back. Nobody told me the word can't. I became immersed in life and stayed enthusiastic because my parents celebrated the successes of my willingness to try.

I do believe that all challenged children should be given this same opportunity. Children need to be included. They need to discover their own unique gifts by using them, by getting involved, by being engaged. Some modification may be necessary, but what I see instead is overprotective smothering to the point of exclusion. Nothing hinders the growth and development of a child more. Too often what I hear of are special circumstances that border on imposed prison as any curiosity is stifled in the interest of safety. Remember, loneliness for a challenged child, especially a blind one, is the worst prison they can have. Even worse is the environment that allegedly protects the child's self esteem by eliminating any "perceived" possibility of failure at all. The truth is, even for "normal" kids, the only failure is not trying. If enthusiasm and willingness are present, then encourage the effort and celebrate the success, even if the success is nothing more than having tried in the first place. Don't leave room for the negative to creep in. You'll do far less damage to a child's self esteem this way than if you never let them try at all.

I know every parent is trying, with all their heart, to give their child every advantage and opportunity. I salute you all and encourage you to push this envelope. You, your family and most importantly, your child, will all reap the benefits.

8
Positive Expectations

The single greatest benefit of my parent's decision to just raise a kid was that it established in me a very strong sense of positive expectation.

I'm sure if you were to ask them, they would tell you that it was much more an intuitive benefit that it was a focused outcome but that really isn't important. What matters is that it has been such a major factor in the success I have known and there are lessons there that we can all take away.

As I look back now, I realize that I never had any doubt about being able to do things. I never heard any doubt expressed, any questions about why I wanted to try something. I never heard that confidence draining, demoralizing question "What makes you think you can do that?" which is asked by so many parents, friends, colleagues and managers. At least I never heard it from my parents.

As a result, I never had any hesitation about trying things. I welcomed new experiences. I just figured that if Ian could do it, or my Dad could it, or Mom could do it, or Blake or Matthew or Nellie could do it, then so could I. And, because hesitation and doubt were not part of my mental makeup, I simply expected to do things well. The expectation was positive.

As an athlete, positive expectation was critical to succeeding. A clear mental image of myself performing well was critical to my development. Producing results that came closer and closer to that image in my mind fueled my determination and my passion.

Reaching that image in my mind produced satisfaction and desire to set the bar higher and try again.

As my life transferred to the business world, I found that not much changed, just the image. Instead of blasting down a hill at fifty miles per hour, I would see myself speaking to an arena filled with twenty-five thousand people, for example.

As I spoke to larger and larger audiences, I became more confident, more effective and happier. I expected my speeches to be well received. As my speaking career evolved and my focus became more about my craft than the size of my audience, I began to get the same, if not more, satisfaction from speaking to one hundred people as I would from ten thousand. Today, I am always blessed, honored, and humbled to speak to any audience, big or small. My craft as a speaker continued to improve because I had this steady, positive progression in the direction of that perfect image I held in my mind fueling my career.

All this happened because of the sense of positive expectation that my parents decisions instilled in me.

What I have also noticed over the course of my life is that I am not very different from most people, except in one way. My expectations are positive and my mental images are inspiring.

We all have a mental image in our mind that we measure ourselves against. I firmly believe we have one of these images for everything we do, from brushing our teeth to driving our car to doing our job to what makes us happy to making Hamburger Helper. It doesn't matter what you do, your mind has created this image. This image needs to be a vivid, clear, positive picture of ourselves performing well. In fact, I believe it should be an image of you performing perfectly, on your terms. If it is not, you are, either consciously or subconsciously, constantly measuring yourself against a benchmark of mediocrity. How inspiring can that be?

I suggest you take charge of this process because it is happening to you anyway. Perfect those images of yourself and then expect to resemble them in reality. It won't happen overnight, it might never happen but that's OK. The key to success and happiness, as I see it, is to make small but constant, incremental and never ending progress towards that perfect vision. Take note of your progress along the way and celebrate it. Then go back and get even better.

You will experience more success, more personal growth, more professional growth, better relationships and more happiness than you will find from any other focus. I promise.

Oh, and all you managers and bosses out there, understand this. You will produce better, more successful, fulfilled employees by helping each of them achieve their perfect vision than through any other management technique you will ever try, but remember...it has to be their perfect vision on their terms. Do you know your people well enough to help them get there?

If they clearly understand what you expect of them, on their level, and then experience success on their own terms while delivering what you need of them, then there is nothing you can't accomplish.

9

Welcome to my New World

"Craig, you'll never be able to see again."

I think I was five before someone, a doctor or nurse, actually gave me a straight answer, or at least before I actually heard it. I had never really admitted to myself that I was blind. I had persisted in asking nurses and doctors over and over if I was ever going to see again.

Maybe they were afraid to tell me. Afraid of making me angry, or worse, destroying my spirit. Maybe they did tell me, but I wasn't paying attention. On occasion, doctors had probably indicated that my condition was permanent but I didn't know what permanent meant.

Even when I finally heard the truth, I don't remember feeling sad.

Until then, the idea that I was blind was just a foreign, uninteresting, vaguely harmful concept that I had filed in some dark mental recess of my child's mind. I covered it up with toys and friends and endless days of happy play.

I was too busy trapping and fishing with my dad. I was climbing trees and playing cowboys and Indians with Ian and my friends on the bluff. I'd be riding my bike and my horse and running with my Golden Retriever Blondie. I was picking berries and baking pies. I was learning to swim. I was going to kindergarten with other kids. I was active, to put it mildly.

My brother Ian, and I, had a great childhood.

Blindness had hardly intruded on my life at all.

I remember when the kids started to learn to write in kindergarten and I couldn't. That made an impression on me. I was disappointed but when Mrs. Martens would tell me that I would learn my own special way of writing next year, the impact really didn't sink in.

Mom and Dad waited until the summer, after kindergarten was over, to broach the subject of me going to a different school. When they did tell me, it really didn't mean anything. I was just turning six years old. It was summer vacation. Yeah, maybe I was going to have to go away but I wasn't leaving just then. I still had all summer to tear up the countryside with my buddies.

None of this became reality until reality set in.

Reality came in the form of the Ontario School for the Blind, which, a few years later, became W. Ross MacDonald School for the Blind in Brantford, Ontario. It would become my home for many years.

It was the day after Labor Day, September 3, 1968. My world, physically, emotionally and soon to follow, spiritually, changed that day. It started almost before I realized what was happening. Dad had the car packed and waiting while Mom was saying her goodbyes. She couldn't make the trip with us. School started for everyone that day. Mom had to stay home with Ian and she had her own school year starting, teaching a new class.

I like to remember Mom that way. Happy, strong, practical, and positive. Maybe she just would have found it too hard to say goodbye to me in Brantford, and then deal with the memory for an eight-hour drive home. I couldn't judge things like that back then. The emotion had not set in for me, yet.

Next thing I knew Dad and I were on the road. It was early, very early. We had a long drive ahead of us but Dad had a longer day ahead of him. Not only did we have a 465-mile drive to Brantford, but Dad had to be back in time for work the next day. Just another in the huge list of sacrifices they made for me.

The drive itself was a good time. Most car rides with Dad were. My dad was fun. He had a way of making these long drives to and from W. Ross MacDonald some of the most cherished memories of my life, and that wasn't easy. Remember, he couldn't distract me with scenery or sites along the way. Let's face it, when you're blind the scenery never changes. It was Dad's personality and compassion that made it all so special.

The trip to Brantford was a little longer, too, because we made a regular pit stop. My Grandpa and Grandma Jefferies lived in a little

Grandma and Grandpa Jefferies

town called Nairn Centre, which is just outside Sudbury. It was on our way and I always wanted to stop. On that first trip I really wanted to see them before I left for such a long time. It was a perfect break. We had breakfast and I debated the upcoming NHL hockey season with Grandpa. His Montreal Canadiens versus my Boston Bruins. We were probably the only two English speaking people in the entire region who didn't cheer for the Toronto Maple Leafs. It seemed Dad and I were leaving almost as soon as we arrived. It buoyed my spirits, especially their parting words, "see you soon, Craigie." No mention of school or being gone for so long.

This became a regular pit stop on my trips to school. I always looked forward to it.

Now it was a right turn in Sudbury, five hours south to Toronto, another right and an hours' drive to Brantford. That was the long part of the trip. Dad and I talked about hunting and trapping and fishing and hockey and horseback riding, and like I said, it was fun, but it could not take away that sense of how far we were travelling. With each passing mile, I felt so much further from Ian and my friends, Blake, Matthew, Rebel, the bluffs, the house, Desbarats, everything.

That was my reality check.

What I remember about finally arriving at the Ontario School For The Blind was being overcome by the strangeness of the place, by how big it seemed to my ears. The W. Ross MacDonald campus is bigger than some colleges and even at age six, I could sense it.

The playground too was a little intimidating at first. Not because of the size, I grew up in the country so the big outdoors was not an issue. It was the noise. It was deafening. There were so many of us. All six, seven and eight years old. All in a new place. All excited and, me in particular, filled with a sense of adventure.

I was excited sure, but there was also a sadness that I was feeling. Maybe in that exact moment it was more like apprehension, but I was six. How would I know? All I really knew was that it was almost time for my dad to leave. I had spent my entire life under the watchful, caring wing of my mom and dad. Now I was about to leave that nest. Imagine, I was being left in a strange world, on my own. It is so hard for col-

The Ontario School for the Blind, 1968.

lege age students to do this, in their late teens. I was about to do it at age SIX!

Dad stayed a couple hours. He helped me get situated in my room up in the junior school and to get my bearings at least a little. It wasn't long, though, before we were walking through the playground again and he said, "it's a long drive home, I should be getting on my way soon." I knew he was getting ready to leave.

I guess I have a tendency to ignore the low points in my life. I believe that is one of the reasons that I've been successful. I don't dwell on bad things.

This, however, was a moment I couldn't gloss over. No doubt one of the lowest of the low moments was the day my dad had to walk away and head out for home, leaving me behind at the school for the blind.

Suddenly I felt devastated. I felt lost. A tear, many tears, rolled down my cheeks. I sat there thinking, "Am I ever going to see my dad again?"

"What if something happens to him on the way home?"

"If I do get to see him, how long will it be?"

These questions were boiling up in my little six-year-old brain, brewing an emptiness in my belly. I knew in my heart he wouldn't be gone just a day. It wasn't going to be a week. I knew it was going to be at least a month, maybe longer. At that age I couldn't even begin to imagine what a month or two might feel like. Would it feel like a million years? Would it feel like forever?

My dad was my last link to home. That link was about to break. He walked me over to a swing. I got on the swing and he pushed me a bit and tried to help me get comfortable with my new place, to kind of break it in. Then, the shock in the finality of it engulfed me.

Geez... When he's gone, he's not a mile away or 20 miles away. He's eight hours away. In that moment I experienced what that would be like. My dad gently touched my shoulder and I felt the rough hand that had set steel traps and skinned moose and chopped down trees and built a log cabin... Now that hand grew soft as it squeezed me.

"Brave soldiers don't cry," he said, his voice calm but choked.

"Okay, Dad. I'll try to be brave," I said.

I tried not to let any more tears come into my eyes.

"I hope you're safe going home," I said. "I'll be talking to you soon. Okay?"

I hope that sounded brave.

He said, "have fun, son."

He was off. His words hung empty in the air.

Fun? How could I have fun, all alone, stranded, away from home, with so many people I knew nothing about?

The ironic thing is, my dad couldn't have left me a better parting line. Before long, I was very busy discovering ways to have fun!

Initially, I felt angry, resentful, hated my blindness for the fact that it was the reason I was there. That anger could have consumed me. I could've slipped into a state of self depression easily and given up on the school for the blind. Fortunately in that first hour after Dad left, I caught a huge break. I met Eric.

Eric was one of my roommates, but more importantly, became my best friend and my partner in crime for 10 of the next 12 years. We clicked almost instantly. After running into each other, literally (there seemed to be a lot of that going on in those early days) on the playground, we talked a little and then got down to the serious business of playing.

It was weird playing with Eric. That was the first time I had ever played with another blind kid but I was just so excited to have a friend. I really wanted to show him my radio. It was the same one I kept under my pillow back home so I could listen to the Boston Bruins' games, on WBZ radio 1030, when I should of been sleeping. It was up in our room and I took Eric there to show him.

As we entered the room, I ran smack into another kid who was leaving. "Hey, why don't you watch where you're going?" I yelled. Eric laughed out loud. "He's blind, Craig, he can't watch where he's going."

Now that was a reality check! Welcome to my new world.

The kid leaving the room, who turned out to be our classmate Roger, was a little on the pudgy side. I said, "Geez, you got a big belly." Roger responded, "who said that?" I answered, "Eric."

And so it was. I was stirring up monkey business and on my way to being a ringleader. Causing havoc. My reputation as the persistent, calculating mastermind of mischief was already beginning.

You think kids pull pranks on each other in regular school? It seems like that's all we ever did in blind school. If we could scuttle someone or take the wind out of their sails, we never hesitated to do so.

As well as being the ringleader, I also had a lot of guts. My years on the farm and in the woods made me tough. I was always a rugged, aggressive kid. I wasn't timid. I wasn't hesitant.

Eric, who grew up in the country north of Bowmanville, Ontario, was much the same. When you put us together, the combination was deadly. We started with little things. In first grade, I locked the teacher out of the classroom. When she went out for something, I just snuck up to the door closed it and turned the lock.

She knocked on the door for someone to let her in. Someone did.

"All right, who did that? I want to know this instant," she said. I blurted out, "I didn't see anyone."

Well it might have been the right thing to say in the sighted school, but totally ineffective at the school for the blind. I mean, think about it for a second. Who was going to know? I could slip up to the front, close the door and get back to my seat and no one else in the room could see me. The teacher I did this to, Ms. Mannings, was a dynamite teacher. I wasn't doing it because I disliked her. I thought she was terrific. I was just doing it because I was mischievous. I was always looking for some prank to pull.

We had other pranks. When we were walking into a class, threading our way between the desks, we just kind of reached over and smacked a guy on the back of the head. We might not know exactly where he was, so it might be a glancing blow, but other times it would be a home run, full palm.

Sometimes we moved another student's books from the right-hand side of their desk to the left-hand side and they would be looking for it.

Some of this was to get under people's skin. Some was pure rebellion. At W. Ross MacDonald, we were taught table manners, so we didn't eat with our fingers. I was up on that because my parents raised me like any other kid. They taught me how to hold the fork and cut the food from an early age. At school sometimes the meat wasn't that tasty but they always wanted us to try a few bites. "Take a bite..." they'd say.

Naturally, that set me off. "You've got to take two bites of meat," they'd always say. I used to throw it under the table. I could cut it. I just didn't want to eat it. I didn't like the way it tasted. You could have put a new sole on my father's work boots with that meat sometimes.

Sometimes I tucked it on the ledge underneath the table. Hey, after about a month I'd have a heckuva wad of meat under there. Then I'd sneak a dried out hunk of it on to another kid's plate.

My pranks, in the early days, were in large part to keep me from thinking about home. I craved the adventure of hunting and trapping and fishing and riding my horse and riding my bike and climbing trees. Well, maybe not climbing trees, climbing is one thing I did often at school. I also missed Mom and Dad, although they did go to great lengths to try and save me that heartache.

Mom and Dad made a huge sacrifice shortly after my arrival at W. Ross MacDonald. They actually sold their home in Desbarats and moved to Brantford to be close to me. It was hard on them. In Brantford Dad had difficulty finding steady work. He did find one job in a refrigerator company but he said, "This job won't last. By Christmas they'll be cutting way back and I don't see anything else. If we were home I'd be trapping and other odd jobs. At least we'd have something to fall back on."

Mom had challenges, too. She was a school teacher but the school year had already begun and all the jobs had been filled. She didn't see much chance of landing permanent work for several months either.

Then there was Ian. He was miserable. He was a country kid transplanted to a city school. He would say, "none of the kids here want to do anything I like, and there is no place to do any of the things we did back home."

Truth is, here were three country people trying to transplant themselves into a small city, just because they were worried about me. In fact, the two months they spent in Brantford would be the longest time Dad ever spent away from Desbarats. He was born there. He grew up there. That rugged, rural, remote way of life was all he knew. It was where he thrived.

I do remember coming home one day and saying to Mom, "It's okay if you guys want to go back home, I'll be all right here." I'm not sure why I said it. At age six I hardly had the emotional maturity to make judgments about my mom and dad's state of mind. I do know this. Coming home to them in Brantford was great because we were together as a family but it wasn't the same happy, energetic place that home was in Desbarats. Maybe I knew they were unhappy. Desbarats was home in their hearts and maybe I just wanted them to be there. Then, I could look forward to my trips back to the utopia that Desbarats was, in my imagination anyway. It didn't matter. All I knew was that this wasn't working.

My parents were torn. They were willing to do anything for me and Ian. In this case, the move proved to be too much. I have always loved the memory that they were willing to go the extra mile for me. In the end, it proved better that I go the 465 miles to them. They moved back to Desbarats after just two months.

Life at W. Ross MacDonald carried on pretty much the same. I got adequate grades, best I could do with minimum effort, and with Eric as my partner, continued to strive for legendary status as pranksters. By the time we entered seventh grade, a certain maturity had begun to creep into our mischief.

By then we had learned to time the night watchman's rounds. I knew once he passed our room, we had forty-five minutes to create unbridled mayhem. Thanks to our climbing skills (I told you about the trees right?) we could escape the dorm and run wild between rounds without ever being detected.

Our room was near the corner of the dorm building, on the second floor. I don't know who the genius was who designed the dorms at W. Ross MacDonald, but as I grow older I understand this was the case in many buildings. The afore mentioned genius used that criss-cross pattern of bricks sticking out on the corners. I'm told it looks cool, but it is even better for climbing.

Eric and I could be on the ground within seconds of the night watchman's passing. Once on the ground, we could go anywhere we wanted. Our navigation techniques were so refined by that point, and let's face it, who needs the sun?

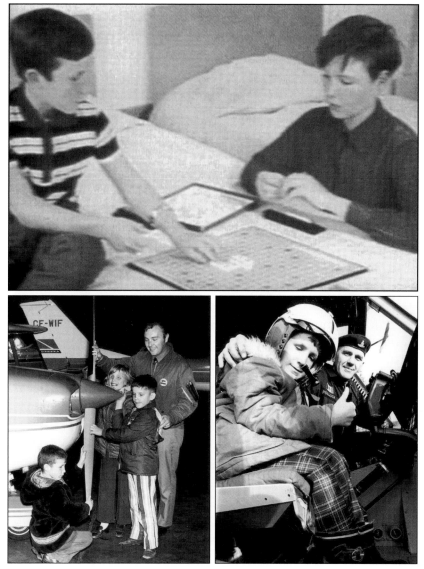

Life at W. Ross MacDonald was always a hands on experience.

Some nights we would go to the girls' dorm. We couldn't actually get in, that was beyond us, but we could certainly climb to the second floor and flirt with the girls. Other nights the music wing was our target, sometimes the security office itself. We learned to defend ourselves by using apples as weapons, throwing them when we were detected, which was rare. I actually connected with a counselor, one night, hitting her right in the neck. I knew this because she went silent in mid-scream as she had been chasing us around the building. By the time she started screaming again, we were back in home territory. We didn't mean anyone any harm but that defense technique was particularly beneficial to us. After that, the authorities always assumed the culprits could see, at least a little, which cleared us from further scrutiny. Ironically, the majority of the kids at the school for the blind had some limited vision. The totally blind kids like Eric and I were in the minority.

By seventh grade I was also coming to grips with my blindness in other ways. I was always determined to make my way back to the sighted world. I grew up in that world for my first six years and I belonged. I never thought it was unreasonable to think I would live my life there, I just needed a few adjustments, and techniques.

One technique I became very effective with was sonar. I became very good at navigating while clicking my tongue off the roof of my mouth. I would emit sounds that would bounce back to me. I could sense the location of trees, posts, walls, even people by the echo that came back, kind of like a bat's radar. Sure, I still had my share of incidents, mostly with low-lying things like benches and chairs, but I became so good that I could walk down the center of the hall when almost everyone else was following the wall.

I also became the master of teasing older kids, getting them so upset that they would chase me, then ducking behind a tree or a lamppost and letting them crash into it headlong. I would run away laughing hysterically, proud of my rep, but knowing I would be facing a "talk" with higher authorities.

I could recite so many stories about our mischief at W. Ross MacDonald, but you get the idea. Anything to stir the pot, any victim, no exceptions. We didn't pick on teachers because we didn't like them. No, usually the opposite, the teachers at W. Ross MacDonald were great, but we couldn't pass up an opportunity.

This rebellious reputation did become somewhat of a pain in the side to the administration at W. Ross MacDonald. My grades were good enough that I was beyond dismissal or being expelled. That didn't mean that I was getting a free pass, just that the school considered some exceptional methods of toning me down.

One strategy was to call my parents. Even the school administrators realized that despite my independent streak, my parents were my idols and I would do anything not to disappoint them. Of course, I thought they might be proud of some of my exploits, being as I was taking on blindness without self-pity, but the school didn't know everything.

The school called home and, concerned for my reputation and good standing, Mom and Dad decided Dad should come and have a talk with me. Of course, they didn't tell me.

No, instead they decided that Dad would drive the 465 miles to the school and catch me by surprise, maybe even red handed, and of course, so that I didn't have time to contrive any answers to explain my behavior. Fair enough tactic, but by then I had evolved in at least one way they didn't anticipate.

Dad arrived, unannounced, and proceeded to my dorm. He entered the building, climbed the stairs and exited the stairwell on my floor only to find me walking toward him, holding court with all my friends around me.

Not wanting to make a scene in front of my friends, he just walked past me in the hall, didn't say a word. Without skipping a beat, I turned my head and said, "So, when did you get here?" It freaked him out. He was spooked.

It wasn't that great a trick. By then I knew the sounds of Dad's boots on the floor even better than I knew my own. I knew his cologne. I even knew the way his keys jangled in his pocket. Maybe I am blessed with exceptional senses to compensate for the lack of sight but I think I just learned to pay more attention to them because I relied on them so much growing up, when, of course, Dad was always right there. How could I miss him? C'mon, I deserved more credit, even then.

I wasn't a bad kid. I wasn't a mean kid anyway. I was determined however, not to be labeled. My grades were good enough and my reputation outside the classroom became legendary. To the extent, in fact, that everyone wondered how I would take out the superintendent each year in the annual student–staff tin can hockey game.

Yes, we had an in-house hockey league at W. Ross MacDonald. We played the game using a tin can instead of a puck so that we could hear it. We would use the can until it got all beat up. It would develop sharp edges and get smaller and smaller until we finally had to replace it. We had to wear helmets with masks, kind of like a football helmet, and when the can got small enough to fit through the mask openings, we would go looking for a new one. Of course, the mask only protected our faces. As that can got more and more jagged, it would really hurt when it hit you, but we didn't care. There was so much slashing and cross checking and stick work in our games that we were always getting bumps and bruises.

Like any kid growing up in Canada, I loved playing hockey. I was competitive by nature and got good enough to lead our league in scoring most years. Of course, I did have an advantage.

There is no off-season for hockey in Canada.

In the 1960's, W. Ross MacDonald was the only School for the Blind in all of Canada. It just wasn't possible to supervise an entire country's worth of students seven days a week. For that reason, the school policy was that if your home was within three hundred miles of the campus, you went home for the weekend. With W. Ross MacDonald being located in southern Ontario, the most populous region of Canada, that meant the majority of students went home. Only a small contingent of students and a skeleton staff was left behind. As Desbarats was 465 miles away, I was one of the few left behind.

W. Ross MacDonald became a totally different place on weekends, but that didn't diminish my sense of adventure, or my reputation. The games just changed, and so did my compatriots. Eric went home every weekend but Darryl, Tim and Walter proved to be equally playful partners to carry on with.

We spent most of the weekend time playing hockey. We would be on the ice eight hours a day, Saturday and Sunday, five months a year. It's the Canadian way. That's where I developed the ability that let me lead our league in scoring. I simply practiced more hockey than anybody else in the league. Isn't that how Wayne Gretzky got so good too? That's what he told me anyway.

Playing hockey builds up a huge appetite and that lead to some of our other, more infamous exploits. You already know what I thought of the cuisine at W. Ross MacDonald. No lack of food, but a significant lack of flavor. After dinner, we were always craving something more, something sweet, not to mention we had burned so much energy playing hockey that we really felt we needed a sugar rush.

We didn't have a convenience store that we could run to for chocolate or candy or soda. We did have a canteen that sold snacks but it was rarely open on weekends. What we did have, however, was a Home Economics room and I got the bright idea to raid the baking supplies.

It started out as a lark one night. After the night watchman passed by, we would be on the ground in a heartbeat and on our way to the new school. That was our name for it but in reality, it was a massive, three-story, quarter mile long behemoth. It housed everything from the gymnasiums to the indoor track to the music studios to the auditorium to the woodworking shops and cafeterias to all the classrooms and, of course, the Home Economic Lab.

Anyway, getting into the building was easy. We always tried to have a door rigged so that it didn't lock but that wasn't a huge deal. You could always find a way in, if you looked long enough. During my exploits with Eric, I had learned one very valuable trick that I used throughout my time at W. Ross MacDonald. It involved my trusty comb and door locks. I had developed the skill of using my comb by prying it between the door and frame in a downward motion. If you got the angle just right, it would trip the latch. We used this technique so often that we were able to open virtually any classroom door on the campus. So when we decided the Home Economics room was of interest, I didn't have any worries.

We learned the pattern of how to find the room from a few girls we were friends with and found it relatively easily. We were in within seconds and, using our home field knowledge gained from our friends, and our fine tuned hearing to listen for the motors on the refrigerators, found the supply cupboard almost as fast.

It took a leap of faith to put our trust totally in our senses of smell but within minutes we were scarfing down chocolate chips and baking chocolate, candy balls and sprinkles and my personal favorites, raisins and shredded coconut. We never stole anything, at least not in the sense that we took it back to our rooms, too much chance of getting found out that way. In the beginning we just pigged out and scooted back. Our equivalent of raiding the cookie jar.

Of course, word spread around campus and through our friends that someone seemed to be raiding the HomeEc room. We started hearing about the goodies we were missing out on. Seems our friends were in the habit of leaving their work in the refrigerator. Once we knew this we searched it out and struck gold, sort of. Sometimes it was fool's gold, but it was still a major discovery. That refrigerator would, invariably, be filled with cakes and pies and tarts and cookies and cupcakes and muffins that our friends had attempted to bake during class the previous week.

We loved it. We would gorge ourselves. Mostly, it was all delicious, too. We discovered the occasional failure and more than a few "science experiments" but not enough to discourage us. It was a treat worth looking forward to. At one point I remember even having the bright idea of leaving behind a list of requests. It would have been in Braille so nobody could have traced it, but better judgment set in. These were good times, why ruin it?

The good times, unfortunately, did not extend to learning Braille. That was a different story altogether. At first, Braille seemed so incredibly complex to me. I thought I'd never master it. Braille is a system of dot patterns you use to create letters and numbers. The Braille alphabet has twenty-six letters, just like the sighted one. After you learn your letters, which is called Grade One Braille, you must master 198 contractions, known as Grade Two Braille, like a form of shorthand. As you probably know, a blind person "reads" by passing his or her fingertips over the raised dots.

What a sighted person may not realize is how cumbersome the system can be. You can pack a Reader's Digest in your pocket. In Braille, it's four volumes in a box.

Braille seemed like an unbelievable thing to grasp when I first got to school. By the time I reached seventh grade, I was able to take dictation of the teachers lectures using a "slate and stylus," with which you punch every dot of every Braille letter onto a piece of rather stiff Braille paper.

There was one time when Braille did come in handy, as usual, in executing yet another of my continual descents into mischievousness. We had a classmate named Robert who was an absolute whiz at math. Our issue with Robert was that he took pride in telling us all how he was the best and I felt it was time to bring him back to earth. Our math teacher, Mr. Barney, was in the habit of putting our tests out on the desks early and then going off to the staff room for a break before class started. On one of these occasions, I snuck into the room after Mr. Barney left and rubbed a few Braille dots off Roberts test. You could easily change a 7 to an 8 or a 6 by removing just one dot. Mr. Barney was incredibly taken aback by how poorly Robert scored on the test and Robert, of course, was devastated. It was hilarious to listen to, if you knew the real story.

Even though I loved learning new things, I just wasn't ready to do the type of work I needed to if I wanted to be at the top of my class.

My best efforts were still reserved for athletics and pranks. Athletics, which I'll talk about later, became my vehicle, my means of proving myself and earning my way back to the sighted world and, in my eyes, the chance of a normal life.

Pranks were my release. I had energy, resentment, vision, ambition; all built up in my young body. When I wasn't on a wrestling mat, which couldn't happen often enough, I was always drawn to playful endeavors. I was the type of kid who couldn't sit still.

Eric, or course, was my partner in crime throughout. It is the rare story of a prank that doesn't start with the words "Eric and I." We perpetrated our mischief in every corner of the campus, and nobody was off limits, including ourselves.

Sometimes we executed elaborate plans, like the time we decided to teach Arthur a lesson (he was about four years older than us and kind of a bully) or the multitude of food fights we started out of boredom or the collisions with calamity that came from our seeming inability to ever sit still. Even our teachers were victims in the midst of our calamity. Once I actually exploded a grape in the ear of the lunch room supervisor, from forty feet away no less. Not a bad shot for a blind guy.

The best example of the Craig and Eric show happened one day when, for reasons I don't remember, we were banished to the supply room adjacent to our class, instead of being sent to the office. All I can think is that sending us to the office had proved entirely futile so maybe the idea was to give us a time out, like sending your child to his or her room. We were in seventh grade by that time and they were always trying new ways to tone us down.

It proved to be poor judgment in any event. We closed the door back there and in our explorations found a number of pieces of indoor-outdoor carpet that had been cut in the shape of the Canadian provinces. They all fit together to show blind kids how Canada was formed.

They also flew very well when flung like a Frisbee. We tested all the provinces and got to playing with Manitoba. It flew the best but, unfortunately wound up being flung behind a four-foot high filing cabinet. We had to get it out to prevent being discovered but the cabinet was heavy and, to make matters worse, was piled high with stuff on top. There was no way one person was going to move it.

Eric started pulling at the bottom and I went to work up top. The bottom didn't move, but the top lurched forward as soon as I pulled. I had no idea what all that stuff was on top but I found out all too soon.

An entire gallon jar of Bond-Fast glue smacked Eric right on the head. Mrs. Tinkus heard this ferocious crash and came rushing through the door within seconds, only to find Eric in a puddle of glue and glass, out cold and looking quite dead. I was covered in glue too and told, not surprisingly, I had a look of absolute terror on my face.

Thankfully, Eric was out only for a second. He came to and we scraped him up off the floor, but not the same can be said for the glue. I think they are still scraping remnants of that adventure up, even today.

I appeared to be on top of my world at that time. Actually, there was a huge void in my insides, especially on weekends. My main link to my parents was the telephone. I usually got one weekly call from them on Sunday.

In my first few years, if that phone call were a minute late, I would think that something had happened to them. If the call was supposed to come in at 10 a.m. on Sunday and the circuit might be busy, or the line might be busy on our end, it just crushed me. I always waited down the hall for that phone to ring and I was always hoping it was ringing for me. When it got near 10 a.m., I'd always be anticipating that phone ringing. They come and get you if the call was for you, but I always had an ear cocked on my own, just to make sure.

Of course, when summer holidays rolled around and I did get to go home like everyone else... well, that was heaven.

Rebel. Blondie. Ian. My friends, Matthew Hunter, Blake Marcel, Randy Barber, all those people. Glen Moore, Scott Hatton! We were back playing cowboys and Indians up on the rock, swimming and ripping. Playing with my cousins, Todd and Jamie, Kim, Bonita, Robbie, Kathy and Paul-roughhousing in the hay mow. It was torture to leave but every fall, I'd return to W. Ross MacDonald. As I got

My pets always welcomed me home.

more used to it, the school became "my domain." I began to appre-ciate what a fantastic place it was.

If you had to be sent away to a school by yourself, this definitely was the place to be. In fact, there was little doubt that W. Ross MacDonald was the finest school for the blind in the entire world and remains one the world's elite schools for the blind. As a keynote speaker, I have had the pleasure to be invited to all kinds of blind fa-cilities in America. Nothing holds a candle to my former school.

I can't imagine how hard it must have been for my parents to leave me at school 500 miles from home.

Yet, I was getting awfully antsy staying there. In fact I began to feel the urge to leave this "blind world." I felt I had to go test my-self in the sighted world.

That was really what I'd been striving for, ever since age 6, the second I got to Brantford. I was struggling in every way I knew to leave or to prepare myself to go. There were times when I got terribly frustrated with my blind-ness and its supposed limitations. I was struck sometimes by the way blindness was a prison for so many of my friends. I think that's why I developed such a forward personality, always pushing, always striv-ing. It was just a great need to infuse myself with confidence, to use confidence as a jackhammer to break out of that prison. I felt I was meant to be able to move and live in the "real" world, the sighted one. I truly thought I was ready to handle anything any sighted per-son could do. I didn't have any idea how difficult it was going to be to leave W. Ross MacDonald.

By the end of eighth grade, I told administrators at Ross MacDonald that in ninth grade I would be transferring to Central Algoma Secondary School. It was a huge public school located in my home town, Desbarats. Central Algoma actually had a student population that exceeded the population of Desbarats itself. It drew from the rural regions, and neighboring towns, servicing a vast area and accordingly, a huge number of kids.

I was going home! I would be with Mom and Dad and my brother and my horse and my dog and all my friends. I would escape the limiting world of the blind at W. Ross MacDonald. I was finally going to break the shackles of blindness. Not just a little during wrestling competitions. Always!

I picked up a little additional motivation as I left W. Ross MacDonald. It seems that not everyone saw my decision as a positive move. One teacher outright called me stupid, told me I'd be a failure and I'd become a dropout if I left Ross MacDonald. Others considered me a traitor for turning my back on the school that had been my home for so many years.

I know now that they didn't understand my determination to become part of the mainstream world. Their focus was on learning to cope with a disability. Mine was on succeeding in that arena where I would have to live the rest of my life. The interpretation didn't matter then. All the comments just fueled my desire to show them, to show everyone, that I belonged and could succeed in the "normal" world, without labels and special conditions.

I had a busy summer that year, representing Canada at the Olympiad for the Physically Disabled. I won a silver medal and was, I think, just expecting to ride the wave of that victory and the associated celebrity into my new life at Central Algoma Secondary School. It didn't happen quite that way.

Yes, I had some celebrity. People at Central Algoma had heard about me in the media. I'd started to have some athletic success beyond Brant County, where W. Ross MacDonald was located. I'd been on television a few times, been written up in many papers and, of course, as the local kid doing well, had been the subject of many conversations around the little town of Desbarats.

That kind of reputation also brings with it some challenges, which I was about to learn for the first time. I didn't understand jealousy and suspicion at that time in my life. I thought that if you were the best, you should be treated that way. Not put on a pedestal necessarily, but given a modicum of respect for the work you had done.

Respect never entered the picture. I had the recognition, yes, but I wasn't given any credit for my reputation, not right away anyhow.

I did know that I would have lots of eyes on me. I expected that. The only blind person in a school of 700 kids doesn't exactly have any place to hide. I expected scrutiny too, even curiosity, but not outright jealousy and resentment.

People know if you're as good as you've been portrayed. They'll know in short order if you can cut it or if you can't. Some are bound to test you, especially those challenged by your presence. I say all this now with the benefit of 20/20 hindsight but maybe I should have expected it. I was coming in with a highly touted athletic background and that did cause some animosity among my fellow students, particularly my new wrestling teammates.

Don't get me wrong. Some of the kids were absolutely splendid and enormously helpful. And my new wrestling coach, Mel Prodan, was tremendous. He knew of and respected my record and was excited to have me on the team. The same couldn't be said for all of my new teammates however.

It turned out that some of the guys didn't want me on the team. At the very least, they wanted to test my abilities. It didn't take long to find this out first hand either. The gauntlet was thrown down on my first day, at lunch in the cafeteria.

Not being the shy retiring type, I searched out my teammates that first day at lunch and sat down at the same table with the rest of the wrestling team. I thought I'd hear a few introductions and maybe a comment or two about what to expect at practice that afternoon but the first thing I remember one of my teammates saying was:

"Pretty clever how you cut your food like a normal guy, when did you learn to feed yourself?"

Not exactly a welcoming greeting, especially to a guy like me who had been striving to prove himself everyday for years. I reacted, not with grace or humility, but impulsively, with no tolerance and certainly without backing down.

"Been doing it as long as I can remember," I said. "How long have you been a jerk?"

That brought absolute silence.

That comment had come from the top, in the person of Tim Golick, captain of the wrestling team. When the shock of my response had passed, he got in my face. "You and me," he said. "We got to get it on."

"Sure," I said. "You want it right here, right now?" Male machismo at its best, even in ninth grade.

"Practice, today!" he said.

"Anytime, buddy," I answered, "Anytime at all."

Frankly, by the time the challenge was thrown down, I was ready. I had been hearing banter in the halls all morning. Some good-natured, some insulting, some just ignorant. All the same, I was starting to feel like a sideshow and I was ready to make a statement.

I had worked my tail off for eight long years to prove I belonged in the sighted world. Now I was here and I wasn't about to let anyone take this opportunity away from me.

I went to practice that afternoon, knowing I wasn't just trying to win a medal or a match. No, this time I was fighting to prove my worth and identity, both as an athlete and a person.

The cafeteria, as in most high schools, also doubled as the auditorium. It had a large stage area and that is where wrestling practice took place. Today, it wasn't just going to be practice. It was a performance. Word had gotten around about Golick and me and a pretty large crowd had gathered in the cafeteria. No problem for me. I was used to wrestling on the big stage by now. I just changed into my wrestling stuff and started up the stairs to the stage.

That was the moment. Some loud mouth in the crowd yelled out, "Hey blind boy, Let's see what you're made of!"

So that was how it was going to be. First day of school and my reputation, my credibility, my sense of self-worth and belonging were all being challenged, not just by the wrestling team, but it seemed by the entire student body. It may have been the best thing that could have happened to me. It didn't intimidate me, I'd spent years feeding off of other people's taunts and their ideas that I was limited. This time I could make a definitive statement right off the start. I belonged here. Just watch me.

As it turned out, I didn't even square off against Golick first. Another kid, Jack MacIntire, jumped in. Maybe he was trying to ease the tension, or just joking around, but it was a mistake on his part. By then I was totally serious, focused. This was beyond gold medal time for me and getting in my way was not a good idea.

I dispatched with Jack post haste. I pinned him quickly and easily and then paraded around like I hear professional wrestlers do these days. I acted like Jack was a joke, daring them to bring on a real wrestler. That was all the goading Tim Golick needed. He walked on the mat. I could tell his pride had been pricked. I had challenged the honor of his team by dispatching Jack so quickly. Now Tim had something to prove, beyond just putting the "blind boy" in his place.

I have often wondered if I brought this scene on myself. I was, after all, an aggressive kid with an attitude and something to prove. I didn't think I came across that way when I entered school that morning, but I was certainly that kid now. As far as I was concerned, Tim was trouble.

Tim turned out to be a good wrestler. He was quick and tough and over my time on the team I would come to respect his ability. That day, however, I showed no compassion. I pinned Tim just as fast as I pinned Jack and I jumped up ready for the real fight to begin. Coach Prodan, before anymore fireworks ensued and much to my surprise, brought calm to the conflict almost instantly.

Before my breathing had even returned to normal, the entire team was now crowding around me, slapping me on the back, welcoming me. In fact, the first guy to shake my hand was Tim.

That first day at Central Algoma was a real lesson for me, an "eye opener" if you will. Yes, I did come in as a cocky kid with something to prove, and I was called on it. I had to, as they say, put up or shut up. I demonstrated that I was exactly what I was reported to be, nothing more, nothing less. It gained me acceptance, maybe a little respect and certainly some friends.

What if I had been a fraud? What if I couldn't wrestle up to my reputation? I would have been no different than all the people in this world who over promise and under deliver. I was on a mission in those days to be more than people expected I could be but I also learned, after much time in reflection - most of it in conversation with my mom - that it was important to never claim to be more than I was. Even more important to me became the desire to be more than I claimed to be. It is an important principle that I learned to live by, Under Promise - Over Deliver.

The rest of my arrival at Central Algoma met with varying degrees of success. I had profile, but not the same high profile and status I had at Ross MacDonald. There I was a ringleader. Here I was a rumor, a recognizable one, but still just a rumor. Outside of wrestling I still needed to establish myself, and learn my way around too.

Central Algoma was not built with blind people in mind, at all. Architecturally, it is apparently spectacular, for a high school anyway. Unfortunately, multi level indoor courtyards with unmarked steps and randomly scattered benches made my "facial perception" abilities less valuable and unexpected collisions more frequent. Hallways full of sighted students were a new adventure, too. They walked wherever they wanted, no discipline of sticking to the right side of the hall. As much as I disdained that rule at Ross MacDonald, I missed it at Central.

I learned the turf quickly enough and my episodes of tumbling over desks and falling up unexpected steps (not staircases, those I could detect, just the two or three steps between the different wings of the school and the levels of the courtyard) diminished over time, but the pranks, yes the pranks continued, played by my classmates preying on my sightlessness never ended.

The best one happened after a wrestling match. I was walking with Tim Golick, yes that Tim Golick - we became good friends - and I was ahead. Tim said, "Just keep going, I'll tell you when to turn." He did, but not where I should have turned. Instead of entering the boys change room, Tim led me into the girls locker room. I was startled to hear the shrieking and then taken aback by the giggling that followed. I had walked in on a team meeting of the girls basketball team. As soon as they realized it was me, the tension was gone. "Nice to see you ladies, looking lovely as always," I said. "Oh, don't you wish" was one of the replies. It was a funny moment.

Apparently, I turned beet red, which had the girls questioning if I was really blind at all. "Are you sure you can't see?" one of them asked. "Unfortunately, No," was all I could say. When I turned to leave, another girl said, "don't be shy, since you can't see, come back and visit us sometime." I never did but I know the rest of my team was envious.

Academically, Central Algoma was a different story. I maintained a "B" average but it was not as easy as I expected, complicated by the fact that my Braille books didn't arrive until May, one month before the end of my freshman year. It never would have happened without my Mother's tutoring and patience. I discovered what a wonderful teacher my mother had been to all her students over the many years of her teaching career.

Brailling notes wasn't so bad but there were advantages, in a learning sense, that Ross MacDonald had offered that Central Algoma didn't provide. They didn't need to, I was the only one who would have benefited from them. More about that later.

Aside from School and Athletics, I was reveling in being home. It is true that Desbarats is boring compared to Brantford. Desbarats has 400 people while Brantford had 70,000 so, as you can imagine, there is a lot more to do in Brantford. But in Desbarats I lived at home with all the room to make my own fun, and that made all the difference.

I did find my moments of excitement, however. With Desbarats being such a small place, that excitement often came on the weekends, when my friends would all get together and take off to Sault Ste. Marie. They were great about involving me, but sometimes I think they may have had second thoughts. Take our bowling excursion for example. It was a Friday night and it seemed that my entire social circle was craving some action. We decided that bowling would be a great way to burn off some of that steam. I insisted that I throw my own balls, no help or special conditions, but that just proved to be frustrating. The competitive juices flowed everywhere, even here. I had been posting frame after frame scoring one point, three points and as often as not, zero points. Finally, when my turn came up again, I grabbed a ball and instead of trying to roll it precisely down the middle of the lane, I just heaved it with both hands as hard as I could. The next thing I hear were all the pins crashing into each other. I had scored a strike and that brought a stunned silence at my end of the building. Not because of the strike but because I scored it three lanes over to my right. A second later the entire bowling alley erupted in laughter. Even the manager came over and congratulated me. I'm told the regulars still talk about that night.

I rode Rebel endlessly, and played with my friends and even found some jobs to keep me busy and my pockets jingling. I was a hard worker but sometimes an accident waiting to happen. I always claimed it was my unbridled enthusiasm but there were some I could just never convince that I wasn't accident prone.

Take my buddy, David Stobie. I was hired, with David and Blake, to pitchfork the manure out of Ed Karhi's stables. Simple job except that, in my enthusiasm, I mistook David's boot for a hard,

Bowling wasn't our only pastime

dried up piece of manure and spiked my pitchfork right into his foot. He needed stitches, but fortunately he stills walks just fine. He forgave me but still claims I am accident-prone. I guess I have to give him that.

I was happy. I was home. I was wrestling and running and still winning. I was maintaining a decent academic standing and I had my family and friends. I thought life was good. This was where I wanted to be.

Unfortunately, as happens sometimes in life, for reasons I have never understood but have come to respect, when things seem too good to be true, they are!

Tragedy struck my family on February 26, 1978. That is a day that will be forever imbedded in my memory. It was late evening, around 10 p.m. We were all sitting around the house, watching television and reading.

All of a sudden Ian jumped up and shouted, "The barn is on fire!"

We all leapt to our feet and grabbed our coats, franticly trying to put on our boots. It was extremely cold out and the ground was covered in snow. We could hear the fire sirens already. The Desbarats volunteer fire department was already in motion and rushing to the scene. They were there in no time at all and actually did a great job. Unfortunately, our barn, like most in that day, was a tinderbox. It was old and weathered. The wood was as dry as kindling and it was full of hay. The most the fire department could do was make sure that the fire didn't spread to the house.

There was no way of saving the barn, or anything in it. The hay could be replaced and some of the equipment repaired but Rebel, and Ian's prize Appaloosa colt, not to mention all the chickens and rabbits, were trapped inside.

I remember Mom and Dad yelling at Ian as he tried to rush inside and free the horses. I heard beams and pillars crashing and falling and Ian was almost hit. He escaped, thank god, how would we have dealt with that, but he wasn't able to free the horses. It was an eerie feeling to stand there listening to the crackling fire, feeling the intense heat, knowing that Rebel was trapped inside there.

By then, it seemed the entire town was there. They were holding and consoling us as we watched the barn burn and come crashing down to the ground. We lost all the chickens, the rabbits, the hay and the tools, but losing the horses devastated us. I'm not sure which of us was more heart broken, me or Ian.

Ian had saved and saved to buy that colt and put his heart and soul into raising her. He was inconsolable. Nobody could get a word out of him for days. Nothing could replace his loss in that moment.

As for me, I don't have to tell you what Rebel meant to me. He was everything. He had been my best friend since I was six. Always there when I wanted him, always willing to listen, never questioning my decisions, always obliging when I wanted to ride, just the best friend anyone could ever want. To make it worse, I was old enough by then to understand what kind of agony he must have gone through. Rebel died of smoke inhalation. A painful, choking, lung searing agony that he couldn't possibly have understood. It made me cry to think of my friend, all alone, in such pain. Even writing about it brings a tear to my eye now.

I don't know how much that night influenced my next big decision, but as I finished out the school year, I found myself wanting to leave my new life in Desbarats, my newfound freedom at Central Algoma, my hard-won superstar status among the sighted. I had proven to myself, and everyone else, that I could make it in the sighted world. I had passed all my subjects, continued winning in track and wrestling, carved out an active, fun social life, and was comfortable. I could have stayed and been quite happy.

Happy, yes, but apprehensive too. I was entering my Junior year and, as always, was concerned about being ready for transition to an independent adult life. Maybe I was looking to maximize my advantages, but of all things...and it astounded me at first...I longed to go back to Brantford.

The idea really began to sink in with me that spring. W. Ross MacDonald was where I had been truly the most free. I had carved out a life for myself there where I could roam at will. I knew every nook and cranny of that place. I'd learned and achieved things that I hadn't at Central Algoma. I was a better student, for one thing. Ross MacDonald has special things like raised maps for learning geography. Academically speaking, that sort of help really makes a difference. Even the athletic facilities gave me an advantage. Ross MacDonald had an indoor track that I could run on alone. I could ramp up my training in ways I simply couldn't at Central Algoma. I thought I was going to find independence in a sighted school but many of the methods set up in Brantford actually gave me more freedom to learn. I missed all those hours on the outdoor rink playing hockey with the tin can and our tin can hockey league, something I didn't have in Desbarats either.

I hated to admit it, but the teachers who said I'd miss the place were right. Hey, I also missed the attention that I received at Ross MacDonald. I had popularity and acceptance enough at Central Algoma but that wasn't like being King of the Hill. Not even close. Let's be honest, maybe I just wanted to go out on top.

More than anything, I missed the special closeness I had with my former classmates at Brantford. I made many friends at Central Algoma but my classmates at Ross MacDonald were family. A friend in Desbarats could live one mile, or thirty miles, away. Some you only ever saw in class. In Brantford, we lived together. Nobody went home after class, some maybe on weekends, but we had a special closeness that came from being together literally day and night, 24/7 as they say. I didn't realize until I left how much I thrived on it, and how much I would miss my best pals - Eric and Doug and Roger. I would come to learn that they missed me as well. Not just my buddies but Coach Howe, the faculty, even the administrative staff. It seems that I had been part of the fabric of their lives as much as they had been part of mine. I was welcomed back with open arms, maybe not by every last person, but by most. Fortunately, I hadn't burned my bridges.

I felt good returning to Ross MacDonald. I didn't come slinking back in with my tail between my legs. I had done what I set out to do at Central Algoma. I'd won acceptance. I'd demonstrated I could operate in a sighted environment with a high degree of proficiency. I had blended in socially, mentally and, needless to say, athletically.

My return to Ross MacDonald was actually triumphant in some respects. I was elected student council president in both my junior and senior years. I was beginning to put the lessons I learned in wrestling and hockey, about giving back to others, to work. I worked to gain more trust from the faculty. I lobbied the staff to allow us the same flexibility other fifteen, sixteen and seventeen year old students had. Things like a decent smoking area for the students who did smoke, more freedom to choose our wardrobe and more respect when the school conducted its tours.

That was important. I learned through my work on council that these tours of outsiders, consisting of politicians, educators, religious leaders, business people, were important in raising money and interest in the school. The downside was that many of us felt like freaks in a side show when the tours came through. I fought hard to get the school to find ways to treat the students more respectfully during these tours. Both sides were happier as a result. That was one of the more rewarding public battles I took on.

Wrestling and athletics remained my priority even after my return to Ross MacDonald but once I was back in my environment, I was able to get into an academic groove as well. As happy as I was to be back, I knew I had to get ready for life after WRM and after wrestling. I took full advantage of my return. I set myself on course to pursue a post secondary education at Carleton University, but that is another chapter.

Do the Work

Hard work is no guarantee of success, but a lack of hard work is an almost certain guarantee of disappointment and frustration.

I'm not saying that there isn't tremendous value in learning to work smarter, in refining your techniques or your delivery or your methodology. There is always a benefit from improvement but if you ever expect to use the edge you are developing to gain a higher level of success you need to do the hard work first, and keep doing it.

In the words of the legendary salesman Frank Bettger, "Sales is the easiest job in the world if you work it hard but the hardest job in the world if you try to take it easy."

The hilarious book, "Murphy Was an Optimist," says "No matter what you want to do, you'll have to do something else first." That something else is the work!

Opportunity is often said to come disguised as hard work. Luck is commonly defined as preparation meeting opportunity and preparation always consists of hard work.

Are you starting to see a theme here? If not, consider it this way.

Have you ever heard that you have to be willing to pay the price necessary to reach your goal? You're not paying that price in dollars. It is an investment mind you, but it comes in the form of hard work.

Maybe you know the phrase "there is never a traffic jam on the extra mile." Do you know why that is? It's because most of us are too occupied with looking for a short cut that we never do the work necessary to develop the stamina, physically or mentally, to get to the extra mile in the first place.

Why are quick fix weight loss programs so popular? Why does every new miracle exercise program that comes on the market tell you can have a world class body in three 15-minute workouts a week? Because most people are looking for the shortcut.

I can't comment on your experience but I can tell you that in mine, the short cuts don't work. There is no magic bullet. There is no magic closing line or technique. There is no magic weight loss food. There is no miracle management technique or parenting style that will replace hard work and experience.

Here's the reality. The miracle edge is your experience. The miracle edge is learning from your experience and applying those lessons in a never ending program of self-evaluation and improvement until you reach the point where it appears you know the secrets and have magic techniques that makes success look easy. The short-cuts that everybody seems to be looking for actually come in small incremental gains in skill, knowledge and awareness that accumulate to become a great advantage. It is the difference between having 20 years experience vs. one years experience 20 times.

At the same time, if you didn't do the work necessary to have the knowledge, or strength or energy needed to create the foundation necessary for such a self-improvement program, you will always be frustrated.

I promise you that if you were to sit down with the people you know who make success look so easy, you'll be amazed at how much work they did before they became so good.

There is no replacement for the work. Let me use my experience to explain.

My success as a wrestler didn't come because I had a magic, trademark move that nobody could stop. Far from it. My success came from the extra sit-ups, the extra pushups and the extra laps that created my foundation of strength and stamina. Then there was the endless repetition of practice match after practice match until my muscle memory reached a point that I didn't have to think about the moves anymore. They were unconscious and my focus was on taking advantage of opportunity (remember - preparation meeting opportunity) on the mat and outlasting my opponents. I'm not saying that this was all a grand plan from the beginning but I learned along the way. Regardless of how good a wrestler I became, my advantage came from all the work.

I didn't win the U.S. Blind National Skiing Championship because I was a superior skier with brilliant technique. I won because I had done so much hard work as a wrestler that I was able to push my body for four months and, through sheer repetition, develop the muscle memory to fly down the mountain on auto pilot. If I hadn't done the work to develop myself physically, I could never have taken on that challenge. I had an advantage and by that point in my life knew how to make the most of it. I'm sure the rest of the field would have been shocked if they knew how hard I had trained all my life. I also doubt any other blind skier ever trained as hard for a single event, but look at the results.

Of course, sometimes you don't have 20 years.

Intensity, and focus on improvement, with practice, can dramatically shorten the curve. That is not a short cut. It simply means that you have to be a person of action, and be prepared for more "action" than you've experienced before, instead of reaction. Of course, by "action" I mean work. You decide.

I didn't just magically figure this out.

I spent more than 18 years as a good will ambassador for the Edward Jones Investment Company. My responsibility was the development of positive brand recognition and a positive corporate culture.

I came to realize this early in my business career when I found myself spending so much time in the world of Financial Advisors and I was struggling to develop rapport with them. After some soul searching conversations, I came to realize what was missing. If I wanted to connect with them, and connect them to the company, I needed to learn how to think like them, I needed to learn what they already knew, and I needed to adapt that knowledge to my style if I was going to have credibility with them. That, to me, meant I needed my Series 7 license. That is the license needed to be a stockbroker. To receive it, you must complete a 250-question, six-hour exam, which I had to take orally.

Problem was, I needed it now. I needed ten years of experience and personal growth and I needed it in ten weeks. Even more daunting was the reality that it started with my obtaining a license no other totally blind person had ever held.

That is when the real lesson of winning the United States Blind Snow Skiing Championship hit me.

I went from being a novice skier to a National Champion in four months. If I could do that on the slopes, why couldn't I develop the knowledge base and understanding of the skills of a successful Financial Advisor in the same amount of time?

Let's think about that. How did I catch up to the field to be able to win in Alta? The competition, the group I wanted to be equal to, had anywhere from ten to twenty years skiing experience. With the skiing season averaging maybe twenty weeks a year and most skiing one or two days a week, on the weekends, that would be approximately 200 to 300 days or 800 to 1,200 hours.

If that was their body of work, then I should have thought of myself as having 10 years experience also. When I hit the top of the hill in Alta I had been skiing everyday for four months, averaging six to eight hours a day on my skis, being mentored by a successful coach. That's 120 days at, say seven hours a day, or 840 hours of actual skiing experience. When you add two to three hours a day of mental preparation and visualization, all compressed into four months, you have a substantial body of work that produced tremendous results.

Now, I do believe there is one more reason why I was able to accomplish so much in such little time. I started with a specific goal in mind. I had a reason why I was doing all this and I measured myself against that goal every day. Was I getting closer? What did I learn today? How did I improve? Was the improvement enough? There was no casual experience. Everything was measured and everything had a reason.

With that mind set, I think my experience accelerated me beyond skiers with many years on the slope. I had to get better and the better I got the more I wanted to do and the more I did the better I got. As a result, I am certain I skied more in four months than most people did in ten years. Not only that, but I learned and improved as a matter of routine, not just residue from simple time and repetition.

Once I understood the reasons behind my skiing success, I was able to transfer that mindset to my Series 7. I completed the training and obtained my license in two and half months. There are no Braille training manuals for the Series 7. My course of study was to tote around 88 hours of training material on cassette tapes. Jim Weddle of Edwards Jones actually had to make special arrangements for those tapes to be recorded. I listened to and memorized the material while I maintained my full travel and speaking schedule. Of course, I was assigned a coach from the training department. I continually challenged her, not only to ensure I understood the material from a licensing standpoint, but I challenged her about how it applied to the work of the Financial Advisor. I related that to my training and experience in communication and relationships (my equivalent to the sit-ups and pushups that prepared me for wrestling) and soon was asking much better questions of the Financial Advisors I worked with. I became exponentially more effective at immersing them positively into the culture and fabric of the company. The results for all of us, the Financial Advisor, the company and me were tremendous. So good, in fact, that I remained with the company for 18 years.

Why did I tell you all of this? Because it is vital for you to understand that the application of the knowledge gained from very hard work produces substantial results. It's not just going through the motions of the work, but the quality of the work that ultimately makes the difference. The work required by your circumstances is unique and you must figure out what that is. You must also take charge of the variables if urgency matters to you. Totally submerge yourself if necessary but you must do the work. Nothing great is accomplished without it.

Of course, there is still reason to respect age and time and length of service. There is one awesome asset you want to have but that you cannot accelerate. It only comes from applying yourself effectively and learning over an extended period of time. What is it?

WISDOM

If you could, ask John Wooden about the value of hard work. His UCLA Bruins won 10 NCAA National Basketball Championships in 11 years. Yes, he had extremely skilled players but he made sure that they were capable of running a full court press for the entire game. They did the work, to the extent that even on nights when their skill was not shining at their best, they still won simply because they were in better shape, they could wear down their opponents and eventually win because they had the stamina to play in the extra mile. It's not the only reason he was so successful, trust me – he was a brilliant coach – but all that work gave his team a distinct advantage and they made the most of it, over and over again.

Roughhousing By The Rules

I've often wondered, what would have become of me if I had been left as that un-channeled, over energized, rebellious bundle of mischief that originally arrived at W. Ross MacDonald.

Fortunately, for me I believe, the world never found out.

I was a high-octane kid who needed a release. I'm sure that was part of my teacher's thought process, although maybe I really did show potential, at that age who knows? For whatever the reason, in the fall of second grade, I was one of only four kids from the junior school to be invited to join the wrestling team.

This was a big deal, for more reasons than I understood at the time. In my little second grade mind, I was getting a chance to leave junior school. Wrestling practice took place in the gymnasium in senior school and I couldn't wait to roam further. To me it was a field trip to unexplored territory.

Once I got there, though, that attitude got adjusted. I went from a curious kid on a new adventure to an intimidated kid in the midst of a struggle. I was a ringleader of mischief in Junior School, even in second grade, but now I had been called up. This was the big leagues with big kids who could play the game as well as me.

I liked the roughhousing, loved it actually, but here we were roughhousing with kids bigger and stronger than us. Suddenly, I wasn't able to pick on the other kids.

Other kids were picking on me!

Practice could be such a battle. I wasn't the only high-octane kid on the mat but I was one of the smallest. There could be up to forty combative blind kids all on the mat at the same time. I would get bullied by other kids who were up to eight years older. You would be on the mat, trying to follow the coaches orders, doing your sit-ups or whatever, when a couple guys beside you would start horsing around. Next thing you know you've been kicked in the face or a body forty pounds heavier would land on you. Just as you're thinking, "Hey, I'm not supposed to bend that way," you'd get slapped upside the head. It was like a demolition derby. Fun when you delivered the blow but infuriating when you were on the receiving end. It was not for the faint of heart, that's for sure.

At first, I wasn't sure I wanted to do this. It was painful and, at least initially, not a lot of fun. Eric had been chosen for the team, too, and I kept going because he kept going, and vice versa. We were still at it after a couple of months when I found my first real motivation to stay with it. Our coach, John Howe, thought I was ready to experience some competition and entered me in a tournament at the Brant County YMCA. The thought of getting on the mat at an outside facility made me nervous until I found out that I was going to be competing against sighted kids. That made me come alive. I had no idea that would be possible, but when it became real, something inside me woke up. To be able to compete against them was important. I was still a little annoyed about being at Ross MacDonald. It was a fine school, but that didn't compensate for the fact I didn't think I should be at a school for the blind, period.

In my young mind, if I hadn't been played a mean trick, being blinded, I wouldn't be there. Now this wrestling was a way to lash out against my blindness. It was a way to get back at the sighted world for putting me where I was, a long way from home. Even more, it was a way to gain acceptance to the sighted world I so resented, and yet, wanted to join.

That first tournament was in February of 1970, just two months after I had started wrestling. I had such a hard time falling asleep the night before. I was nervous, scared, hyper, anxious, all at the same time. I really had no idea what to expect but I knew it was going to be a big day. I think more than anything I was afraid of embarrassing myself. I just didn't want to be a failure.

We had to get up very early Saturday morning to go down to the YMCA and weigh in. It was foreign to me. We got on a little bus at the school. John Howe drove. We arrived, walked up some steps and went into the YMCA. Inside, it was a sea of humanity. A lot of parents and kids were there. Imagine your eyes being flooded with an array of flashing lights. That's what filled my ears, indistinguishable noise.

Weighing-in seemed to me like a silly ceremony, too, in the beginning. The lightest weight class in Junior wrestling was 60 pounds. I weighed 52. We went to the change room. You're supposed to strip down to your underwear and get weighed. Heck, I could've weighed in with my shoes and jeans on and still made it under 60 pounds, but coach said everyone had to do it. John Howe took me by the hand and led me up there. Confident as I normally was, I was scared this time.

There was no way I was going to make it to the scales on my own. Shoot, there were probably 100 people there in the room between me and the scales, not to mention gym bags and equipment scattered all over the floor. I didn't know the space or configuration of the room. For me, it was just total confusion. There was too much noise for me to "hear" my way around as I was used to doing.

For once I wasn't so certain of myself. I wasn't so full-speed ahead. Maybe afraid is a better word. This was my first taste of the fear of failure.

I got on the scale and some guy said, "Fifty-two pounds." I stepped off. Now my competitors, or at least their coaches, knew they would be wrestling a guy almost eight pounds lighter. Eight pounds seemed like so much back then. That reality just made my head spin more with apprehension.

I was totally off stride but the electricity in the room jolted me in a good way. I may have been scared and nervous but I was also excited because it was getting more real every second. I was going to wrestle with the sighted kids. I really was! We got our stuff back on and grabbed a bite to eat. My fear may have been turning into excitement but I was still so nervous I didn't want to eat anything. Coach Howe said, "well, you have to. You won't have any strength." I ate a bowl of cereal. I hardly tasted it as it went down.

My weight class was up first in the competition. We came back, changed into our wrestling shoes and uniform, a singlet they called it. The nice thing about being in uniform was that even if I wasn't good enough, at least now I looked like I belonged, at least for the moment.

We went out near the mat and sat on our team bench. The place smelled like old sweat but there was a lot of kidding and laughter on our bench. When they announced the first matches, coach Howe came over, rubbed my shoulders, loosening me up and told me to do some jumping jacks and stretches. Then they called my name and I had to go to the center of the mat. These kids in my weight class were all fifty-eight, fifty-nine and sixty pounds. In those days, we shook hands and then locked arms. When I felt my opponent's arm, I thought, "God, how much bigger than me is this guy?"

It was frightening, but I wasn't psyched out. I was nervous, had butterflies, of course, but the energy had shifted from that initial fear all the way to enthusiasm now. Even though I was so young, I felt I had something to prove. I thought if I ever was going to get out of that school for the blind, this would be the springboard. This was an arena I could do it in. Wrestling is the only sport where a blind person can compete with a sighted person on an equal basis.

You probably think such thoughts wouldn't cross the mind of someone so young. I promise you they did. It wasn't that I was so mature for my age or had any great understanding or insight. It was just a longing and a hunger to get out of the school for the blind anyway I could. I sensed, on some deep down level I didn't even understand, that I had to make the most of this chance to escape.

My enthusiasm was also fueled by Grandpa Jefferies. Back at Christmas, he told me, "Craig, give them hell from the start. That's the secret to winning." He was one of the people who mattered most in my life and I really took his words to heart. The one thing I wouldn't be, going into that first match, was timid. Like everything else in my life I was on full throttle from the first whistle. It worked too. That first match took 24 seconds. I pinned my opponent.

It wasn't all skill and brilliance mind you. In fact, I had been losing to that point. He got an escape and a reversal, so he was up on me by a point but then we went off the mat. When we started again he just kind of walked into a move and I wound up pinning him. It was a very short match, but a ton of action. It was spirited from the first whistle and, somehow, I had won. I was flushed with pleasure. A deep sense of satisfaction swept through me. Give'em hell. Grandpa, you were right.

A sense of satisfaction might be too mild for what I was feeling right at that moment. I remember that winning was a rush, even then. When the referee took my arm and lifted it over my head for the first time, it was just the best thing I had ever experienced. I wanted to get right back on the mat and do it again. John Howe has since told me that I came off the mat that day and told him, "Coach, someday I'm going to be a champion."

Someday turned out to be that day. That afternoon, I was the champion. It took four more matches working through my bracket,

including one particularly memorable match that has stayed with me until this day. I remember it so well because it was a real wake up call to just how hard other guys would fight me to win. The other guy in this case was Richie Dawson who was so aggressive that he bit me. His dad was the referee. Richie got disqualified!

I remember. I was pinning him and Richie, who didn't like to lose any more than I did, bit me on the arm. I slugged him right in the face. It was just a reaction, part of my rough-and-tumble nature. I would've done the same to Ian. I didn't even think about what they might do to us.

Winning may not be everything, but it did feel good.

The whistle blew and the ref ripped us apart. I showed the bite marks and Richie was disqualified. That first tournament helped establish my habits on the mat. I wouldn't take anything from anybody. That was the start of the mental toughness that would define the rest of my athletic career.

So did winning!

Winning that first gold medal was spectacular. When I went to bed that night I clutched my medal tight in my hand until I'm sure my knuckles were white. I slept with it in my hand. I slept with it under my pillow. I put it back around my neck. I tried it every way, seeing where I liked it best, where it seemed most comforting or prolonged the sense of exhilaration that I had on the mat.

That medal became a very tangible symbol of hope. I could touch it and bring back that sense of achievement I felt. It may have been my first experience with visualization, not that I knew that's what I was doing. When I held it I could see myself winning in my imagination. That image just grew stronger and stronger, until I reached that state of mind where I just expected to win, every time. It also stood for something more. It was something I had achieved against sighted opponents. It touched the core of me, into my soul. Winning that medal clearly was a turning point in my life. It catapulted my spirits into thinking I really could be competitive in a sighted environment. It wasn't the biggest or the fanciest medal I ever won, but it was by far the most important. It represented hope and served as my link to the world I so wanted to be a part of.

After dinner, back at Ross MacDonald, and all the excitement of telling my buddies about my triumph, I was back in my room still riding the adrenaline rush. Adrenaline is a powerful drug for most adults. Imagine how this overdose was affecting me at age seven. I wanted to talk about it, continue to feel it. I didn't want it to end. There was no way I could wait to tell my parents the next day on the phone. So I didn't. I phoned them that night. Collect. They were thrilled. If I hadn't called them I think they would have called me. They were as anxious to hear about my day as I was to tell them.

By the time we returned to classes on Monday I had come back to earth. That made it all the more surprising when I was called into the office of Mr. Armstrong, the school superintendent. We're not talking about my guidance counselor now, or even the principal. Mr. Armstrong was the head of the entire school. He was the Big Kahuna, if you will. Being called to his office was serious business.

My first reaction was dread. That feeling of, "OH NO!" What had I done this time? My pranks and misbehavior were almost daily occurrences but I couldn't remember any current crimes. I couldn't imagine that I was in any trouble although it wouldn't have surprised me either. Maybe I was doing so much wrong that I couldn't keep track of it. All I knew was that I had to go see the head of the entire school. How did he even know who I was? I have to tell you, I was scared.

I walked down the hall to his office. I had more butterflies swirling around in my stomach than before any match I ever wrestled. I almost sneaked into his office, like I was hoping nobody would notice I was there. To my total surprise, he met me with a handshake, used my name and lifted me off the floor with big hug. He didn't scold or lecture me at all, as I'd been expecting. Instead, he congratulated me. "Hey, that's really terrific what you did in the wrestling tournament. We're so proud of you," he said.

He didn't parade me up in front of the student body at an assembly, but he might as well have. I thought this was as big an acknowledgement as any student at Ross MacDonald could have asked for, and maybe it was, but the maximum dose of encouragement came later that evening.

Mr. Armstrong invited me to eat at his house. In his house! He lived on the school grounds and that evening I ate in his dining room. No cafeteria food for me. It was a real, meat and potatoes, home cooked meal. I'm talking real potatoes, just like home. If I didn't know better, and I didn't until I was older, I could have thought they called home and asked Mom what my favorite food was. When you're away from home, a meal like that means everything.

What I did know is that I liked how this made me feel. If this was how people treated you when you were a winner, then I wanted to win some more. I was determined never to lose another match.

Mr. Armstrong became like a second father to me. He would attend matches when he was able, drop by on practice once a week or so, check on me and encourage the team. He was continually looking out for me, particularly on weekends. There were numerous other dinners, too. Mr. Armstrong would actually laugh out loud when I regaled the dinner table with stories of my pranks. He would admonish some of my more audacious or outrageous escapades and sometimes suggest I tone it down a touch, but he respected the spirit of my adventures and never sought to break my spirit. Instead he guided it.

I was told years later, off the record of course, that Mr. Armstrong would come to my defense on occasion in staff meetings. He defended my escapades and defused the intentions of some staff members to take over the top disciplinary action against me. I'm sure these were the same times that he would invite me for dinner or take me aside at practice and give me words of wisdom, often urging me to focus my energy on wrestling instead of wasting my precious opportunity goofing off.

Mr. Armstrong was a major influence on my formative years. I have no doubt that much of my character and work habits were ingrained under the guidance of Mr. Armstrong's tactful but firm hand. I wonder how much more he might have taught me if I had not lost him so very much too soon.

Two years after that first victory at the Brantford YMCA, Mr. Armstrong died of a massive heart attack. The administration at Ross MacDonald knew that Mr. Armstrong was well liked by the entire student body and staff alike. When he passed away at the hospital, they called an immediate student body assembly to tell us of his passing. I had no warning what was coming as I entered the auditorium, but I could hear the somber music coming from the pipe organ. I wasn't prepared for such a devastating message but I knew bad news was coming. When they told us, I was crushed. I just sat there, maybe an hour or more, tears rolling down my cheeks. I had no experience with such tragedy. I was only in fourth grade and I had just lost, aside from my parents, my biggest fan. Mr. Armstrong had become my mentor. I looked forward to his hugs and our conversations. As I look back now, I see that I lost a dear friend, despite the difference in our ages and position. He'll always have a place in my heart.

Under that watchful eye of Mr. Armstrong, and of course, Coach Howe, my wrestling career got off to a roaring start. Fueled by a warped combination of loving to win and a total fear of losing, I won my first 27 matches in a row. I was already in third grade before I lost for the first time and that was to a fifth grader who was about 10 pounds heavier.

It wasn't a tournament match. By then Coach Howe had me wrestling in exhibition matches to keep me challenged and continue my development as a wrestler. Even though wrestling went by weight class, often in dual meets, John Howe would have me wrestle an extra match in addition to my normal matches. The extra match would be against someone bigger and stronger. He said it was just to gain experience.

It was an excellent strategy for improvement but on the day I lost my first match, I wasn't so impressed. Inside I was really boiling. I mean, I guess you're not really supposed to think you're invincible, but tell that to an eight-year-old kid who has won twenty-seven in a row.

Coach Howe explained that it was making me a better wrestler, which excited me, and a better person, which in third grade I quite frankly didn't understand. It was making me work harder, which I thrived on. Eventually, I think that being forced to stretch during those seemingly invincible days did teach me what it was to win with humility, to lose with dignity and always give my best shot in every situation, not just on the mat. I appreciate all that today, as an adult, but back then, that first taste of losing was terrible. If that's what failure tasted like, then I didn't want to taste failure at all. As a matter of fact, I'd rather have eaten liver!

I think I succeeded early on because I had an enormous fear of losing. It wasn't so much about losing the match or a fear of being humiliated or losing my special perks or my status. It was about losing my opportunity. When I lost, rare as it was, I felt as if my chance to get home, to get back to the sighted world was slipping away. I had to keep winning to keep that hope alive, because when you have hope, you have everything. That's why I was always willing to put in a little extra to do better. I wasn't a braggart at heart. The arrogance people saw was just a façade I tacked up over the uncertainty and fright I had of failing. I also didn't want to use blindness as an excuse if I lost.

The harder I worked, the more success I experienced. That was natural and to be expected, if not by me, then by my coaches and mentors. In me, it manifested as a hunger, an absolute thirst to be the best I could be. Wrestling against sighted kids just fueled that fire. It set the bar higher. Winning against those kids would get me noticed and give me credibility. It also meant that I didn't just have to be a good wrestler, I had to be faster and stronger. Grandpa's advice worked but I learned that I also had to be able to "give'em hell" for as long as it took.

I started building myself up to the point that, at nine years old, a lot of days I was doing 500 sit-ups and 500 push-ups. Not all at once, but, during the course of the day, I would do 500 of each. I had built myself up to 80 pounds. When I was 11 or 12, I could do 500 sit-ups in a row no problem. Push-ups? I could do a couple hundred straight.

I would get up at 5 a.m., do my sit ups and push-ups and be back in bed before anyone knew I'd been up. I didn't want people to know how hard I was training. I was a maniac. I was fighting for an opportunity to be treated as an equal. In my mind, I think I was fighting to get back home. I was fighting to be accepted in a sighted world. I think it would be safe to say I was on a mission.

Between meets, I drove myself to prepare for that fleeting moment of competition. I never did weights to build myself up at the time; just push-ups and sit-ups. The only exception was my legs. As I began to mature, somewhere around eighth grade, I could repeatedly do 600 pounds on the leg press machine. My legs were the main source of my strength. I was blessed naturally by God to have that.

I also did all this because wrestling is an individual sport. You don't phone home for help. Your teammates and your coaches can't help you, or at least not much, once you're on the mat, anyway. You can rely only on yourself and you have to have the reserves to sustain yourself. You can know all the moves, and perform them perfectly but if you don't have the strength, the energy or the stamina to deliver in the crunch, it doesn't matter. Wrestling develops tremendous character and tremendous individualism. Those lessons were great preparation for my entire life.

Wrestling consumed me. I would daydream about it in class. I'd think about new wrestling moves and couldn't wait to test them in the gym. Class wasn't that important to me. I did what was necessary to get the grades I needed to stay on the wrestling team, but wrestling became an absolute priority. It was the vehicle I was going to use to achieve my goal.

Mom and Dad were definitely my biggest fans.

Wrestling seemed to drive my every waking moment; when I wasn't thinking up pranks and getting in trouble with Eric, I dreamed about gold medals. I lived for victories with the losses haunting me in between. I learned to never take winning for granted.

My name started to spread outside W. Ross MacDonald and outside Brantford. In fact, I had developed my reputation to the point that, between my eighth and ninth grade years in 1976, I was picked to compete in Canada's first national games for the physically disabled. My performance at those games lead to my being chosen to compete for Canada at the first international games for the physically disabled.

By that time, my athletic ability had extended to the track as well. I was beginning to excel in the sprints, the 60-meter, 200-meter and 400-meter dashes. I was winning almost every race I ran and I honestly don't remember ever finishing lower than third. I don't think I ever finished out of the medals.

I was brimming with confidence by now.

This was all happening at the same time that I was preparing for my transfer to Central Algoma Secondary School. I truly thought I was ready to handle anything the sighted world could throw at me.

I was going to find out how difficult that could be as several of the biggest incidents in my life were about to unfold.

First, we lost my Grandma MacFarlane. That was in September 1975. She lived next door to us in Desbarats and I very was close to her. Remember, walking to her house was one of my early, great adventures in independence. Hearing her voice when I arrived was always a wonderful reward, not to mention the cookies. Now that voice was gone.

Eight months later we lost Grandpa Jefferies.

I was at a three-day regional competition in wrestling and track and field, which qualified you for the Ontario provincial champion-ships. I had won a gold in sprinting before Mom and Dad left to see Grandpa Jefferies in the hospital. They handed him the medal and they tell me Grandpa grabbed it so hard that he wrinkled the ribbon and scrunched it up in his hand. They said he would not let go of it.

It was an emotional tournament for me. I was extremely torn about what to do. I wanted very badly to go and see him. Everyone seemed certain that he wasn't going to make it. If they were right and I didn't go, it probably meant I would never see him again. That was an impossible idea to grasp.

If I did go it meant forfeiting any chance to compete at the Provincials, which meant no chance at a National championship or making the National team.

Mom and Grandma were insistent. They wanted me to stay in the competition. They told me to stay for Grandpa. They told me that he wanted me to stay and win for him.

I didn't fight with them. I took them at their word. I stayed and won gold, in wrestling and sprinting. Immediately after I won, Ian and I jumped into a taxi, raced to the train station and caught the first train headed for Sudbury, which would stop in Nairn Centre. We made good time, but by the time we got there, it was too late. Grandpa had died.

His funeral was a few days later. It was the day before the pro-vincial wrestling championships for the blind in southern Ontario, so once again I found myself rushing off. This time to the airport. I had to hop onto a plane right after the funeral because weigh-ins were being held the next morning, followed by the competition. It was all so emotionally devastating, especially for a thirteen year old. I felt bad, guilty even, about not being there before Grandpa died. Now I was rushing away without a moment to stop for him. I was a wreck.

The weigh-in was nothing more than a ritual. I was just going through the motions. I didn't feel the burn. There was no fire in my belly. For the first time in my life I really didn't want to compete. In fact, as I stood on the scale, I can honestly say that I just didn't care.

My first match of the day should have been a stroll. I was wrestling somebody I knew well and had defeated easily many times but this morning I was floundering. At the end of the first round, I was actually losing. Even then, I found myself between rounds questioning whether I really wanted to be champion that day.

Coach Howe had his arm around me. He knew I wasn't myself. He wasn't yelling at me this time. He knew what was going on inside. I was still thinking about Grandpa when, in an instant, unexpectedly, it hit me!

That old saying grandpa used to give me all the time.

"Give them hell on the start, Craigie!"

Suddenly, I felt I had really let my Grandpa down by not trying my best the first round. If he was watching me from wherever he was, he must've been totally disappointed with my effort. My muscles got tight. I wanted back on the mat that instant. I found that Eye of the Tiger I had been missing.

I went out for the second round with purpose and pinned the guy before he knew what happened. Hello!

With Grandpa's hand on my shoulder for the rest of the day, I went on to win Provincial Championship and a couple weeks later I also won the Canadian Blind National Championship.

That set the stage for a pretty big summer.

At age fourteen, I carried the Canadian Flag in the Olympiad for the Physically Disabled in the Toronto suburb of Etobicoke. I was the youngest member of the team. I might also have been the most passionate. I took representing my country very seriously. I saw it as a great honor, to the extent that I actually got into a couple of scuffles in the change rooms with kids from the U.S. team. They were really rather minor dust-ups, just shoving matches actually, but it seemed inevitable. The atmosphere was intense.

I also received a rather startling lesson in humility during training camp at the Olympiad. It was about one week before the competition and we were taken on a tour of the Blind Olympic facilities, which included the pool where the diving events would be conducted. As I listened to the guide explain how high the ten-meter diving platform was, which is about thirty-three feet, my mind drifted off. I had been listening to the Montreal Olympic Games on TV and I 'd heard them talk about Greg Louganis doing a "double back flip with a twist in the pike position." I had no idea what the "pike position" was but that didn't matter. I got energized at the thought of doing my own dive.

I took off, running up the tower, shouting "Hey, coach, watch," as I ran. I took a huge leap backwards off the top of the tower and started trying to flip and twist through the air. Honestly, not flipping would have been harder. It was also hard to judge the distance to the water. I wound up twisting around and over rotating into about two and three-quarter flips and landed – square on my back.

They say that when an elite diver executes perfect form, hitting the water from the ten-meter platform is still like diving through a sidewalk. I'm here to tell you that is the absolute truth. I felt like I had split myself in two when I hit the water. It knocked the wind right out of me. I came out of the water gasping for air and doubled over in pain. I could barely walk the rest of the day and my back was red for a solid week.

My sense of invincibility definitely suffered an attitude adjustment that day.

You already know about my initial rite of passage, or should I say acceptance, onto the wrestling team at Central Algoma. That set the tone for the next couple of years. Those who challenged my arrival soon became some of my closer friends. Tim Golick actually became my roommate for road trips. In later years, I was saddened to learn of Tim's death in an auto accident in Northern Ontario.

To make the message even sadder, Jack MacIntire was killed in the same accident.

Once I settled in, wrestling life continued, pretty much as it always had.

There was a tournament somewhere almost every week. Sometimes we travelled overnight, sometimes it was just a day trip but we always wrestled. The discipline was still good for me, I al-

ways thrived on competition. I continued to win the majority of my matches and tournaments, but I have to admit that for a little while, some of the fire diminished.

Maybe it was the atmosphere of Central Algoma. Maybe it was trying to adapt to the social life of a typical teenager, maybe it was the new challenges of maintaining adequate academic numbers in a sighted school, but I was distracted. I also think that to a certain extent I had let down my guard. My mission had been to return home and establish myself in the sighted world. I was doing that and reveling in the life of a "normal guy," rather than one who was always defined by his athletic prowess. I don't know the reason but I knew inside that I had lost a degree of interest. You could say I had lost my edge.

The pursuit of trophies and medals had begun to lose its meaning for me. I had been winning them since I was seven. They didn't shine as much anymore. Maybe it was because I had won so many, maybe it was because I achieved my primary objective and didn't have the same sense of purpose driving me, but even though I was still successful on the mat and the track, (I never lost my fear of losing). I just wasn't attacking competition with the same zeal. I missed that. One day at Central Algoma I tried to inject some usefulness back into those trophies, and I learned a great lesson in the process.

In the ninth grade I won a big wrestling tournament in Detroit, Michigan and I was given a large marble trophy. I decided rather than take it home, show it off, and add it to my collection, I would give it to a ten-year-old boy in a wheelchair who had been watching me and cheering for me loyally for five matches. I felt that his loyalty should be rewarded. Fans like him had been so valuable to me over the years. I thought this might be a nice way to pay those fans back. I also thought it might give this particular fan a greater sense of hope. He would never be able to win a trophy like that, but maybe it would remind him of what someone else with an alleged disability was able to achieve despite what had happened to him.

Whether it was rational or subconscious, I did give him that trophy with the hope that somehow it would bring greater meaning to my wrestling again. Please don't get me wrong, though. I'm

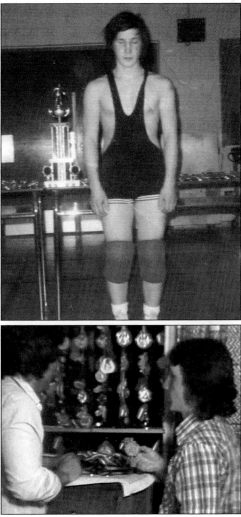

I didn't mind the medals and trophies, but my objective was to get back home.

not claiming that I became the world's greatest humanitarian that day, or that I am now. I was very much a work in progress at that time. I can tell you however, that I got tremendous satisfaction from giving that trophy away. I thought my reasoning was sound and the emotion it brought to me confirmed that. I can still remember the excitement in his voice when I handed it to him. I realized at that moment that it meant a lot more to him than it would ever mean to me.

This was a significant step for me in my maturation, both as an athlete and person. I had spent my entire life struggling to be independent, avoiding help from others as much as I could. It did me good to feel what it was like to be a helper, to realize that satisfaction and reward could come in other forms. It forced me out of my comfort zone and made me a better man. Helping others and making opportunity live for others became somewhat of a cornerstone of my life as I grew up from that point on, eventually becoming a focal point of my speaking career and of my foundation, but I still needed time to realize all of that, spiritually and professionally.

Not all my athletic endeavors were as successful as wrestling and sprinting. I also tried my hand at discus, javelin, and briefly, high jump. I learned high jump, like everything else, through tactile trial and error. In the beginning I would feel the stanchions and the crossbar, get a measurement of the height clearly fixed in my mind, back step three strides, then sprint those three strides and jump. It was a good strategy but limited in terms of the height I could clear. I gradually extended my back steps to four, then five, six and eventually seven strides. That was the limit of the room I had to work with, at least the way the high jump pit was positioned when practiced in the winter. With each additional step back, I found I could clear higher and higher settings, but once I was limited at seven, I started getting frustrated. I wanted to go higher. Then I got the bright idea that I could get an extra step if I approached the jump on an angle. Creative, maybe, effective, not so much. During my first approach on the angle, I am certain I came at the jump faster than ever, but the angle affected my judgment. I took off and as I reached the peak of my jump, cracked my head off the stanchion. I spun like a helicopter blade, knocking over both the crossbar and the stanchions. I picked myself up, wiping blood from eyes and was promptly taken to the doctor for seven stitches in my eyebrow. That was my last high jump attempt.

In the meantime, life, and athletics, continued. I may not have been exactly burning up the wrestling mat that year, but I did rekindle my competitive burn in another national blind competition, on the track. In the summer of 1977 I had become a big favorite to win the 200 and 400 meter gold medals at the blind nationals. With this expectation I overcame my little competitive swoon and got cranked up for those games.

Of course, you can't run in the Nationals unless you compete in the Provincials. I was used to that routine, I did it every year for both track and wrestling.

What I was not used to was extreme heat.

At the Ontario Provincial Championships that summer the weather took a rare turn for Canada. The temperature soared to a record 107 degrees, even more when you calculate the humidex but what did that matter? 107 was still plenty hot, humidity or not. Hot enough, in fact, to cause me to change my race strategy.

I had always paced myself for the first 200 to 250 meters, staying with the pack but saving my all out kick for the last 150, which it seemed was always where the race was won. On this day I was worried about having any kick left and decided I would try and take charge right from the start. I was hoping to surprise my competitors and build enough of a lead to carry me to the finish, even if I did tire out. I did take the early lead but I couldn't hold it at the end. I lost in a photo finish by one-hundredth of a second. I'd actually fallen behind by 20 meters and had to fight back but just didn't quite have enough to be first at the tape.

Fortunately, all three medal winners were taken to the Nationals so there was a chance at redemption.

The Nationals were held in Edmonton, Alberta that year and the temperature was much more forgiving, only 85 degrees, which was just fine. I ran my usual race and won pulling away at the finish line.

I learned a valuable lesson in humility that summer too. I had begun to believe my press clippings, as they say, by the end of my first year at Central Algoma. I was living my dream of independence in the sighted world, continuing to win in virtually all my athletic endeavors, developing a large network of friends and the associated popularity that goes with it. I was a National champion in wrestling and the fastest blind sprinter in the country. All good things except that in the mind of a fourteen year old, all that can lead to some warped thinking and that summer I was guilty, and got called out.

By the time I reached Edmonton my ego was in full bloom. I thought I could do no wrong. I decided I was above the rules and on the last night of the competition, with nothing left to rest up for, decided to go out on the town, totally disrespecting the curfew.

The team manager was waiting in my room when I got back. "MacFarlane," he said, "I'm taking your medals and your uniform. You're suspended from the team."

At first I was livid. Who did he think he was? In my mind I had earned those medals and the uniform was my souvenir from the Nationals. I was the fastest blind sprinter in Canada. I proved it that day, how dare this guy challenge me!

Then it hit me. This wasn't just some guy who didn't like my latest prank. This was management, in effect, and had the authority to really bring consequences to my actions. This time in a way that had never struck home before. We were in Edmonton, 2,500 miles from home, and my parents were there too, in the same hotel. They had taken the time off to come along and watch me and now I was about to disrespect them on a National stage. My ego was, although I was too young to understand it, about to cause my parents an unfair embarrassment. That made me stop dead in my tracks. I realized in that moment that I had been wrong. I backed down, made my apologies and was able to retain my medals and uniform. I was also able to uphold my parents honor. I learned, through the tough love of one disciplined manager, that I wasn't above the rules. Pushing the envelope in the heat of competition was highly encouraged, but that ended when the games did.

TOP Dalton, Craig, Patti, Derek, Ashley, and Morgan September, 2013.
BOTTOM LEFT Just another walk on water!
BOTTOM RIGHT Patti and I at the Neuschwanstein Castle in Germany.

To Craig McFarlane
With best wishes, Nancy Reagan

TOP Receiving an award from First Lady, Nancy Reagan.
MIDDLE Gordie Howe and I carrying the Olympic torch through Washington, D.C. 1984.
BOTTOM One of the highlights of my life, meeting Pope Benedict XVI.

TOP LEFT Derek, Ashley, and Morgan with mom and dad at a wedding in Canada 2010.
TOP RIGHT Visiting with Wayne Gretzky at the Canada Cup, Ottawa 1996.
BOTTOM The Netherlands is an awesome place to visit.

TOP Surprising Patti with a Disney sculpture for her birthday.
BOTTOM I enjoyed some Kiwi hospitality during a speaking tour of New Zealand.

TOP The sounds and visual descriptions were fabulous after my speaking engagement in London, England.

BOTTOM Another special moment with the President and First Lady, George and Barbara Bush.

TOP LEFT   Does it get any better than this? Sanibel Island, Florida
TOP RIGHT   Take a ride on the wild side! 1985
BOTTOM   What an amazing city...and oh so much history. Rome, 2006

Craig MacFarlane
Cypress Gardens, Florida
September, 1994

TOP   I loved the culture, people and food in Munich, Germany. 2007
BOTTOM   Living on the edge!!!! Cypress Gardens, Florida

TOP On one of my numerous trips to the White House to visit President George H.W. Bush. 1992
BOTTOM LEFT—Sharing another laugh with Steven Tyler. 1994
BOTTOM RIGHT The National Sportsmanship Award Banquet, St. Louis, MO, 2005

TOP From left: My parents, Joyce and Earl MacFarlane and Patti's parents, Diane and
     Don Everson, Canada 2010.
BOTTOM Another special family moment at Disney's Animal Kingdom in January, 2012.

TOP   Sharing the stage with Arnold Schwarzenegger in Los Angeles, 2013.
BOTTOM   I was honored for my work with the youth of America by President
George W. Bush.

TOP My parents, Joyce and Earl MacFarlane near Desbarats, Ontario, overlooking Lake Huron. 2011.

BOTTOM Derek holding Morgan with Ashley beside them. Easter 2007.

TOP LEFT   Dalton MacFarlane before one of his MMA fights in 2013. Photo by Lou Sirianni.
TOP RIGHT   Dalton and I at one of my speaking engagements in Los Angeles, 2013.
BOTTOM   "Hello, Hello, Can you hear me?" Ireland, 2009

LEFT   Do the lakes in Northern Ontario ever warm up? Diamond Lake, 2013

TOP RIGHT   Michael Theisen and I getting the royal treatment from some Gladiators.
Rome, 2007

BOTTOM RIGHT   A Magical Moment for Ashley, Derek, and Morgan at Disney's Epcot.
January, 2013

TOP LEFT   This has always been one of Patti's favorite pictures of me.

TOP RIGHT   This picture has no special meaning, but here it is.

BOTTOM   Wrestling is the sport where blind people can compete on an equal basis with sighted opponents.

TOP   With my childhood hero, Mario Andretti at the Indianapolis 500 in 1994.
BOTTOM   I'm always honored when I'm invited to speak in Hawaii.

TOP My Canadian/USA tour. 1993
BOTTOM LEFT Always ready to conquer another mountain.
BOTTOM RIGHT Zurich, Switzerland 2013

The events of that weekend would come home to roost with me many times over the balance of my athletic career. John Howe would be particularly instrumental in helping me develop the emotional maturity needed to deal with success, accomplishment and notoriety. I learned that, while I had earned a few privileges through my hard work and success, that it came with a price as well. If I wanted to continue to reap the benefits of my position, I had to be an example, a leader, even a teacher on occasion. I had to be aware that people were emulating me, whether I liked it or not, and if I wanted to stay on top, I needed to be someone who was worth it, not some egomaniacal kid who put himself first. I didn't figure all that out in an instant. In fact, there were still a few lessons I had to learn through experience over the next couple years, but it seemed that the focus of my athletic success shifted that day from medals and glory to responsibility, and maturity.

That was the most dramatic summer of my track career. I continued to run throughout high school and stayed competitive enough to win the blind nationals, in one race or more, every summer until I graduated. Winning the gold in track carried a certain prestige and notoriety that kept my competitive fires stoked. It also kept me focused on training during some of the emotional struggles that were to come. The emotional times started during the school year following Edmonton. That was the winter the barn burned and I made my decision to return to Ross MacDonald.

The idea of returning to the Ross MacDonald wrestling team was exciting but as I re-entered that world, it became daunting as well. Life was different when I returned. I was beginning to mature and had interests beyond just athletics. My involvement in school politics took up a great deal of time. It was my first serious foray into the world of helping others and giving back to those who helped me. I was taking it very seriously and reveling in it. I was also starting to think about life after high school, which made academics more important now than ever. I felt I had so many demands and other distractions now that I couldn't give wrestling the focus it deserved.

I was so wrapped up in so many things that I actually dropped out of wrestling for a few weeks. I wanted to be very good at my new endeavors and thought I needed to throw more time at them to succeed. Wrestling took a lot of time, and besides, it was hard work too. Giving it up so I could dedicate my time elsewhere made sense in my thoughts but in my heart I felt guilty every time I missed practice. Since the age of seven I hadn't missed very many practices at all, only if I was ill. All along I had believed that every extra sit up, every extra pushup, every extra mile I ran was just one more the competition wasn't doing. In the late rounds, in a close match, in the final stretch, I counted on that dedication, that drive, that hunger, to pay off. And it did, so many times. Now, in my heart, it felt that I was tossing it all down the drain.

I was in the student lounge that first afternoon that I missed practice. I was hanging out with a few of my friends who weren't athletes, having a couple of laughs. It wasn't long, as I sat there, before I heard those familiar footsteps climbing the stairs to the lounge.

"Craig, are you up here?" It was John Howe. "Where are you supposed to be right now?" He asked.

"Practice," I said sheepishly.

"Then why aren't you there?"

"I'm confused coach," I said. "I feel overwhelmed, maybe a little burnt out."

"Let's talk," he said.

So off we went to his office. That old familiar room where he had been such a friend, father figure and brother to me. That room where I had done so much soul searching, so many times. That safe haven where I could open up and let the bundle of emotions come out.

We talked at length. He realized that, at age sixteen, it would be natural for my interests and ambitions to be expanding beyond the wrestling mat. He also realized that I wouldn't have much time for my new found interest in student politics or my

Raising the bar

growing desire to excel academically with

my typical training schedule. I usually worked out in the morning, did some kind of physical activity at lunch and practiced after school. After that there was dinner and homework. No wonder I was finding life so physically and emotionally exhausting.

Coach Howe talked about how I'd let my teammates down. He reminded me that I was a leader and they looked up to me. I had no idea they cared what I was about until Coach Howe told me.

"My door's open when you're ready to walk through it again" was how he left it.

Those two weeks were difficult. Coach Howe was my physical education teacher as well. I really appreciated that he never once in that time pressured me in any way. I learned from Eric later how John Howe had told the team that when I made my decision there wouldn't be any questions. They gave me space and I respected them immensely for it. I guess that's what teamwork and camaraderie are about.

I was fully immersed in my new pursuits but by the end of the first week I was coming to realize that something that made me complete was missing.

Wrestling!

After one week away I started secretly getting up at five a.m. and doing my sit-ups, pushups and running just like I did in my earlier years. I didn't tell anyone but I didn't want to lose that step. My edge. I didn't want to fall behind my teammates. I thought I was making up my mind but I think it might be closer to reality to say my mind made itself up. By the beginning of that second week it was a foregone conclusion that I would continue to wrestle.

I prayed a lot that week. I prayed that God would help me find the balance between athletics, academics, politics and my social life. I know not all prayers are answered in the timely fashion we would like, but in this case the answer came with perfect timing. Of course, when you pray regularly, turning up the volume like that occasionally does lead to a clarity of thinking that many people struggle to find because they never pray at all.

I was back in routine finally, gradually finding that balance I so dearly needed. My athletic moorings came back slowly. I was still evolving through that struggle between ego and responsibility and that brought on another lesson in maturity because of my selfish actions.

I don't know if it was purely ego driven in this case or if it was a touch of boredom creeping in. Maybe a bit of both. I got in a bad habit that year. The habit of toying with my opponents. If a guy had a sister or his family or a girlfriend at the match, I wouldn't pin him first chance I got. Instead of going for the win right away, I'd rack up a lot of points first just to show off how good I was. In fact, we once had a bet among the team members to see who could run up the highest score on an opponent. We each put up two bucks and then, because I didn't like to lose bets either, I went out and ran up a score of 34-0 in one of my matches. I kept getting him down, letting him go, then scoring on him again and again.

When Coach Howe figured out what was going on he was livid. And he should have been. It was a terrible thing to do. The way he handled it, though, taught me another major lesson in how I should behave, and why. He didn't scream and yell at us or make any kind of a scene. Instead, he told me he wanted to see me in his office as soon as we returned to Ross MacDonald.

Another meeting in his office. I went in expecting to have a strip torn off me. I wasn't afraid or nervous. He'd been my coach too long for that but I knew how angry he was and I expected to catch the brunt of it, but it wasn't that way at all. He was calm, but stern. He asked me what I was getting from this juvenile endeavor of ours. Then he asked me what the rest of the team was getting from it. He reminded me that I was seen as a leader on this team and pointed out that my teammates were following my lead, even though many of them weren't good enough to give their opponents second, and third, chances on the mat. He asked if that was what I wanted them to learn from me. Was that the legacy I wanted to leave with them? He also pointed out that actions like this could easily spill over to the rest of my life. That I could tarnish my image and reputation as Student Body President. How would that affect a future in politics should I choose to go that way? Maybe some teachers would resent me and want to challenge me the same way, toying with me in their classrooms. How would that affect my academic standing and my desire to go to College? He made it clear that even this petty behavior on my part could seriously affect my life, and maybe even my future.

He also challenged me. If I wanted to stay on the team, he told me that it needed to stop. He also told me I needed to do it in a way that sent a message to the team that it was unacceptable! He challenged me to be the leader I was seen as. He also told me that if I didn't, he would have no choice but to cut me from the team. Just as in Edmonton, I came face to face with the reality that I wasn't bigger than the team. My role was no longer just to win medals and pad my own stats. My role was, in fact, to set an example that younger students, not just wrestlers, could follow. I was there to be a positive impact on my teammates. If I couldn't do that, if my presence was negative, or abrasive, or condescending, instead of encouraging and constructive, then the team was better off without me. I was the one with everything to lose. That was a major wakeup call and my first true lesson in leadership.

At the same time that I was dealing with these challenges to my attitude and maturity, I was feeling enormous pressure to win. If I lost, the only question I ever heard was "How'd that happen?" It was like I was never expected to lose. My enemies, the ones who thought I was too confident, would be saying, "Serves him right." And when I lost, I also felt I not only lost face with my teammates but with all my friends. I always had a fear of losing, but it was becoming amplified now.

The only way to quell my fear of losing was, obviously, to win. That old, persistent fear of failure continued to be my driving force. I became more and more driven to win, not for the glory, but to avoid the stress that came with a loss. As the year progressed I became driven to win the biggest challenges. I thought this would demonstrate leadership, but it was also a means to make sure nobody knew how much I was afraid to lose.

The biggest challenge that year was one I created for myself at the Blind National Wrestling Championships. The challenge wasn't winning a national title. I was very confident that I could do that, in my usual weight class anyway. No, the challenge came to mind when I discovered that three national champions would be wrestling in the 125-pound class. I wrestled at 136 pounds.

In my mind, if I could get down to 125 pounds, I could go head to head with my biggest rivals over the years and we would decide, once and for all, who really was the best. This instantly became a mission, if not an obsession, in my mind and I checked out of life for the next fifty-two hours, focused on qualifying for the 125-pound class.

Over the next fifty-two hours I lost eleven pounds by eating almost nothing, drinking just enough water to stay alive and exercising to near exhaustion. I let Gordie, Pat and Eddie take the scales first when it was time to weigh in. Then I stepped up and the attendant announced, "One Hundred and twenty-five, even!" Everyone in the room was shocked that I had lost the weight, but not me. The biggest challenge was still ahead.

Gordie had been undefeated over the past two years in blind competition. I was fortunate to pin him in the second round. Next

Just after my match with Pat.

up was Pat. In a hard fought match, I outscored him fifteen to nine, which set up the showdown for gold with Eddie. Four national champions in one weight class; only one would walk away victorious.

At the end of the first round I was leading Eddie five to four. Then, with just a few seconds to go in the match, we were tied at ten. I was struggling now. I was literally tasting my own hunger from the loss of weight I had put myself through. I could taste blood in my throat. I was dizzy, and weak. The whistle blew and by the grace of God, I scored a one–point takedown on Eddie as time expired. I had won, by a score of eleven to ten. I think that was one of the ultimate payoffs for all the extra training I had done all my life. When I felt like I had nothing left, the residual, with a little help from God, let me perform right to the end.

I had done it. It was one of the most special medals of my career but it came at a high price. With that medal around my neck, I spent the night in the hospital hooked to an IV.

Yes!

My most memorable match after returning to Brantford wasn't quite so dramatic. It was actually one that I lost. It was against my arch rival Jeff Nunn, who attended North Park High School. He had never beaten me although we had some major wars.

In this particular match I was, uncharacteristically, whipping him pretty thoroughly. I was leading 14-0. I was so far ahead that I got lackadaisical and wound up pinning myself.

I tried a new move that I'd dreamt up in English class. Not such a good idea against someone like Jeff and certainly not in a competition where the shoulder blades only have to touch the mat for one second. The ref's hand slapped the mat and I had, in essence, pinned myself with my new move.

Technically, Jeff had pinned me, but it was the nonchalance of my move that gave him the opening. I knew he was good enough to take advantage and I still can't imagine why I let my guard down and gave Jeff such a chance.

He went ballistic. You'd have thought he won the Super Bowl. He ran around and around the mat hooting and hollering and inciting the crowd to higher and higher cheers.

I was headed off to the change room and dejectedly into the shower. A few minutes later, Jeff came into the shower too. "Well, I finally beat you, you blind s-o-b!" he crowed, laughing hysterically.

I didn't say a word. I just flew at him, fists whaling. I swung with everything I had, as many times as I could. I wanted to tear his head off. The feeling was mutual. There we were, buck naked, toe-to-toe, neither giving an inch, blasting away at each other. Several coaches and other people heard the commotion and it took all of them to finally pull us apart.

No, I never did lose the fire for winning.

My final act of infamy, at Ross MacDonald, came on the final day of my senior year. I had one last book report due, and had made arrangements to deliver it to Mrs. Tinkus by simply sliding it under her door early that morning as I was catching an early bus to the airport. I wrote that final report on the "Brantford Telephone Book," concluding that it had an extensive cast of characters but a monotonous plot. Apparently my efforts were discussed in the staff room a final time that afternoon. I had succeeded once more in provoking a "rolling of the eyes" and an involuntary chuckle. There is nothing better than going out on top and, true to my style, I left in blaze of glory. Sometimes I miss those days.

It was always an honor to represent my country at international competitions.

In 1980, I left W. Ross MacDonald to travel with the Canadian team to Arnhem, Holland to compete in the Worldwide Olympics for the Disabled. I competed in wrestling, sprinting and "goalball."

Goalball is a game developed for the blind in Europe. It uses a ball that is bigger than a soccer ball, with bells inside of it. There are three players to a team with each player blindfolded to ensure a level playing field. Many of the athletes in blind competitions are legally blind but in reality are only visually impaired, having some minor degree of sight. Not in goalball, here the blindfolds made sure everyone was equal, totally blind.

It is a heck of a sport. When I was younger the ball would knock me down sometimes. A good thrower could rocket it at more than twenty miles per hour. Unlike soccer, you roll the ball back and forth; you don't kick it.

Holland was a good time, both in and out of competition. I was excited to be in Europe and, being in Holland, I really wanted a pair of wooden shoes. I decided to venture out into downtown Amsterdam, by myself, and accomplished this mission in short order. With my prize slung over my shoulder in a sack, I started making my way back, walking alone with no cane, no dark glasses, no guide dog. I was using the canal as my guide because I knew it lead directly to the hotel and I could tell where I was by the sounds of the water and cruise boats and general conversation around me. I thought I was so clever, until I misjudged where I was and stepped off the sidewalk directly into the canal, wooden shoes and all.

I had better success later. We were wrestling an exhibition match against a local Dutch club. It included some of their blind Olympians, the Dutch champ among them. He was thirty years old. The matches were right next to a strip of bars and drew an enthusiastic crowd of rather liberally lubricated Amsterdammers. It was an exhilarating place to compete, especially compared to the sweaty monotony of high school gymnasiums, where so many of my competitive matches had been held.

I rode the wave of enthusiasm and pinned the Dutch champ in two minutes. Then, feeling pleased with myself, I took off for the change room, got undressed, and headed for the sauna. The Dutch coach said, "Second door on the right." I should have expected what came next, after all it wasn't the first time for this prank to be pulled on me, but I just strode through the door, all excited and confident as usual, and found myself in a hallway full of the same people who had just seen me wrestle, except now they were seeing a little more. Thank god I had a towel around me!

Despite the events, and embarrassments, of the trip, the Olympics themselves were a success for our team. I won a silver medal in wrestling and, as a team, we finished fifth out of twenty-seven countries in goalball, which was a new sport for Canada.

After the European trip, I came home unsure as to where my athletic career was going, if anywhere at all. Competition for most blind athletes ends with high school and I was looking for new avenues of expression for all the fire and energy I had inside. At the same time, my name, and so-called fame, had spread around fairly decently throughout my native land. I'd been the subject of three documentaries on Canadian national television and that would lead me in yet another direction. I found myself taking up a new pursuit, one that would become a lifetime passion for me. It was a new way to harness all that fire and energy. I was constantly being asked to speak to groups about my life, my accomplishments and how I had made it happen. Doing that, I was finding a new way to experience the pleasure of giving.

As I turned the next page in the adventure that has been my life, the transition to my career as an Inspirational Keynote Speaker was getting underway.

There were, however, still a few memorable and event filled athletic quests yet to be pursued.

Knowing Why

"**R**emind me again, why am I doing this?"

We've all heard someone say this, usually in a state of frustration or exasperation, always when they are doing something that challenges them or that they find unpleasant or that they are not very good at, yet.

To me, hearing these words always brings a sad feeling, because almost invariably, even though the person who uttered them thought they were being witty, and probably that they were deflecting attention from their failure, that person is about to give up on a goal.

That's sad because they couldn't have asked a better question to bring them to success.

Why? Why do you want the goal you are striving for? That is the critical question. If your answer is clear, specific, detailed and, most of all, inspiring, to you, on your terms, then you'll know the value of every task required to accomplish it, no matter how minor or how difficult. You'll have the strength, the resolve, the energy to take on every aspect of your plan and your goal will become real. In essence, if your why is right, your how will take care of itself.

Of course, defining "why" is only the beginning. Once you have defined why, once you are excited by "why" you want to achieve your goal, then you have to get focused, you have to get obsessed, you have to get eager and you have to stay that way. If you don't, all the goal setting and achievement advice and strategy is useless.

I don't want to make this sound like I have a magic bullet for setting and achieving goals. You are still going to have to do the work, all of the work. What I am telling you is that if you want to stay the course, keep your energy and remain excited regardless of the task required to reach your objective, the first and most important discipline of goal achievement is the focus on YOUR reasons why.

Please note I said the discipline of goal achievement. That is not a casual comment. So many people that I meet think the power of Why is all about inspiration, but the reality is that the inspiration comes from the discipline. Staying focused on Why is something that you must do with intent and repetition. You need to write your goal down, in detail. You need to spend time with your goal every day. You need to remind yourself daily of the steps you WILL take to make that goal a reality. You also need to celebrate your progress to stoke your internal flame. If you lose your focus, find some creative ways to reignite your passion. Keeping your inspirational reasons why at the forefront of your thoughts is essential, so much so that there is never a need to be reminded, never any doubt, never any second thoughts about the importance of every action you have deemed necessary to reach your goal.

Maybe a practical example or two would help make my point.

Every year I attend numerous sales conferences and conventions over the course of my speaking engagements. I work on an almost daily basis with financial sales professionals and have for more than twenty-five years. I deal with the question of how to increase sales virtually every day of my career. The question I always ask, of every salesperson who ever asked me how to increase their sales, from senior account executives to entry level Financial Advisors, is always the same. Why?

In almost every case, they answer a different question. They tell me they would make more money or qualify for higher bonuses or be able to apply for a promotion. All nice benefits that could result from making more sales, but it wasn't until we got to the real reasons, their reasons, that their sales started to go up.

After they were finished with their initial reasons, I ask them to describe how achieving their goal would change their life? I ask them what their life would look like in a year's time if they were achieving their goal. I ask them how their house will look, what kind of car they will be driving, what school their children will be going to, how would their relationship with their spouse be affected, what type of office will they be working from, where their stress levels will be, how will these things make them feel?

The answers to those questions define the reasons why you want to achieve your goal. They are not the goal itself. That is easy to identify, but the answer to these questions are the inspiration that will take you where you want to go.

If your goal is a new car, you need to know how owning that car will make you feel. What benefits will that car bring to your life? How will your world be better with it than without it? When you are focused on those reasons why, doing whatever is necessary to get there will be simple for you, not necessarily easy, but simple for you to follow through.

If your goal is to lose weight (haven't we all had that one), the focus is not on how many pounds you want to lose, or have lost. The focus has to be on how you will feel when you have achieved your perfect weight. What kind of clothes will you be able to wear? What will other people say? What will happen to your confidence? Where will you go that you may have avoided? How will your health improve and what will that do for your energy? Won't those thoughts inspire you to do the extra sit-ups, run the extra lap or skip dessert more than the thought of losing a pound?

If you want to stop drinking or smoking, move to a new home, earn a degree or a license or a promotion, take a trip, have a child, win the US Blind National Snow Skiing Championship or any other worthwhile pursuit that matters to you, I promise that if you understand WHY and discipline yourself to stay focused on all the good things and feelings that will happen in your life when your goal is achieved, you will get there easier, faster and with less stress.

There is another benefit that will happen for you too. Nothing can give a more positive boost to your self-esteem, to how you feel about yourself, than setting and achieving a personal goal. And don't forget, success breeds success. Finding the discipline to achieve your goal becomes easier the more you do it. Achieving future goals becomes easier as a result and feeling good becomes a way of life.

Remind me now, "Why are you doing this again?"

13

Howe I Came to America

It has often been said, mostly by those who don't understand why, that "The harder you work, the luckier you get."

My sense has always been that those who stand behind this excuse think that, for the most part, success is a matter of luck, or timing, or, as they say, who you know. I have come to understand why it looks that way because so often the big break comes, not as a result of the specific pursuit of the goal, but because of a "lucky" break that happened along the way.

That "lucky" break perception may be true, but in every case I have found that the luck was a result of the hard work of the recipient. They never would have been in a position to be the beneficiary without having given everything to create enough opportunities for the "luck" to find them.

As a guest pastor in Desbarats once preached, "Good things come to those who wait, but only the things left behind by those who hurried." That message got my attention but what really drove his point home was when he paused, took a breath, and spoke directly to every one of us as he said, "Folks, what I'm telling you is that prayer is great, it's essential, but the reality of our world is that sooner or later, You have to get off your knees!"

If you want to get lucky, work hard. I had been working hard since I was seven. Maybe I didn't understand the principle but that didn't matter. Like all the principles of success, if you apply it, the results will come. The principle in the case was that you make your own opportunities.

In this case, my efforts at working hard had everything to do with advancing my career, proving myself and earning the right to something, but they had little to do with the moment. I wasn't looking to create my lucky break, not at that moment anyway, I was just trying to make dinner.

Admittedly, I was living on my own for the first time, and still determined to demonstrate I was capable of an independent life in the sighted world. I was back in Brantford to complete Grade 13, which in those days was a prerequisite for Ontario High School Students to attend university. I don't know what made us so special because no other jurisdiction in North America had such a requirement, but we did. I had taken a junior one bedroom apartment and was, in fact, actually attending arch rival North Park Secondary School because Ross MacDonald didn't offer the grade 13 year. There was no strategy to my method yet. In fact, on the day that the door to my "lucky break" cracked open that first inch I was just trying to make hot dogs.

Why hot dogs? Because even unbridled ambition can't change reality. A blind man, especially an eighteen year old, was not about to stir up a brilliant edition of Osso Bucco or Chateaubriand all by himself in a junior one bedroom in Brantford, but I was certainly capable of boiling water.

My challenge was that I like my buns toasted. I mean my hot dog buns! I had developed a strategy for that. I would put the buns in the oven, under the broiler, which my friends taught me was a left turn of the oven dial, and then rely on my overly acute sense of smell to tell me when they were ready.

That day was no different. Everything seemed to be going fine, the aroma from the oven reached the appropriate scent, I grabbed my towel (it's hot right), opened the oven and reached in. I didn't know about putting the buns on a tray so I was, as always, trying to pluck the buns off the rack. It took me a couple of stabs but when I grabbed the first one it felt good, but the scent had changed. Almost as fast as I realized there was something wrong with my bun I sensed extreme heat beside me. OMG, my towel was on fire!

I came as close to shear panic in that moment as I ever have. I spun toward the sink and tossed the towel, but it didn't help. My shirt was on fire too! I almost climbed into the sink. Thank God I'm not 6'2". I had the water running and was able to put myself out, but my apartment was already full of smoke.

I could hear the fire alarm ringing in the hall and a knock on my door. I made my way down the hall and found my neighbor in a state of panic too. She rushed in, checked me head to toe, and when I turned out to be only singed, she exhaled and offered to order me a pizza. I laughed out loud and said "Sure, but you have to admit I bring a whole new meaning to well done."

She waited with me while the fire department checked the damage and the smoke cleared. She turned out to be a sweet middle aged lady and from that point forward she was always looking out for me.

My burnt shirt became a hot topic among my buddies. They all wanted one but didn't want the experience of making it. They didn't want me cooking dinner for them anytime soon either. I realized too that I shouldn't be cooking my own meals, for both safety and nutritional reasons. I could learn to cook later, but for now I needed a different solution. After all, a steady diet of pizza and fast food was not the way to make weight for wrestling.

A friend of mine came up with a temporary solution by arranging for me to stay in their spare bedroom. They were a great family and I have to admit I needed the help. As much as I wanted to do everything for myself, I was still wrestling competitively and if I wanted to be my best, I had to give something up. I didn't cook anymore after that, and I know I was better for it. My taste buds were grateful for my arrangement as well.

There was another tremendous benefit that came from living there. If you can believe it, they lived next to another great family. Walter and Phyllis Gretzky and their kids who just happened to be named Kim, Keith, Brent, Glenn and WAYNE. Yes, that Wayne Gretzky!

Wayne was already a superstar in the National Hockey League but he was still only 19 years old. Young enough that he still wanted to make it home to Mom and Dad's when he could. I got to hang out with him.

One time he let me sit in the driver's seat of his Ferrari and burn rubber in a vacant parking lot in the middle of the night. On numerous other occasions we would go skating but the best thing was just sitting up on his parent's front porch into the middle of the night, talking.

I told Wayne all about my plans to become a lawyer. About enrolling in pre-law at Carleton University and even how I had been the subject of a documentary on Canadian national television titled "I Want to be a Lawyer."

Wayne was very supportive of my goal to further my education, but he was much more interested in my athletic achievements. It was his opinion that there must be opportunity for someone of my accomplishments to cultivate a commercial opportunity or significant financial benefit in the sports business world. The world of academics would always be waiting but the window to capitalize on my athletic celebrity may be short lived.

I was already enrolled at Carleton for the fall semester and they had no wrestling program so continuing my athletic career in university was not an option. I thanked Wayne for his concern and advice but still thought that education was the key to my future and I pushed on to Carleton that fall.

I earned a B average at Carleton in my first year. By most standards, that was a pretty good first year and I should have been happy, or at least most people told me so. Problem was that I knew I could have done better but I was, as I had been so many times before, restless. If I had poured myself into my studies, done the hard work as I have said, I would certainly have been an A student, but I wasn't ready for that work, not now, and not in the near future. It really doesn't matter what the goal is, if you are not ready to do the hard work, you are not going to achieve the goal. My thoughts, when I entered Carleton, were about a life in politics, or being a sports agent but these ideas just weren't giving me the right reasons why I should pour myself into the pursuit of a law degree, and being top of my class, which I saw as a key to great job. I just wasn't ready, not yet anyway.

I was still thinking about Wayne's comments and my marketable worth in the athletic world. If Wayne was right, there must be someplace where my accomplishments and persona could come together in a rewarding and profitable pursuit. After a year of university, I wanted to be sure I exhausted all my athletic options for a career. I sensed I wouldn't be ready to commit to the heavy lifting required to succeed in law school until I had.

It was about this same time, much to my surprise that I heard from Wayne again. He called and asked if I would be the Honorary Chairman of the Wayne Gretzky Celebrity Tennis Tournament. I absolutely leapt at that opportunity and it was a great experience. It also shifted my imagination back into overdrive.

I decided to hold an event of my own and in 1982 I hosted the Craig MacFarlane Celebrity Tennis Tournament in Sault Ste. Marie, Ontario. This was easily the biggest thing I had ever undertaken and most gave me little chance of pulling it off.

I knew I could do it because this had the right reasons "why." First, I could give something back to the Soo and Desbarats, the place that supported me and my family when we needed it most, and still did, and does. Second, it was, in my mind, a great way to connect with influential sports personalities who could help me explore my marketability. All I needed to do was attract them.

That was going to require credibility and I determined that I needed a major sponsor for that and, of course, for financial support. I set my sights on Molson Brewery and landed an appointment with a regional executive named Bill Juke. It wasn't an ideal meeting. Without going into all the gory details, let me say it was less than a perfectly staged presentation. He knocked on my hotel room door and I met him in a towel (he was early) and I served him a Labatt's beer from the mini bar instead of Molson's (hey, they don't label beer in Braille.) Bill, fortunately, had a great sense of humor and he still let me pitch my tournament. Turned out, he was also extremely generous. He loved the idea and pledged the awesome sum of $250,000.

That was my first ever sales call and I have never forgotten that I got the sale on enthusiasm and commitment. That is not to say there isn't room for more professionalism, after all, you can't always answer the door in a bath towel, dripping wet from the shower, and expect to close the deal, but I seriously believe that you will be more successful if you are firmly committed to your product and share your ideas with personal energy, enthusiasm and passion. That, and provided you actually ask for the order. More from that soapbox elsewhere.

Once I had my major sponsor, and a budget (what a budget) to work with, I set my sights on attracting a major name as my honorary chairman. I set my sights on Gordie Howe. To me there was no bigger name in Canadian Sports. In fact, as a Canadian kid, there was no bigger name in sports, period! Wayne may have been on his way to legendary status but Gordie already resided there. He wasn't just a legend in hockey, he was a God.

It wasn't the first time I had asked something of Gordie, either. When I was in third grade I had written Mr. Hockey a letter:

> Dear Mr. Howe,
>   I think you are one of the greatest hockey players in the NHL. Can I have an autographed picture of you? I am a pretty good hockey player myself.
>   Sincerely, Craig MacFarlane

I wrote my letter in Braille of course, and my teacher, generously, had underlined the script and written in the words.

I was ambitious, even in the third grade, and fully intended to become the first blind hockey player in the NHL. I didn't realize that dream, but I did touch the heart of one of my hockey idols. Gordie remembered receiving my letter. In fact, he had kept it. I was determined to be just as memorable at age nineteen.

Colleen most often related the story. She would later talk about being bombarded with phone calls from me, literally one after another, trying to get Gordie to be my honorary chairman. It was Colleen who finally said to Gordie, "You know this kid is not going to give up, we might as well do it. Who knows, it might be fun."

Colleen's enthusiasm and the fact that Gordie, (despite being the roughest, toughest and possibly meanest player in any professional sport) had a warm, kind, considerate heart, led them to say YES to my tournament. That was a major turning point in the success of the tournament, and as it turned out, in my life. After that everyone else was on board. Restaurants, businesses, celebrities all made donations or agreed to participate in one way or another.

The tournament did run into one major glitch. Air Canada went on strike the day before many of the forty celebrities were to fly to the Soo. We had to make special arrangements to fly them in by charter, which took a significant bite out of the tournament proceeds. Even with that setback, the tournament was a success. We were still able to make a worthwhile donation to charity.

After the tournament, the night it ended actually, I sat up with Colleen and Gordie past 3:00 a.m. talking. Colleen, showing a motherly concern already, was interested in what I wanted to do with my life. I told her and Gordie that I wanted to take my athletic experience and create some form of business path that I could follow and build. I also shared that I didn't know how I was going to do this yet and I was now researching and networking, looking for the right contact or opportunity.

It seems in that moment, I had made the right contact. Most people say I got incredibly lucky that night and at the time I was inclined to believe that, too. Today I recognize that I made my own luck, as I always counsel others to do, especially students. When I look back now, I realize that this piece of luck was a true case of preparation meeting opportunity. I had prepared my entire life to prove myself worthy and when I got my chance, I presented myself with energy, enthusiasm and passion, always totally committed to my ideals and principles. I had actually made this presentation many times. The lucky part was that it was Gordie who saw the potential and responded.

Later that month, Gordie and Colleen invited me to their cabin at Bear Lake outside Traverse City, Michigan.

That day, the Howe's made me an incredible offer. Let me try to paraphrase Gordie's comments:

"My wife was very impressed with Craig," Gordie said. "She talked to him, talked to his parents and asked a lot of questions. The kid was concerned about his future. By the time I sat down with him, Colleen and I had already decided that we should assist him. She wanted to take him back home to Connecticut and virtually adopt him for a period of time. So she helped him get a green card, the work permit and helped him get a job. Colleen did most of the work at that point. When she decides something, the project is already half done."

The Howes actually invited me to come and live with them in their home in Glastonbury, Conn., just outside Hartford. Gordie obtained a position for me with the National Hockey League's Hartford Whalers, in the Community Relations department. I was able to learn more about sports marketing, a field of interest to me, while I got my feet under me in America and got serious about a future.

It was nothing short of unbelievable. The two biggest icons in Canadian sports, think the equivalent of Babe Ruth and Ty Cobb, in Gordie Howe and Wayne Gretzky, had taken an interest in me. They had a powerful, life changing and positive effect on my life.

In September, 1982 I left Canada for Connecticut. That was an emotional moment for me. I was deeply Canadian, I had worn my country's colors in international competition. I had stood on podiums and listened to the Canadian National Anthem with gold medals around my neck and sung patriotic songs. I benefitted greatly from the enormous generosity of the Canadian system and the Canadian people. My heart would always be Canadian.

At the same time, I was excited to be going to a new country, a tremendously proud country, one that offered unlimited opportunity, and that I would be competing on behalf of just a few short months later. I was excited to be going to America, anxious to make a difference and proud to represent the red, white and blue. It was a natural transition for me too, after all, my mother was born near Detroit.

All the emotions aside, it was also unbelievably nerve wracking to be starting a new career and a new life, in a new country. No matter how prepared you try to be, no matter how perfect you try to make your paperwork, you still have to deal with customs and immigration. That will make anybody sweat.

My fears calmed considerably when I got off the plane and heard the words "Welcome to America." It was Gordie, there to pick me up. That made all the difference, even when dealing with the humorless, bureaucratic automatons at immigration.

There is not enough that can be said about my mentor, Gordie Howe. He was probably the toughest, roughest, meanest player ever

A classic Gordie Howe moment.

to succeed in any professional sport. He was also the softest-spoken, most humble, warm hearted man you could ever wish to meet. He and Colleen counseled me constantly, forcing me to ask the tough questions of myself, asking tougher ones of me, all the while guiding me through the transition from the world of athletics to the business world.

I don't want all of this to sound like life was all serious, far from it. The Howes lived a full life and that included lots of wacky moments. I'm just talking of little things but we laughed and smiled a lot. That made me feel like family.

For instance, I would always remind Colleen to turn off the lights when she left a room, even if I was still there. She would laugh and try but she couldn't get comfortable. It obviously didn't matter to me but if I was there, fixing something to eat in the kitchen, or "watching" TV she would just leave, shaking her head. I saw the fun and took great delight in being in a dark room when she entered, giving her a little fright when she turned on the light.

With Gordie, on the other hand, it was less intentional, more spontaneous fun. We spent so much time and grew so comfortable together that it simply lead to silliness. Comments from him like "I'll watch the left side and you watch the right," or "I think you missed a sign back there, Craig" or "let me know when the light turns green," would fall out naturally in conversation, and after a pregnant pause of sorts, we would both burst out laughing. I liked those moments best, not because he was trying to be funny, but because he honestly forgot I was blind. I was just one of the guys to Gordie.

Gordie also has another quality that inspired me more, or made me want to be more inspiring. Gordie has celebrity power. Just his presence, and nothing to do with how tough he was renown to be, could change the way people behaved. One time, just being Gordie Howe probably saved our lives. We were driving home, late at night, after a speaking engagement and Gordie ran out of gas, and in a pretty rough neighborhood, in New York City. Two simple guys in suits, in a long Lincoln Continental, broken down in the Ghetto. Just as I am saying my last prayers and wishing I had a will, somebody stepped up to the car and said "Hey, aren't you Gordie Howe?"

Surprisingly, they couldn't do enough for us to get us back on the road.

It made me think. Maybe this is the ultimate potential value of my celebrity, not that it compared to Gordie, but as a public speaker and motivator. If I could bridge gaps between blind and sighted people, maybe I could also build bridges between people who are separated by color or gender or culture or race or age or religion. As a blind person I can't judge somebody by any of those preconceived prejudices because I don't know they exist until I reach out and make contact with them. Once contact is made 75 percent of the gap has been closed already, and most people are far more the same than they are different. There was a message that I hoped I would be able to deliver effectively during my career.

I sometimes think that sighted people might be better off if they were blind, at least as far as relationships are concerned. There are times when we all need to put blinders on, to step back, to not be "so judgmental" and to take the time to learn. Somebody once told me that I have two ears and one mouth and to use them in that ratio. To me that meant gathering information and learning about the person I was meeting before I spoke too much, before I drew conclusions or stated my position. I can't help but think that if that kind of judgment was always used, instead of "sizing someone up" on first impression, that this would be a happier, more effective, less divisive world.

The entire question of celebrity, at least meaningful celebrity, wasn't lost on the Howes either. Gordie made sure he was worthy of his fame and the benefits that came with it. He set standards in his career and achieved them and expected no less of the people he respected, me included. He challenged me one day. "If you don't want to be just another blind athlete, if you really want to be the best ever, why don't you win 100 gold medals? Why stop now?" He was basically saying that if I wanted to build a career using my athletic success as my springboard, then punctuate it, leave no doubt about it. One hundred Gold medals would be a tremendous milestone. It was a worthy goal and when I considered the accomplishments of the man who suggested it, I was inspired. I was going to do it.

I prided myself on staying in top physical condition, so I was ready for this challenge and decided that the quickest route to win-

Ready to race!

ning seven more gold medals would be in track and field. In that same month that Gordie challenged me, I entered the U.S Blind Nationals in Long Beach, California. Having set the goal, it was important to take action, right away. Otherwise goals have a way of becoming delusions and I have never been delusional.

I was not to be denied and I won four gold medals in California. That left three more to 100 and the next event I could get to was the New Jersey Invitational in November. I went in feeling confident that this would be the day my milestone accomplishment would be reached, but my confidence took a hit early in the competition.

The first event was the 60 meters, which was an indoor event in New Jersey that year. The competitor immediately before me had veered off the course and run head on into a steel post, knocking himself senseless, unconscious actually. I swear I could still hear the post ringing as I was loading myself into the starting blocks. That mental image and sound does not create a confident feeling, particularly when you are expected to hurdle yourself down the same course, at breakneck speed with reckless abandon, in pursuit of nothing but sheer velocity. It affected me. I lost. By three one-hundredths of a second.

That left me with my own mental challenge to deal with. I had a strategy in my mind going into the New Jersey competition. I really wanted to win the 60 meters. That would take a little internal pressure off. It would still mean winning two of the next three events but now, to reach my 100th Gold, I had to win three in a row. I couldn't let that take my focus off the next event. Let's face it, I couldn't win the javelin toss until I ran the 400 meters. I still had to do this one event at a time, but my spirits were down, for a second anyway.

The best-laid plans don't always go precisely the way you would like them to. In fact, more often than not what happens isn't what you hoped for, but it isn't what happens to you, it's what you do about it that matters. I had to find a way to boost my confidence but that, too, was a challenge. Next event for me was the 400 meters, and my energy tank didn't seem to be full that day. Sometimes you have to gut things out and this was feeling like one of those days.

In any race for a blind runner that involved a corner, which for me meant both the 200 and 400 meters, you are required to have a guide runner. Your guide runner keeps you on track around the curves, where it would be impossible to run to the sound of your coach's voice. In a perfect world, your guide runner would be approximately your same height, with the same stride, and hopefully capable of running as fast as you could. You would be connected by means of a short piece of rope, no more than a foot long, and tied in a loop. The blind runner would hold the loop with his right hand, the guide with his left, and the two of you would run in unison, arms and legs moving in sync. Coordinating this technique took a little practice and some strategy but like everything else it ultimately came down to effective communication. When you were of the same mindset, it worked brilliantly.

This day I launched myself into the 400, getting a great start and going into the final 100 meters I had the lead, but not by much. I wouldn't be cruising to the finish line. In fact, I could hear footsteps just off my left shoulder. I reached down for that little something extra but there was no great surge coming. This was going to be a fight to the finish.

I forced myself, stride by stride to keep pace, I wouldn't let up, but my mind was going blank. I was bagged. I just kept lunging forward until I heard my guide runner call out "forty meters to go." I could sense that he was starting to tire, starting to slow down, and in that instant my old friend the Grey Zone, kicked in, sort of... I dropped the rope and was off on my own.

The hand of God didn't instantly reach down and tap my shoulder, turning me into a gazelle with the speed of a cheetah, the Grey Zone didn't work that way. It wasn't a magic power that I summoned, it was more an involuntary reaction to years of mental and physical conditioning. At any rate, my conscious mind slipped out of the equation for a minute, or a few seconds actually, and I went on an awkward form of autopilot. I remember almost nothing about the end of that race. My friends and supporters told me later that I went into a lunging, lurching, exaggerated gait. It looked as if I was striving to break the tape with every stride. Truth is, I had no idea where the finish line was by then. I didn't even stop running until I was 20 meters past the finish, and only then because I collapsed.

I think it came from having always been taught that you can never let up. That's what caused my sub conscious mind to take over that way. As much as I like to win, I was pushed by a relentless fear of failure and in this race I was about to experience both, losing a race while my body failed, and when I was so close to my goal of winning 100 gold medals. That had to be where this desperate form of the Grey Zone was conceived, but I didn't care. I had won the race, by the slimmest of margins, only two feet. Two gold medals to go.

Gold medal number 99 was different. No drama, no epic competition to the finish. This was one of those times, I am sure, where I was simply the beneficiary of my obsessive behavior growing up. I spent hours and hours every summer throwing javelin and shot put and discus events under the watchful eye of my mom in the field beside the barn. She actually became quite adept at helping me refine my technique. Regardless, as had been the case so many times before, my instincts were ready even if I wasn't. I just grunted harder and twisted myself further. I won in javelin.

That left the 200-meter dash, my favorite track and field event. I loved the combination of speed and power, and the full out sprint of the straightaway, my strong suit by far. On this day, I didn't know much would be left in the tank for the straightaway.

I took off like a tiger, a man possessed, and nobody could catch me. It was a picture perfect race. I had an awesome guide runner. We ran in unison, accelerating off the turn, arms and legs moving in perfect symmetry, almost as if we were challenging each other to go faster, and faster. This time there were no competitors footsteps distracting my focus. I was challenged to keep up to him, he was challenged to keep up to me. The rest of the field just couldn't keep up at all. In this race I would not let myself be denied. I did it. I had won my 100th gold medal!!!!

I threw my arms around Gordie and told him, "Thank you for inspiring me to do this, thank you so much."

Gordie taught me one of my most important lessons. Never give up until you're finished. It's important to be fully engaged and leave no doubt right from the start but it's also important to keep pumping through the tape. The start is critical, but the ability to finish is crucial. Capturing 100 gold medals was a goal worth striving for, but it was also a lesson in perseverance. Without perseverance, you can never reach the important goals in your life.

Play the Hand You Were Dealt

One of the best pieces of advice that I was ever given was to "Play the Hand You've Been Dealt."

I've heard the message in numerous ways but over the years I've come to realize that it was always the same message. I've heard it expressed as:

- Don't waste your time worrying about what you don't have.
- Don't pretend to be something you're not.
- Focus on what you have, not what you can't have.

What it has come to mean to me is this; we are all unique and have all been blessed with our own God-given gifts. Our responsibility is to develop those gifts to the best of our ability and not waste our time on false hopes and dreams, thinking "if only."

Now, let me make one thing very clear. There is a difference between having gifts and being "gifted." You have gifts. We all do. We all have passions and abilities that, if we develop them, can lead to incredible things in our lives. The truth of the matter is that you must take responsibility to develop those gifts, or nothing will come of them. You are responsible.

This advice, in a very direct manner, is another confirmation of the importance of knowing yourself. Lao Tzu once said, "Mastering others is strength. Mastering yourself is true power." In simple English, isn't that what Playing the Hand You Were Dealt is all about?

In a very practical sense, that is what has led to the success I have experienced in my life. I learned early that I had some qualities that were valuable to my desire for a "normal" life. I developed those qualities with a focus on my goal. Even at age eight or nine, I wasn't languishing in self- pity waiting for a miracle or dreaming about what life would be like if I could see. I thought I had found a means of achieving my goal doing something that was available to me.

The fact is that I was strong, durable and energized. I craved physical activity and someone in my life had the sense to recognize how that fit with wrestling. Once I was connected, I focused on developing those gifts of strength, durability and energy so I could best take advantage of my opportunity. For me, that focus on developing the gifts I knew I possessed in that moment paid huge dividends and led to more opportunity, as you are reading about in my stories.

Some of you are going to say, "sure, but you got lucky. Somebody else thought you could wrestle and it just worked out for you." For those of you who are thinking that way, there is another piece of advice I received just as often that I also want to share with you.

"You make your own breaks and opportunities. You don't wait for the world to come to you on a silver platter." Remember, I saw an opportunity in wrestling that nobody else did. It wasn't handed to me. I had to make it happen for myself. I think I succeeded because I tried so hard to make the most of what I could do, without fretting over what I couldn't.

I may have been exposed to wrestling at an early age, but the people who saw my potential as a wrestler didn't see it as the opportunity I saw. They didn't do the sit-ups and push-ups and running and practice. I did that work. They didn't see how wrestling could be my ticket home, my way out of W. Ross MacDonald. Only I saw that. I played my hand and developed the gifts that allowed me to become a winning wrestler because it was my best opportunity at the time. Finding a cure for blindness would have been a better solution to achieve my goal, but it wasn't an option. I played the hand I held at the time, with wrestling being my trump card, and it improved my life.

That's not the only example in my life of playing the hand I was dealt. Other trump cards became apparent when I saw opportunity while serving as Honorary Chairman of Wayne Gretzky's tournament and recognized that my circumstances lined up perfectly to run a similar tournament of my own. Why? Because I knew who I was, that I had a comfort factor with people that would let me pursue such a goal, and a passion for helping those less fortunate than I was. I was always looking for opportunities where I could capitalize on my personal strengths. This turned out to be one of the best examples of how I did that.

The same results came from living with Gordie Howe and learning where other cards in my hand had value, like getting on skis once and recognizing I had the physical dexterity to succeed, even though I needed to develop it. Similar results came from music, water skiing, and public speaking. In every case you could say I got lucky, but I disagree. My eyes, or maybe I should say my ears, and imagination, have been opened to many opportunities over my lifetime. I have been able to take advantage of these because I have tried to develop my unique gifts, and I was ready for action when opportunity arose. I attribute all the good things that have happened in my life to learning those few simple lessons. Let me repeat:

- Play the Hand You Were Dealt
- Don't waste your time worrying about what you don't have.
- Don't pretend to be something you're not.
- Develop your God-Given gifts to the best of your ability.
- Make your own breaks and opportunities.
- Always speak from the heart!

Notice I didn't try to become a great racecar driver. I did buy my own car, which I backed into several ditches, and I burned rubber in Wayne's Ferrari a couple times in empty parking lots, but that was the limit of making that dream real. I also didn't pursue the dream of becoming a star hockey player, or an expert marksman or a thoracic surgeon or a dentist. All ideas that I would have loved to pursue but not possible in any meaningful way, considering the hand I'd been dealt. I stayed within myself and the results speak for themselves.

What are the trump cards in your hand? What untapped asset do you possess that could change your life if you did tap into it? What are the God-given gifts that you should be developing? What are the opportunities around you that align with your assets? What great things could you make happen in your life if you took the action now to match your gifts to your circumstances? What are the gifts your kids, or your grand kids, should be starting to develop now? How can you use your gifts to help them find theirs? You don't want to be one of those people we all know who say, "I should have, I would have, I could have."

If you don't want to be one of them, then start listening. Start asking. Your family knows what your strengths are, your friends know, your colleagues, too. I'm sure at your core, if you listen closely, so do you.

Who is your Coach Howe, your Wayne Gretzky, your Eric, your George Spangler, your Gordie Howe?

What opportunities are circulating in your life right now that you are not recognizing, or not seeing the connections to?

I urge you to start listening, watching and feeling all the elements of your life. Develop your inner strength, learn to pull from it. Start learning and developing those gifts you possess that will allow you to make opportunity happen, to pursue your goals with passion and excel as you bring those goals into reality.

Soon, people will be saying you got lucky too, but you'll know, you made it happen for yourself. You have it within you. You have your own unique, personal dynamic, in the form of that special combination of gifts God gave you! Do you know what your gifts are? Have you fully developed your gifts? Are you even trying? Why don't you start now?

Go Ahead and Jump

Snow skiing started out as my way of dealing with the competitive burn at age 20. It turned into an obsession and a pursuit that was successful, but ultimately it left me feeling unfilled. After all, we won the Blind National championship, and that was amazing, but not being named to the national team after all that time, training, effort and sacrifice put a disappointing finish on a storybook adventure. I skied in excess of 50 miles per hour, I developed new training methods that are still used to train blind skiers, I overcame a devastating injury, but I didn't get what I deserved. I should have been on the national team.

Of course, there was still the opportunity, if I wanted to play their games. By the fall of that year I was back in Connecticut and certainly could have made my way to the slopes in Vermont and continued training. I never doubted that I could have won another Blind National championship, and in doing so, forced the selection committee to pay attention to me. I could have paid my dues and eventually had a chance to ski for a world championship, but my spirit was broken. I have always been a big believer that people should be selected and rewarded on merit. I had already earned my way onto the world stage. I didn't have the burn to do it again. In fact, I never snow skied competitively after that.

So there I was that fall, back in Connecticut, licking my wounds, when I received a rather unexpected phone call. It was from Cypress Gardens in Florida. They were looking for a spokesperson for the blind national water skiing championships in late November. That set off bells. I was honored, of course, but immediately I thought, Spokesperson? Heck, let me compete too!

We came to an agreement instantly and I was in the competition. That meant I had one entire month to train for the national stage. Not a big deal, I already had the formula.

Find the best available coach, commit my days to non-stop training, immerse myself in the fine points and mentally prepare each evening, work relentlessly without rest and take a break when the competition was over. Simple, and in this case, I thought a little easier than snow skiing. At least I had been on water skis before, even if it was at age eleven. I was certain that my snow skiing experience would help too. I also thought the collision factor would be lower.

That coach turned out to be John Swanke of Danbury, Connecticut. Once we connected, we immediately went to work on Lake Zoar, or more appropriately considering the time of year, Lake Brrr. That didn't matter to me. I certainly wasn't going to let that break my spirit.

I've always had a mind-set when it comes to things like that. It wasn't always spring like conditions in Brantford at the school for the blind, but that didn't stop me from my five a.m. run every morning. When you really want something, when you are serious about a goal, then a little hardship or inconvenience doesn't get in your way. If anything, it becomes a factor you take advantage of, that you overcome and in the process use to develop deeper character and greater intestinal fortitude than your competition. If you want the goal you have to do the work and you do not let circumstances stop you.

Of course, it always helped to have an incredible coach, and John was just that. He was patient, talented and terrific. He had skied competitively so pushing the envelope came easily to him. He even taught me how to bare-foot which totally enhanced my confidence, and no doubt my ability.

John was so cool to work with but as great as John was in the world of water skiing, that was not his primary claim to fame. He was much more famous, and in demand, as a set designer on Broadway. He spearheaded the team that designed and built the set for the famous Broadway musical CATS. On what was virtually our only day off from training he took me to the theatre. I was actually able to stay backstage during the performance that evening. That was awesome!

I have been blessed with so many experiences like that. It is amazing how high you can rise, where you can go and who you will meet when you commit to giving your all in everything you do.

That night was like a tonic that kept me charged right through to late November. By the time I boarded the flight for Orlando, I was confident and ready to test myself on the big stage again. I was also very ready for some warmer water to ski in.

I was so impressed with Cypress Gardens and excited to ski there. I became even more impressed when I found out on the morning of the event that TV shows such as "P.M. Magazine" and "The CBS Morning News," not to mention numerous other shows and media outlets, were there to cover the event. Several of them did stories on me later that afternoon and there were many more of those to come.

Finally, it was time to compete. The event was simple enough. Every skier, and there were a lot of us of all different ages and backgrounds, would make four passes of twenty seconds each, the objective being to cross as many wakes as possible in that time. You would get more points if you did it on one ski instead of two. Guess how many skis I used? You got it. I skied on one.

We would all make our first run, consisting of two passes, and then regroup and go again. When everyone had completed their first run they announced the "half time" scores and, much to my surprise, I was in the lead, and by a considerable margin. That was exciting to hear, but I had learned from experience not to make too much of it. You can never make assumptions about the circumstances of your competition. There might be a miraculous comeback brewing in the pack, like mine at Alta, so you had to compete to the end, never letting down. I just proceeded to get ready for my second run. After all, if I lost my focus and wiped out, it would all be for naught anyway. Without a successful second run myself, my great lead would mean nothing.

I pushed hard through my third and fourth passes and by the time I was back at the docks my quadriceps were burning and my arms ached. I let go of the rope a little too soon and actually crashed into the dock instead of skiing up smoothly. It looked much worse than it was, just a couple bruises, but somebody said later it was the appropriate way for me to finish. I guess I looked close to crashing all day, which I took as a compliment.

Nonetheless, my strategy paid off. I held onto my lead and had won the event.

Can you imagine, there I was in Cypress Gardens, the water ski capitol of the world, a long way from and much warmer than Alta Utah (not to mention Desbarats, Ontario), and I had just become both the U.S Blind National Snow Skiing Champion and the U.S. Blind National Water Skiing Champion in the same year, seven months apart in fact, and during my first year in the United States. Nobody else has ever been able to claim that. Not bad for a Canadian, eh?

Why then did I feel a little empty as I was called to the podium and awarded my Gold Medal? Honestly, I didn't feel like I had done much for this. The competition was really very simple. There must be a more demanding way to test the abilities of a water skier, even a blind one. Then, they announced that I would be representing the United States at the World Blind Water Skiing Championships in Oslo, Norway. That made my spirits leap. I didn't feel empty any more.

That's the moment when someone in the crowded yelled out, "Hey MacFarlane, Have you ever ski jumped?"

Ski-jumped? Now there was a challenge that would test my abilities as a water skier. I yelled back "No, but I'd love to!"

That was enough. A buzz started running through the crowd. I heard one person yell, "Yeah, let's see him do it!" Then somebody responded, "no way, he can't, he'll kill himself." Kill myself? I doubted that but there had to be an adrenaline rush attached if the crowd was thinking that way. I had to try this!

I got my wish. Ricky McCormick, a world water skiing jump champion, lived nearby. Ricky had been so successful as a water ski jumper that he had even appeared on Johnny Carson (for those under the age of 26, look Johnny up, he was the king of late night TV. Many think he still is!) They brought Ricky over to Cypress Gardens. I couldn't believe how fast he got there and let me tell you, meeting Ricky was a rush. I felt like I'd met my match. I was an energetic, outgoing guy, but here was Mr. Energy personified. This man had a heart of gold and knew water ski jumping like the back of his hand, or bottom of his feet. He lived it, he breathed it, and he was excited to share it. I knew instantly I had just found my Cliff May of water skiing.

Ricky was totally into the idea in a moment. Almost before I knew what was happening he had Donny Croft pull up the boat and we were on our way to inspect the ramps. It was as if Ricky had been in touch with George and Cliff. He seemed to instinctively understand how to take the imaginary vision of a blind person and turn it into a tactile reality. He started teaching right away.

I can't say enough about Donny Croft either. Ricky was an amazing teacher, but we also had the best boat driver in the world. Donny was incredible then and he's still there now. Legendary wouldn't be an understatement to describe his status.

So to the ramp we went. No skis, no equipment. We just climbed out of the boat and walked around on the ramp. I was able to get a sense of how wide it was, how long it was, even how high it was, and even what it was made of. I tested the approach of the ramp to see how much was submerged in the water where I would enter. I even jumped off the end to get a sense of what kind of drop to expect. Of course Ricky explained that I would go higher in the air due to the speed of the approach but it was still vital information for me to have. Now, I could start to develop a clearer mental picture of what would be expected of me.

Within minutes of meeting Ricky, I actually had hard knowledge that I could use to envision and translate what he was about to teach me. That proved invaluable because this was all happening at such a whirlwind pace, literally just moments after the medal ceremony. I doubt I could have connected all the information Ricky started to feed me with what I was physically about to attempt if I didn't have the physical reference from my tour of the ramp. Understanding what was expected of me before I tried to do it was always critical. It helped me harness the nervousness and pent up energy. I would refocus that through visualization and my confidence would start to grow. And remember, too, I had no idea what a ramp looked like. I seriously needed this reference. Of course that makes us seem like geniuses now. In the moment, it was all instinct but once I realized why it worked, I never forgot the lesson.

Instructions seem to be coming fast and furious:

- Make sure you're not leaning too far back or you'll fall on the ramp
- Make sure you're not leaning too far forward or you'll face plant
- Keep your skis together or you'll become a whirlybird
- Remember the boat will pull you to the right, so compensate

Ricky was telling me all of this as he and Donny took me back to the dock and helped me into a set of jump skis. They were wider than normal water skis and I was surprised how heavy they were, but they felt solid. At that moment, in the midst of all that frantic activity, a touch of solidity was reassuring, somehow.

The buzz from the stands was growing. It was as if nobody had left. In fact, it seemed that a bigger crowd was assembling to watch the "blind kid" try and kill himself. More people were there now than had been present for the Blind Nationals. Even "PM Magazine" and "The CBS Morning News" and other shows were still there. They had set up again and had their cameras rolling. I am certain they really must have thought there was serious risk to life and limb, mine in particular. Why else would they stay to film a lark like this?

Donny fired up the boat again and we were off. Ricky skied beside me on a separate rope, the same length as mine obviously, and was going to guide me into the ramp. He would give me a five-four-three-two -one countdown, - one of those again - and I'd be off. He kept shouting last-minute instructions to me, repeating everything we already covered, but I really didn't hear him now. I was waiting for the countdown with just two instructions in mind:

1. Jump
2. Don't die!

I never really expected that this was going to result in any horrible tragedy. After all, it was just a ski jump. I'd jumped hundreds of headwalls in snow skiing and practically landed them all. I couldn't see my landing point then either. I just expected the skills to translate. (I have always found positive expectation beats negative expectation every time.) Ricky didn't express any serious concerns, either. If he had, maybe I would have hesitated, but this was a go in both our minds, right from the beginning.

If there were any concerns, it was too late now. Ricky started the countdown. FIVE...FOUR...THREE...TWO... I barely heard him say ONE. I heard the chatter of my skis across the ramp and in an instant I was airborne.

It wasn't a long flight. I splashed down almost right away and not in a terribly graceful manner. My skis hit the water and my butt

Airborne!

splooshed right down on top of them. Fortunately for me, I had the strength (residual benefit of the years of training as a wrestler) to fight my way back to my feet and ski away. What a rush, I had just landed my first jump.

A cheer went up from the grandstand. Good to know they were excited for my success. I was hooked on that sound as soon as I heard it. It just added to that adrenaline rushing through my system, but not as much as Ricky's reaction. He was beside me again in a second, giving a high five and embracing me, at least as much as he could considering he still had a rope to hang on to.

"That was just awesome!" he yelled.

There wasn't much time to celebrate. There was another ramp at the other end of the water-ski show area and we were going to take

that one, too. I heard the count-down, hit the ramp and, well, I lost this one.

In the excitement of landing my first jump, I hadn't fully re-grouped and was leaning a little too far forward when I hit the second ramp. I flew in the air like an eggbeater, arms and legs going in every direction. I tried to keep it together, but no chance of that.

Safe Landing!

Both skis went flying as I hit the water in what must have been a spectacular wipeout.

All I could think in the instant was to immediately stick my hand in the air to show the driver, and the crowd, that I was al-right. That's another thing Ricky taught me. I did as instructed, and laughed out loud. This was all such a thrill.

Ricky skied up saying, "It's OK, it's OK, everyone does that. We'll get it. You've already stuck one."

I wanted to do more. I was hungry for another try. I knew what I did wrong. Ricky didn't have to tell me. I called out "Give me another shot."

No issues there. Ricky and Donny were ready to go. They were both so excited for me and I fed off both of them, using their energy to supplement what I had left of my own. As I got back into my skis Donny kept saying "man, you were amazing, you did it, you're gonna nail these next two, I know it, just stay confident, you're gonna stick it." Whatever "stick it" meant, it sounded like a good idea. "Let's go" was all I could say.

I didn't exactly stick jumps three and four but they went well. I landed both of them without getting my butt wet and skied away cleanly each time. It was still thrilling but it was also time to get back to the dock. The old adrenaline drain was kicking in and I could feel my energy bleeding off quickly. Physically and mentally,

I was spent. It had been a long day of skiing for a kid who had only started seriously skiing a month before. This would be enough for today.

As I came to a halt on the docks I was absolutely besieged with questions, from both media and spectators. The questions were fast and furious but not anything insightful, just excited curiosity really. Then I heard a comment that caught my attention.

A reporter said to me, "Despite the odds, you did it."

I turned in his direction and replied, "If no blind person has ever ski-jumped before, then who the heck set the odds?"

This was a sensitive issue to me. People are always trying to "set the odds" for you. In effect, always judging you before they know you. They are always saying "What makes you think you can do that?" or "You're too short" or "You're too tall" or not smart enough, or mean enough, or strong enough, or good enough. People had been setting the odds for me all my life. It has always felt like I am on a mission to prove them wrong.

In reality, they are not odds at all, they're challenges. They are effectively the indirect questioning of your ability and the suggestion of your limitations. When people "set the odds" the thing to do is laugh. Then go to work.

I wonder, how often do others set the "odds" for you? How did you respond?

By the end of that day I was totally infected with the water-ski jumping bug. Truth is, nothing I had done before had brought as great a rush, generated such an adrenaline pump or stirred as many butterflies as this did.

I wanted to do it again and my new friends, Ricky and Donny, were more than happy to oblige me. With Donny driving, Ricky and I were back on the water the next day, this time jumping between regular shows of the Cypress Gardens Water Ski Spectacular. We landed a lot more than we missed, and a few of them were very clean, with my ankles barley even getting wet. That's what Donny had meant by "stick it." Land in perfect form and just ski away.

This was more than just a novelty. This was seriously fun. As a matter of fact, this was the most euphoric experience I had ever had.

So much so that I was thinking in the back of my mind that I should move to Florida so I could take it up as a serious pursuit. It turned out I wasn't the only one thinking that way.

Before the second day was out, the executives from Cypress Gardens approached me about becoming part of their regular ski shows. They told me I was the first "totally" blind person they knew of to water ski jump. I figured they would know. After all, Cypress Gardens was the water ski capitol of the world. They featured the best-sighted water skiers and jumpers on Earth, stars equal to the Wayne Gretzky, or, the Michael Jordan, in their sport. Four shows a day. Seven days a week, beginning January 1, 1984. I would be paid the handsome sum of $5,000 a month plus free lodging in the hotel across from Cypress Gardens Gates – meals included.

My ultimate dream was coming true. I was finally a Professional Athlete. Forget the fact that I would have been overjoyed if they had only offered $5 a month (but I never told them that.) My athletic ability was about to bring me a decent living wage and a sense of financial independence for the first time in my life. Financial Independence had been my goal since I graduated from high school, maybe even before and to have achieved it through an athletic pursuit was almost too good to be true. I realized, years later, that I may be the only totally blind athlete, in history, to ever achieve professional status.

I officially joined the water ski team at 8:00 a.m. on January 1, 1984. The team came together at that time every morning to stretch, run, get loose and get ready for shows at 10:00 a.m., noon, 2:00 and 4:00 p.m.

I was part of a professional team at the age of 21. It is so hard to explain what that meant to me. I had always wanted that. I had always wanted to fit in and contribute to a team, to belong, to enjoy the camaraderie and chemistry that comes from working closely with others. As I've said, participating in team sports is difficult for blind athletes so I had always been a solo competitor. Being part of this team took my athletic career to an entirely new level and this was a great team to be part of. Right from the moment I arrived everybody went out of their way to make sure I felt like I fit in, like I belonged.

They were also a remarkable group of athletes. The water ski show may be an entertainment production. It takes incredible athletic ability to make those routines look so gorgeous and effortless. Every one of my teammates was exceptional in their own right and it was a privilege, as much as a thrill, to be included in their company.

I didn't miss a single jump on that first day as part of the Cypress Gardens water ski team. Yes, I struggled with a couple landings. I got out of line once or twice but I managed to pull up every time skiing away just like the plan called for, waving to the crowd as if it was "business as usual." It was tremendously satisfying. I really felt like I was part of the show. I didn't need any special consideration, I was just one of the guys.

It's really hard to describe how thrilling it is to ski at Cypress Gardens. Yes, of course waterskiing is always a thrill, with the sound of the motor, the spray of the water in your face and the sensation of speed. Now, add to that the aroma of flowers coming from the gardens themselves and the murmur of a thousand people watching as you performed stunts that most people would never even try. It brought the exhilaration to an entirely different level. I became addicted to it. I loved the idea of being watched, performing in front of that crowd. The pressure to not disappoint brought one more adrenaline rush and you just can't have too many of those.

Now, at the same time I'll be the first one to admit that I probably didn't deserve to be there. Merit-wise, I was the Blind National Water Skiing champion but experience-wise, maybe I hadn't earned the right to have such an amazing job. I may have been there because

Practicing at Cypress Gardens.

I was in the right place at the right time, but there was one thing I could promise. I was willing to work as hard, and probably harder, than anybody to prove I deserved to be there.

Every morning we worked on our routines and it wasn't long before I was becoming a regular part of the show. I was soon doing doubles and trios and even skiing in pyramid formation. This was an incredible learning experience, and so satisfying to succeed at. The coordination and concentration required was demanding. Imagine, not only was I water skiing, but in pyramid formation, I was doing it with somebody else on my shoulders. Often it didn't stop there. With the guys forming the bottom layer, we would be carrying three or four tiers of skiers on our shoulders before we were done. I was making every effort to "earn my keep" and not just be the token sideshow. The Cypress Garden shows were a true acrobatic extravaganza and I was working hard, getting better and becoming someone my teammates could rely on. Soon it felt like I belonged.

Cypress Gardens was an amazing place to work. It is hard to describe, but the experience of running through the Orange Groves at 8:00 a.m. on a spring morning, when the trees were in full bloom, with all the blossoms christening the air with that delicious fragrance. It was an intoxicating experience of heaven on earth that made all the events that follow more than worth the price.

Of course, inspiring my confidence sometimes comes with consequences. As a person who suffers from unbridled ambition I was, and still am, always looking to push the envelope and my experience at

Finally, part of a professional team!

Cypress Gardens wasn't any different. As I became more skilled and more dependable I wanted to add more elements of excitement to my performance.

One day I got the brilliant idea that I was going to try a helicopter jump. That's where you wrap the rope around your waist and attempt to do a full 360-degree rotation before you complete your landing. I don't know how it happened but I got off center in the course of my spin and wound up cracking Mark with my skis. Not only did I break his collarbone but I practically drove him to the bottom of the lake. My helicoptering experience ended there, just as soon as it began. I felt horrible about it but that didn't mean I wasn't ready to try more.

Before long my next bright idea came to me. I decided I was going to try a back flip off the end of the water ski ramp. Little did I know that when you are in the air rotating, it becomes incredibly difficult to judge when to pull out of your spin without the use of sight. I had an excellent teacher in Scotty Clack, who was a world champion freestyler and who would be my partner as I attempted this stunt, but unfortunately, that wasn't enough.

I did this live in the show. No rehearsals, no practice. I think I knew that this was a seriously high risk stunt. If it was going to be a one-time thing, why not let the paying customers get the benefit?

I got the countdown to the ramp and went into my rotation. I may have had too much speed, too much enthusiasm, or maybe it was just a judgment thing but I did a 390-degree rotation instead of 360 degrees and I got off my axis and got my axis kicked. I smashed into the water in a horrific, cart wheeling, out of control crash. I bent my body in ways it was never intended to bend, and that came at a price.

Instantly I knew this was bad. I heard a voice from the crowd, a kid saying "Look Mommy, he's hurt!" and I thought, "you don't know the half of it, kid!" This wasn't a small hurt. I felt like my body was totally paralyzed.

As I had done so many times before, I shortly found myself on the way to a hospital, this time in Winter Haven, where my worst fears were confirmed. My ribs were cracked, my collarbone was broken and my hamstring was torn completely away from the bone. Incapacitated was an understatement.

My skiing career at Cypress Gardens came to an end that day. I wasn't much use to Cypress Gardens in my incapacitated condition. As has always been my way, I refused to be a burden or take advantage of others when I didn't feel I was earning my share. I'm sure I could have hung around, stayed at the hotel and convalesced, maybe even returned to the show when I had recovered, but I couldn't let myself just sit on the payroll for months doing nothing. Not me. If I wasn't going to be skiing I'd find something else to do. It didn't take long. I was hired by Eagle USA Wetsuits as a spokesman and found myself moving to Houston.

Healing took a very long time. It took me April, May, June and into July to really start feeling better. Even in July, when I started attempting to train for the world championships in Oslo, I was doing it on one good leg. I still couldn't use my injured leg effectively.

The impact of my injuries showed and I finished fourth in Oslo that year. Fortunately, I had some other exciting pursuits happening in my speaking career to keep me busy but such a disappointing finish did leave a bad taste in my mouth.

I decided to give it one more try and was back in shape and healthy by November when I won the U.S. Nationals again. Now I was back in the hunt for the worlds in August of 1985.

My trainer through the first trip to Oslo and the second U.S. Nationals had been Ken Ransom, a vice president at Eagle USA Wetsuits. Ken and his wife, Tricia, had asked me to dinner one night, and, as they told people later, "the guy never left." Through the first trip to Oslo, I lived with them in their home in Woodlands, Texas. Ken, a transplanted Englishman, had more patience in training than anyone I've ever met.

For this second trip to Norway, Ken and I trained at a Boy Scout camp north of Houston called Camp Strake. It wasn't exactly heaven on earth to me because I'd heard about the alligators living there and I had no plans to make the sequel to Crocodile Dundee. I was constantly in fear of running into a future piece of luggage with the jaws and teeth still attached.

The first thing Ken and I did when we got to Camp Strake each day was a Gator run. We circled the lake, looking for alligators and on more than one instance we found them towards the ski dock end of the lake, often very close. Ken would try chasing them with the boat toward the other end.

Skiing in a lake with alligators may sound crazy, but it had one advantage. It provided a tremendous incentive for staying upright on the water rather than in it.

We did encounter a few of these prehistoric creatures during the course of our training. Fortunately, whether by pure blind luck or because our communication had become so fine-tuned, these encounters were little more than high-speed passes. Of course, I also had the benefit of being blind. On more than one occasion, when we got back to the dock, Ken would say, "Thank God you're blind, you really don't want to know what you just missed."

I sometimes wonder if I might have panicked and made matters worse if I had seen what I just flew past. I realize in this case that what I didn't know could hurt me, but at least I didn't hurt myself.

Throughout our escapades, Ken was the perfect coach, always reassuring, always encouraging, always thinking. He even video-taped me and the films help me refine my technique as we skied day and night, yes, sometimes at night, relentlessly preparing for the worlds.

And, as usual for me, hard work paid athletic dividends. My skiing improved dramatically. This time I went to Oslo brimming with confidence, maybe too much.

I wasn't overconfident about my skiing, I knew full well what a wipeout on skis could do to me, but maybe I was overconfident about my intestinal fortitude. For some reason, I didn't bring a wet-suit with me, to of all places, Norway. Heck, I'd even been here before but I misjudged my memory of the weather, thinking that last time I was in Oslo the chilly weather wasn't really Oslo weather. That proved to be irrelevant anyway. It turned out that we were competing in a tiny town called Beitostølen, on a Fjord well north of Oslo. It may have been August, but it might as well have been December.

The Norwegians thought I was nuts, or at least had a couple screws loose. As acclimatized as they were to the local conditions, they all wore wetsuits. You couldn't blame them. The water temperature was just over 50 degrees Fahrenheit. This is one time I wish I had a greater sense of self-preservation.

It didn't matter, I was on a mission once again and this time everything clicked. Attribute it to all of Ken's training, to the fact that I was healthier, to the fact that I was fully focused this time around, but I reconnected with my old friend, the Grey Zone once again. There is a point in time where the Grey Zone almost becomes an irresistible force for an athlete. Many people, none of whom have ever been in the Grey Zone, dismiss it as a gift that some athletes are just lucky to find, by chance, at times in their career. I disagree. The Grey Zone comes to an athlete when physical and mental preparation, it takes both, are refined and focused through repetition and hard work until excellence becomes involuntary. This time I had done the work, and it paid benefits.

On my first run I nailed seventeen crosses in my twenty second first pass and on the second pass went whizzing back and forth like a crazy man. I had no idea how many crosses I'd hit. I had gone that quickly, like I was in a trance. They announced I had hit a perfect twenty.

The second run was pure autopilot. If I could have gone faster, I can't imagine how. I hit twenty crosses again on my third pass and actually increased that to twenty-one my final pass. They said twenty was perfect so I guess twenty-one was just a bonus. Whatever it was, it was enough. I had my world championship!

Skiing in Norway without a wetsuit, brrr!

After the medal ceremony, one of my competitors, from Italy I believe, came to congratulate me and said that next year he wasn't bringing a wetsuit either. Everybody laughed.

I had to call the states right away. I called a friend of mine in Houston. He was a DJ named "Moby" and was emerging as one of the most prominent morning men in America. He had a rather prominent sportscaster working with him, too. None other than Hanna Storm, well on her way to NBC Sports by that time.

Moby put me on the air right away and, fortunately, Ken Ransom, who had not been able to come to Oslo because of business commitments, was listening in his car. Ken told me later that the excitement in my voice was so high that he couldn't help getting choked up himself. He had to pull over.

There was more than just winning the event that contributed to my excitement and Ken's emotion. We had discussed this day many times. I wanted it to be my last athletic competition but that could only happen if I won. As much as I was ready to move on, I knew I could not settle down if I didn't go out on top.

I was certain, right at the moment of winning, that my competitive athletic days were over. I'd been a champion in wrestling, medal winner in the Blind Olympics, track and field, snow skiing and now water skiing. My body had taken a pounding since I was seven years old. Mentally, and physically, I was weary of it now.

I had 137 medals of one kind or another, 104 of them gold. It was deeply satisfying that I was going out as I had begun, when a visionary teacher selected me for the wrestling team, seventeen years earlier, as a winner.

It was time to move on, to focus on a business career, maybe start a family, to reap the rewards and take advantage of the opportunities that my athletic career had exposed me to. My speaking career had begun to gather serious momentum during the past year and now it deserved my full attention. In fact, when I left Norway, I was on my way to speak to more than 21,000 at the Lions International convention in Dallas, Texas.

Mediocrity

I have spent much of my career challenging individuals and audiences to elevate their world, to lift their performance, to make a positive, meaningful difference, not just in their own lives but in the lives of those around them.

I challenge everyone to take responsibility. To set standards of achievement and behavior and to discipline themselves to maintain them. I share my experiences and the lessons that have allowed me to do this in my own life and speak with thousands of people a year about doing the same in theirs.

Setting standards of achievement and behavior has always been my means of having a good life. Surprisingly, to me anyway, the majority of people I meet don't seem to have the same interpretation. The most common subject I am asked about is not how to live a good life but "How to achieve greatness?"

I always tell people that I don't know. I tell them that my standard is to be "GOOD!" Of course, if you are going to set a standard for yourself, you need a yardstick to measure yourself against. Here's mine:

I heard a talk many years ago that has stuck with me ever since. I forget who the minister was but I'll paraphrase his comments and hopefully they will stay with you as well. He had referenced the Book of Genesis as he compared God's opinion of himself with how we think of ourselves as humans. He said it this way:

"God created a tree and said it was GOOD. Man invented the automobile and said it was amazing, stupendous, *Great*. God created a rabbit and said that it was GOOD. Man invented the refrigerator and said it was awesome, super, *Great*. Well, the wheels fell off the car, and the fridge broke down, but the tree's still up and the rabbit's still running! The quality of God's work, GOOD."

Now, if God didn't hold himself to a standard of Great, what chance do you really think you have?

In my opinion, greatness, even for those we consider great, is too tough a standard to maintain. In fact, I don't believe it is a standard that is maintainable, let alone obtainable. We do great deeds, have great successes, see great results over time, but we do not live in a state of greatness. Great things are moments that happen and greatness is the accumulation of multiple great moments during one's life or career. We don't live great lives. Albert Einstein summed it up best when he said, "You ask me if I keep a notebook to record my great ideas. I've only ever had one." One idea, but Mr. Einstein's legacy is one of greatness.

Great legacies, that's a different story. When someone aspires to greatness, this is what I believe they mean. The unfortunate reality is that most who aspire to greatness are living lives of mediocrity, waiting for a transformation that is never going to happen. The leap from mediocrity to greatness, whether it is a onetime event or a legacy, is just too far and totally unrealistic.

That is why I subscribe to the standard of GOOD! Being consistently good, day in and day out, without exception, (which is what I mean by standard) is very hard work. It takes discipline, it takes personal growth, it takes intellectual growth, it takes follow through, it takes the patience to do the right things and to do them right. It also takes consistency and dependability.

Being GOOD is all about developing the proficiency, knowledge and resources that enable you to apply your particular skills and expertise in a consistent and persistent manner. It is about being utterly dependable.

If you can achieve the standard of GOOD, then you have accomplished something remarkable that goes beyond just the benefits of a wonderful life. You will have set yourself up for great moments to happen.

When you are good, you are ready to respond to opportunity. You can raise the bar in your life to take advantage of opportunities when they present themselves. The well-known quote suggests that Luck is what occurs when preparation meets opportunity. In my experience, great achievement also occurs when preparation meets opportunity, but only if the prepared is good enough to raise the bar.

When you are good, you are also ready to respond to challenges, problems and the unexpected. History seems full of far more examples of those who had "greatness thrust upon them" than of those who set out to achieve greatness and succeeded. When you maintain the standard of GOOD, you will be ready to raise the bar when called upon to deal with any obstacle that may rise before you, and often experience moments of greatness along the way.

The world of sports is full of examples of athletes having good careers who, in the face of seemingly insurmountable odds, have raised the bar and turned in a great performance that has gone down in history. The ones who did this more often are remembered as great, but even the greatest weren't great every night. In fact, their true character is more often remembered for how good they played when they were not at their best, how they were always good. Think of Michael Jordan or Cal Ripken or Wayne Gretzky or Gordie Howe or Jack Nicklaus. All utterly dependable and consistent, playing at a higher level than most, but not great every night. They were, however, far more capable of giving us moments of greatness because it wasn't too far to go from the standard they maintained.

The world of sports is a great example, but it is also a small and exceptional segment of our world. If you understand the example that Michael or Gordie or Jack represent, then you can transfer it to the business world. History is full of examples of those who, in the face of challenge or criticism or even failure, have raised the bar to develop new procedures, products, programs, companies and even industries that have produced great results. Do your research. You'll find that most of these people were GOOD.

If you think about the world of medicine you'll find the same story. Doctors, researchers, chemists, biologists, physicists, therapists, nurses, who, in the face of challenges, problems, emergencies or just ongoing struggles, have found exceptional answers that have produced great results. You'll find that most of these people held themselves to the standard of GOOD.

So there is my philosophy on being great. Be GOOD, day in and day out. Don't be afraid to raise the bar when you can, or when you have to, but never let your standard drop. And if you truly want a great legacy, never lose sight of those words spoken by Vincent van Gogh, "Great things are done by a series of small things brought together."

Maybe it can all be summed up by this wonderful quote, from Hilary Cooper, that my wife Patti has hanging on the wall of our kitchen.

"Life is not measured by the number of breaths we take, but by the moments that take our breath away."

17

Smoke Gets In Your Eyes

When you travel as much as I do there is one sound you get used to but never want to hear. It is that ear piercing blare produced by a hotel fire alarm.

Fortunately, in most cases, before you've shaken off your slumbering haze and taken your mental inventory (it seems most fire alarms go off in the small hours of the morning) there is an announcement that it was a false alarm.

But, as I said, that is only most cases. That was not the case early one morning in late 1985. I was awoken by that loud staccato squawk that I had become so familiar with. Never taking a fire alarm for granted, my mind did its quick inventory. I was on the twenty-third floor of a Los Angeles hotel. I had a great view, I suppose, but all I could think in that moment was that it was a long way to the ground.

I threw on a pair of pants, grabbed a shirt and forced my feet into a pair of loafers. Fortunately, I keep hotel rooms perfectly organized, nothing out of place, ever. I have to, not in anticipation of a fire, but because it is the only way for me to cope. If I have a five a.m. wake-up call I don't have time to read the carpet, like Braille, looking for my socks.

There was nothing else to worry about. The only important thing to do in that instant is to get out. Of course, I was expecting that calm voice on the intercom telling everyone that this was a false alarm, but it never came. What I heard were panicked voices in the hallway, plenty of them. This was a large hotel and there were a lot of people looking for the exit.

The exit! OMG, I hadn't bothered to locate the exits. You'd think someone in my situation would orientate himself, but after almost a million air miles I had become rather blasé about such details. There was one attitude adjustment I would have to deal with later.

For now, I just exited out into the hall. I quickly realized that if I just followed the crowd, I would be led to the exit. That part of my plan worked. I found the staircase and was on my way down when I realized something was wrong. Not with me, but I could hear something. A voice, a soft-spoken voice but one that was in trouble. Everyone else just kept pushing past, making their way to the ground as quickly as possible. Nobody else seemed to hear this, but I was always hearing things nobody else did. By age twenty-three my hearing had become very acutely developed. Tonight that became more a Godsend than a compensation. There weren't that many people left in the stairwell. We were close to the top floor and it seemed all of the guests were already below me, at least in my stairwell.

I had only gone a couple of floors when I heard this. I couldn't ignore it, but I couldn't find anyone else to check it out. I decided I better do it myself. I exited the stairwell at the next landing and quickly found this voice. It was a woman's voice, coming from close to the ground. I followed the sound and quickly found a woman in a wheelchair. "Please help me," she said. "The elevators aren't working. I don't know what to do."

Of course, you can't take the elevators during a fire, but how was I going to help this woman? I don't think I even took time to strategize. There was no time. I pushed her wheelchair through the door into the stairwell landing, turned her around and picked her up, chair and all. It was the only way I could think to get her to the ground level. There was certainly nobody left to help us at this point. This was all up to me.

"Don't worry ma'am, if I make it out of here, you will too, and I fully intend to get out of here."

It wasn't long before I realized it was going to take every ounce of strength, energy and resolve I could muster to get the two of us to safety. By my calculation, we had around twenty floors to go. It wasn't long before my arms started to ache and I felt my equilibrium slipping away, or at least my orientation. We were going backwards, eight steps, around the corner, eight steps, around the corner. Again and again and again.

I wasn't going to put this woman down. I didn't think we had the time and I didn't want to startle her anymore than she already was. We maybe had ten flights left now, or twelve. How much longer could I carry her? I was in great shape, yes, but I wasn't a weight-lifter. I stayed toned through pushups and chin-ups and cardio. I had to keep going, but how?

I was praying for that calm voice on the intercom. These are always false alarms, right? Maybe we still had to get down these stairs but how urgent was it? Just as I was thinking this, the smell of smoke hit my nostrils. No announcement today. I picked up my pace, maybe a little panic setting in, recognition of the urgency to get out, certainly. And the fear of the smoke. I may have been blessed with the refined instincts to maneuver in the dark, which translated well to a visually impaired, smoke filled stairwell, but that doesn't mean the smoke still didn't burn my eyes too. I knew you could suffocate through smoke inhalation. Yes, I got a little scared, for both of us.

My quickened pace brought with it an adrenaline rush, a small burst of energy to get around those last five or six corners. God, don't these stairs ever end, I thought. Then I felt it. A break from the heat, a blast of cooler air on my back. We hit the final landing. I set her chair down, swung it around and stumbled out the side door onto the street. We were safe.

Fortunately, it was small fire on one of the lower floors that never amounted to much. I didn't get all the details, didn't really want them. I was just happy the two of got out safe and there was still a chance for a couple hours sleep before checking out in the morning.

I have thought, since that night, if there isn't always a bigger plan in God's scheme than we ever realize, or ever could. I may have been the single most qualified, appropriately experienced person, in that moment, to save this woman's life.

I'm not saying this to brag. I'm not a superhero, but I am, or at least was, particularly qualified to perform an athletic deed in a stairwell with the lights out. I was still riding the residual fitness benefits of my competitive athletic days, including those days at Carleton University when I trained by running the stairs of the YMCA Tower in Ottawa. Was it pure luck or some divine intervention that this woman was found by maybe the only man, certainly in that hotel that night, who had run up and down twenty floors of stairs, over and over and over again, for no particular reason than just to be "in shape."

It was as if I had been training my entire life for this night. All the inconveniences were nothing more than training for the most important race I would ever run.

Think about it. The simple, virtually random accident that took my sight at age two, may well have saved another person's life two decades later. The way my parents raised me to be as normal as possible, hunting, setting traps, riding my bike, throwing bales of hay, created a man who was anything but fragile when the chips were down. Those nights Eric and I used to sneak out the third floor of boy's residence at W. Ross MacDonald, then creep along the ledge, and climb down the corner bricks to the ground, must've been preparation for the treacherous flights of stairs I somehow made it down through the smoke. And the strength I was driven to create in my upper body and legs for wrestling – few people in that hotel could've maneuvered that woman in her wheelchair the way I did.

And think about this. A sighted person may well have become completely disoriented when the smoke filled the stairway and visibility went to zero. Not me. I was perfectly equipped to maneuver in the dark, especially walking backwards carrying a wheelchair.

I don't say this to boast. I say it to drive home one point. If I can do it, so can you. If I can live the exciting life I've lived, so can you. And if everything in my life led me to this point, then ask yourself, "Where is your life leading you?" What special duty are your inconveniences leading to? What special duty are you in training for right now?

The question for you is simple. How has your life prepared you to be a hero? How have you prepared yourself? If I can be a hero so can you. After all, I'm no better than you are.

The Power of P.R.I.D.E.

It was quite early in my speaking career that the principles I call P.R.I.D.E. showed up in one my speeches.

I was looking for a compelling way to express my philosophy of life and success. As speaking became a more regular event for me I found that I wanted to develop a format or structure to my

message. I had so much more I wanted to share than just the novelty of "Blind Kid Makes Good." I had tried several different formats for my speeches, with limited success, then one day these principles just flowed as I talked. They came straight from the heart and have remained there to this day.

P.R.I.D.E. became the foundation and backbone of my speaking career and remains so to this day. It embodies and is the essence of who I am. This is what P.R.I.D.E. means to me:

P. The "P" stands for perseverance. It is the backbone of everything we do in life. It's the intestinal fortitude you need to be able to do what you have to do to accomplish goals, dreams and aspirations you have set for tomorrow and on down the road. If you don't have a purpose in mind, I don't believe you ever wholeheartedly throw yourself into something. In wrestling my purpose was to mainstream into a regular school. I had to ask myself, "Do I go to the gym to work four days and then, ah, it's raining...slide on the fifth?" Or do I have the mental strength to push past the moment of decision and keep making myself the best I can be? Perseverance without purpose is meaningless.

For almost eleven years, I built myself up by doing several hundred sit-ups and pushups a day, not because I enjoyed them but because I never wanted to give people the opportunity to say I lost because I was blind. I never wanted people to look at me as handicapped, but to look at my blindness **"as just a minor inconvenience."** We all have inconveniences, regardless of what stage and age we may be at. How you overcome these inconveniences will ultimately determine how successful you are. Not just monetarily, but in attitude, spirit and overall outlook on life.

R. The "R" stands for respect. If you don't have a sense of belief in yourself, how can you expect others to believe in you? It's also about respecting all the unsung heroes who don't necessarily receive recognition - parents, grandparents, coaches, teachers, the ordinary people who take the time out of their lives to do extraordinary things in ours. I'm sure if you think about it you don't have to go back very far to come up with your own unsung heroes who've touched your life.

It's also about respect for authority and respect for those in need. I encourage everyone to never be too busy or complacent to extend a helping hand. Somewhere, someday, you may well be very grateful that someone was kind enough to reach out and help you in a moment of need - even if you think you are invincible, which a lot of us do. I could not have made anything of myself without the helping hands of others. I need to pass that along when I can.

I. The "I" stands for Individuality. This is my favorite. Blindness never gave me a chance at team sports on an interscholastic-competitive basis. I was part of a team but always in an individualized sport - wrestling, track, skiing. But it's OK to stand alone on some things in life. The peer pressure and the decisions we make today could potentially have an enormous impact on the person you become tomorrow and beyond. It takes a much stronger person to walk away from a negative situation than to stay and participate.

The question is, are you going to be a leader? And, if you choose to follow, will you follow the right person, for the right reasons? That takes as much strength of character as leading.

You can't let other people set the odds for you. They can say you're not good enough or fast enough or smart enough or good-looking enough. They may say you come from too limiting a background to succeed. If you're looking for someone to doubt your ability, you won't have far to look. If you want to shift blame for your failures or pass off your responsibilities, you can do that, too. DON'T! Be your own individual. Stand on your own two feet. Make your own decisions, and when you draw the bottom line for whatever you do, ask yourself if you could have done just a little bit more. Did you leave any cards on the table un-played? When I got finished with a wrestling match I often barely had the energy to walk off the mat. I let it all hang out. I left nothing to chance. If I lost, a better person won that day. I didn't want excuses being made for me. I wanted the deciding moment to come down to me, alone.

There is only one person in this world who knows what you are fully capable of achieving and that, of course, is you. Take charge of your own dreams and aspirations. Make them your own. You'll be happier in the long run.

D. The "D" stands for Desire. We are all blessed with an abundance of desire, our challenge is with unleashing it. Desire is what often throws another log on the fire when the flame is burning out inside you. Desire is the eye of the tiger determination that you need to live life to the fullest. Desire is the manifestation of your perseverance. It determines whether you persist or give up. It is what gets you to the extra mile when you want to pull over and rest. It is the ultimate force that you need to achieve your goals and dreams instead of settling for the status quo. Live your dreams. In wrestling, I tasted my own hunger sometimes making weight. If you want something bad enough, you have to be willing to taste your own hunger, to feel that fire burning in the pit of your stomach.

Desire is the spark plug of life but you can't buy a can of desire at your local corner store. No one can give you a handful of desire either. Desire is measured by the size of your heart! How do you measure up?

E. The "E" stands for Enthusiasm. It is that spirit, that zest, that zeal, that passionate attitude that we need to enjoy life every day. I'm not talking about some overt, over the top, demonstrative behavior that is overwhelming. We all demonstrate enthusiasm differently, but in every case it comes across as a quiet, energized confidence that can't be ignored. It shows in your smile, your actions, your posture, your words and your results. It's how the fire in your belly turns you into a breath of fresh air that cannot be denied. It is what separates you from the dull, mundane, downtrodden majority that can't inspire anyone or anything. Enthusiasm is what ultimately carries the day and what will ultimately carry you to realize your goals and dreams.

The day that Gordie Howe and I carried the Olympic torch through Washington D.C., I came up with this analogy. "Inside everyone of us, we have a small little torch. How high you light the flame on the torch inside you can only be reflected by the smile you put on your face as you walk through life each and every day."

P.RI.D.E. has always been a powerful force in my life but as I have grown in my career, P.R.I.D.E. has grown as well. I now refer to this philosophy of P.R.I.D.E. as the Personal version because my business experience has given rise to the Professional version. I believe this evolution of P.R.I.D.E. is a natural progression. If you dedicate yourself to the outline above, and commit to constant and never ending improvement as we have discussed, you will begin to demonstrate the principles of Professional P.R.I.D.E. as well. Here is how I define Professional P.R.I.D.E.:

P. The Professional "P" stands for Performance. Performance is about never going below the threshold that you've set for yourself. Performance is about consistency and dependability. It is about committing to the standard of GOOD and demonstrating it every day in your behaviors, actions and results. It is about continually refining your skills, knowledge and abilities in a program of personal growth and compiling that improvement into that quality we call WISDOM.

Ultimately, Performance comes down to results and how you deliver them.

R. The Professional "R" stands for Relationships. When referring to the success of others, I find so many people are ready to quote from the hip, with the first cliché to be fired usually being "it's not what you know, it's who you know" that determines your success.

It's too bad that most people who fire from the hip that way are usually coming from a posture of jealousy making an excuse for someone else's success or defending their own failure. That's sad because their statement was true. They just don't understand why.

Yes, it does go beyond the "who you know" but it is definitely the people in your life that determine your success, and your happiness.

Your success, in plain and simple terms, is totally dependent on the number of effective relationships that you have in your network, both personally and professionally. You may be the single most knowledgeable, skilled person on the face of the planet, but until you can manifest that knowledge over a wide network of family, friends, colleagues, employees and customers your potential success is extremely limited.

There are two very important words to take note of here. Effective and manifest. I'm not talking about using people or how many favors your friends can do for you. I'm talking about your ability to effectively connect with the broadest number of people, on their terms, to each other's mutual benefit.

When your communication skills have evolved to the point where you not only understand others but can make yourself effectively understood, on their terms, then you have the greatest opportunity to accomplish both their objectives and yours, be they personal, professional or spiritual, in a manner that is satisfactory to everyone involved. The more people you know and can accomplish this with, the greater your legacy is going to be.

Bottom line! Successful relationships are all about Effective Communication!

I. The Professional "I" stands for Integrity. Your integrity is your reputation. It defines what the world thinks of you and how they deal with you. It is at the core of your success. It is how you follow through on your communication. It is what gives your words and your actions the congruency you need to be seen as a true success in every sense of the word. It is what inspires the confidence of others in you. More importantly, it is what inspires their trust in you.

Integrity means that you walk your talk. You do what you say. You say what you mean. Your word is your bond. You under promise and over deliver, every time. You answer your emails and return your messages. You arrive when you say you will. You deliver what you promise, when you promised it. You follow through. You maintain a standard of performance that is unquestionable and impeccable.

Your integrity is the essence of everything successful about you. Take it seriously.

D. The Professional "D" stands for Discipline. Discipline is the cold hard reality of what it takes to be a professional. Discipline is about doing what you have to do, when you have to do it, as you should do it, whether you like it or not. Discipline is integral to your integrity. Discipline is critical to your effectiveness and effectiveness is all about results.

Discipline may be the least romantic of all the principles of P.R.I.D.E. but it may also be the most important. A lack of discipline is the differentiator between success and failure. When you practice the principle of Discipline in all aspects of your life, the results invariably follow.

E. The Professional "E" stands for Excuses, or more accurately, "NO EXCUSES!" Benjamin Franklin once said, "He who is good for making excuses is seldom good for anything else." Isn't that the truth?

There is always an excuse that can be made. Always a reason to delay or change or re-schedule but none of them are ever acceptable. Even worse, if you find yourself leading with an excuse, you are creating a self-imposed mental block, barrier or wall before you even get started. If you have embodied the principles of P.R.I.D.E. you will begin to find that you are rarely confronted with circumstances where you might consider making an excuse. If it happens, remember the Professional E. Find a way to get it done, and learn the lesson necessary to ensure that you aren't confronted with that situation again. Beyond everything else, don't let your excuse be somebody else. Don't blame somebody else when you fail to deliver. Take responsibility for your mistakes. If you're in management, take responsibility for your team. Take responsibility for your results. Above all, take responsibility for your Life.

You will never remotely reach your full potential if you accept excuses, your own in particular.

P.R.I.D.E., when all is said and done, is a comprehensive bundle of principles that apply across the full spectrum of your life. If you make an honest effort to embody them every day, on a persistent and consistent basis, they will elevate you to the level of champion in whatever endeavors you choose to pursue. It's a matter of discipline.

This is how I close everyone of my speeches today.

I can honestly say that, given the opportunity, I would gladly trade all those gold medals and championships that I fought so long and hard to win - I'd gladly give every single one of them just to be able to have my eyesight.

To be able to see how beautiful the colors must be in a rainbow. To see the faces of my parents, something I honestly don't remember. To see my wife and my children. To see those things that you take for granted every day, the trees in the fall or a gorgeous sunset.

But as I travel around, I understand that there are people in this world who are a lot less fortunate than I, who have not been blessed as I have. It is a responsibility for everyone one of us to want to make a difference in the lives of those who haven't been as blessed or fortunate as we've been along life's highway. I have had so many wonderful people make a difference in my life. Now my responsibility is to make a positive difference wherever I can. In fact, the true measurement of your success will not be in what you made, but in what you gave. How are you measuring up?

In the early days of my speaking career, I had started to find my inner self through these speeches. I felt good knowing that I could share what I had learned. It fueled my desire to make a difference, a positive difference, in the lives of everyone who heard me.

The fundamentals of P.R.I.D.E. have sustained my career and my life. They have allowed me to achieve so many worthwhile goals while being happy, and I hope, balanced. If you take them to heart, as I have, they will do the same for you.

The Music Man

"I want a new drug,
one that won't make me sick,
One that won't make me crash my car,
or make feel three feet thick."

Huey Lewis and the News

After Oslo, I suppose I was looking for a new drug of sorts. My drug had been athletic competition. Now that my competing days were over I needed a new outlet for my restlessness. I was looking for a new story to write. I had no idea Huey Lewis would be stepping into the opening act.

It seems everyone can share my next dream. Either overtly or secretly, in public, or just in the shower, we have all had at least a flickering flirtation with the idea of being a successful singer, of bringing down the house with a brilliant performance, inspiring a standing ovation with a magnificent solo, or maybe singing the first dance at our child's wedding. Whatever the dream, I think everyone has fantasized about being a singer. I just took mine a little further.

My dream was for platinum albums, performing to sold out arenas, winning Grammy awards and touring with the full rock star entourage. It's true that I never played Madison Square Garden but I did sell out in Boise, Idaho. I never became a platinum recording artist either, but I did make a couple albums, three actually.

I clearly remember the start of this ride. It was at Fantasy Studios in Berkley, California in late 1985. It was 1 a.m. and I had navigated my way to the cafeteria during a break in our recording session. Recording an album had always been a dream, a yearning desire that I wanted to pursue and now here I was, in the same studios that had been graced by Creedence Clearwater Revival, Journey, The Pointer Sisters, Jefferson Starship, Eddie Money and many, many more. The wallpaper was comprised of countless platinum albums that had been recorded and mastered right there, in that same building. Now I was taking a stab.

Well, at that precise moment, I was taking a stab at getting popcorn out of the vending machine. The music industry may be glamorous but making an album, like any other worthwhile endeavor is more about the hard work than the limelight. It is also about the budget. Studio time was much cheaper overnight, so like many who went before me, and no doubt since, I was laying down my tracks in the middle of the night.

That means no staff in the cafeteria, just vending machines. I had found my way to the right machine, but had no familiarity with this particular beast. I wanted a bag of popcorn, but too often over the years, I punched in what I thought was the right code, but instead of popcorn, turned my last quarter into a pack of Certs.

I could hear someone else nearby, I suspected the janitor, but I called out anyway and he graciously came over to me. I asked him to help me buy my popcorn and, since he seemed like the friendly sort, I asked him to help me with the microwave as well.

He took my popcorn, punched a few buttons and the microwave went to work. While my popcorn popped, the janitor and I made small talk about things like how cool San Francisco is, how brutal these overnight shifts can be and other general stuff. I remember thinking, "This guy is pretty cool for a janitor." So cool that we got totally engrossed in our conversation, completely forgetting the popcorn. Several minutes later, still gabbing away, we heard an explosion and he said, "Damn!" My popcorn had blown up inside the microwave.

"I need to clean this up." He said "Give me a minute, and I'll start another bag for you." I tried to tell him not to worry but he insisted. Like I said, he was pretty cool.

We paid attention to the second bag and once I had my prize in my hands, I really had to get back to the studio. I thanked him again and thought I should introduce myself, finally.

"Thanks for all your help. By the way, my name is Craig MacFarlane." I reached out my hand and he shook it firmly as he replied, "It is an honor to meet you, I'm Huey Lewis."

I swear my jaw dropped all the way to the floor. Sure, I had been around celebrities before but...I didn't expect that. Huey was humble, friendly and totally self-deprecating. No ego at all and just so helpful. He walked back to my studio with me and actually hung out in the control room while I laid down a track or two. Made me feel like a real recording artist. Sweet.

What was sweeter was the next night when he invited me to hang out in his studio. This was the kind of scene I imagined back in my fledgling days as a budding musician at the school for the blind in Brantford, but not even in that wildest imaginative state did I envision rapping with Huey Lewis during recording sessions in the middle of the night.

W. Ross MacDonald in Brantford wasn't a bad place to dream about a music career, regardless of how crazy the dream. I started with piano lessons in fourth grade and became competent rather quickly. W. Ross MacDonald had a heavy emphasis on music and a first-class music wing. There were about 20 individual practice studios and a piano in everyone. I used to hit the music wing regularly and by the time I was in seventh grade, I was much more into playing pieces by stars such as Elton John, rather than the traditional stuff they were trying to teach us, when I could get away with it.

When I wasn't in the studio, or at wrestling practice, I was usually trying to rock the house with my buddies Eric, Kevin and Kenny. We formed a band of sorts and called ourselves The Truckers. We would play Beatles tunes, Rolling Stones, Elton John,

Eric and I, "rocking the house."

all the stuff they didn't teach us in music class. It was great fun. I primarily played keyboards and did some vocals. I loved taking the lead and jumping around the room as I did a song, feeling the beat and doing my best Mick Jagger strut. Not the kind of behavior most expected from a blind band, but it turned out to be the best training for the Inner Vision tour years later.

Attending such a music-oriented school meant that other, more traditional school band instruments were also part of my education. I took up the clarinet in fifth grade and by sixth grade I was playing in the school band. As a side note of interest, Jeff Healey from the movie "Roadhouse," who recorded the hit single "Angel Eyes" also played in that band. Jeff was a couple grades behind me.

When I was at Central Algoma for my Freshman and Sophomore years of high school I added the trumpet, and then the trombone to my experience. It wasn't that I wanted to play every instrument in the band, well maybe I did, but I wanted to be in the fraternity. The Freshman year is, for most students in Canada anyway, the first time they are ever part of a music environment and are usually learning an instrument for the first time. I think I took up the trumpet just to be like everyone else, to fit in.

The trombone proved to be the most fun, primarily because I could create the most mischief with it. I learned to make airplane noises and the sounds of a racecar and would often do them just for fun during the rehearsal of long, boring pieces. Of course, in those days I was the golden boy. Our music director, Mr. Ricci, thought I could do no wrong and always sharply scolded some other member of the trombone section for the noise, while I stood by, biting my lip to keep from laughing.

The fun continued back at W. Ross MacDonald during my Junior and Senior years. Music was great fun but despite my musical fantasies, athletics were still my obsession. The wild dream of a rock and roll career was never pursued seriously, but never left the back of my mind either.

After Oslo, my mind found a little time for my recording fantasy and I started stretching in that direction. It began with a call to Fantasy Studios. I was looking for a producer, someone who could lead me through this process and help me record my first album. They put me in touch with Elliot Mazer. Elliot had done some stuff with Janis Joplin, Neil Young, Tina Turner and Linda Ronstadt, just to mention a few. We hit it off and it wasn't long before we were together in Houston, finalizing plans to record an album.

I never envisioned so much work went into recording an entire project like that. This was going to take months. Of course, we were starting from ground zero so this included everything from writing new songs from scratch to organizing studio musicians, to laying down the recordings, to mixing it, pressing it, getting the cover designed and photographed, writing the liner notes, and more. I know I'm glossing over this, but it was like maneuvering an army. A million details had to be worked out between each of those steps.

We did put together an impressive group of studio musicians to help me record that first album at Fantasy Studios. The bass player was Ross Valery from Journey. Our keyboard guy was nicknamed "Banana," and had played with the Youngbloods. In addition, some of our keyboards would be played by Tim Gorman. Tim had played on one of The Who tours. If that's not enough, some background vocals were laid down by none other than Eddie Money.

I was very fortunate to benefit from this group. If it wasn't for Elliot, I am sure they never would have given me a second thought.

Walking into Fantasy Studios that first night was like taking a side trip from reality. There were four studios at Fantasy and it was a full house, but I was the only minor-league player. Steve Perry was finishing the vocals on an album for Journey in one studio. I think that was the "Raised on Radio" album. Huey Lewis was there, of course, in Studio D working on "Hip to be Square," while Studio A was being shared by Eddie Money and Jeffrey Osborne.

I just kept thinking, "What am I doing here with all the big boys?"

The big boys, however, were very cool. Elliot had given them a heads up about my athletic experience and background and they were, as a result, very engaging. It seemed we had an ongoing give and take, and often longer conversations when time allowed. Steve Perry, I remember, was particularly interested in my snow skiing and water skiing adventures and even just how I maneuvered the halls of Fantasy Studios.

To be honest, maneuvering the halls of Fantasy Studios was a challenge for anybody, not just me. People were always coming and going, the halls were always cluttered with equipment or chairs or even stacks of crates. Once, trying to find my way back to the vending machines for the umpteenth time I knocked over a stack of wooden crates and scored a direct hit on Eddie Money's shoulder. He just shook it off and laughed. "Don't worry, son, I knock things over around here all the time too."

Recording that first album was a fantastic, albeit expensive education. You don't just show up, record a couple of songs and leave. You don't even record the entire song at the same time. I was surprised, and impressed to learn that most of the music on a recording goes down one track at a time. It is a laborious, pain-staking process but when you work with talented people, it can produce absolute magic.

I remember wearing my headphones, doing my lead vocal tracks. You can get the mix any way you want it in your headphones. No background vocals, less guitar, more bass. … it's your call. The engineer can give you whatever conditions you believe will bring out your best performance, but mine came from a different place. I stood there, singing my heart out, imagining all the great vocalists who had stood in that same spot to record some of the most popular music of all time. I think I was trying to channel their talent, hoping I could absorb enough of their psychic residue to become the next platinum selling artist.

We worked on that first album for a couple months before it was finished. I called it "Love is Blind." I didn't become a platinum selling artist with that one, in fact it was never officially released. The "timing" wasn't right, or so I was told, over and over again. Still, it was one heck of an education and, in my opinion, one heck of an album.

I recorded two more albums in pursuit of my rock star dreams. I say that casually but it wasn't just a dream, it was a passion. I was now in the working world, pursuing a business career and music had replaced athletics as my outlet, my passion, my pastime. It is where I went when I wanted that euphoric high I used to get from competition. Recording the albums was just my way of "doing the work." As in my athletic career I wanted to be sure that if my preparation met up with opportunity, that I was ready. Isn't that what getting lucky is all about? Recording those albums was part of "doing the work" to be ready if my big break ever came. It was also a ton of fun.

My second attempt came in 1987 when I recorded ten songs in Toronto, with the help of Bill Pugliese, who was a real champion of mine and lent considerable financial support to this project. Although the album was never officially pressed, I felt these ten songs were some of the best work I ever did.

I actually had financial help with both albums, Bill with the second project and donations from numerous friends for the first. It seemed my friends felt I would conquer the world of music like I conquered athletics. I am so grateful to all of them, and sorry the albums didn't provide a return on their investment. Of course, I also invested a huge amount of my own cash in these projects. The total cost of "Love is Blind" exceeded $50,000 and the Toronto project was in the neighborhood of $40,000. That was a lot to spend but we weren't done yet.

I took one more shot at the album thing and invested another $50,000 to record "Inner Vision." This effort could easily have cost a great deal more if it were not for the fact that it was produced by a dear friend of mine, Arnold Lanni, who owns Arnyard Studios in Toronto. Isn't that a cool name?

Arnie was a star in his own right. He wrote "When I'm With You," which was a No. 1 Billboard hit for a group called Sherriff. He also was the lead singer for a group called Frozen Ghost which had several big hits in Canada.

We often worked sixteen-to-eighteen hours a day on that project. It was absolutely grueling and ran the full gamut of high and low emotions, but to live out this dream was certainly worth every ounce of energy.

To mix the album Arnie brought over Steven Taylor from England. He'd worked with people such as Rod Stewart, Tina Turner and RUSH. He was one of the industry's premier engineers.

The result was an album that I am still very proud of to this day. It was sold in parts of Ontario and became the foundation for my Inner Vision tour in the summer of 1993. That tour was special. Playing in front of hundreds, sometimes thousands of people is something I'll never forget.

Making albums and performing in concerts was a great thrill. Yes, I admit I have always been disappointed that my music career didn't produce more success. When I set my mental compass I was used to arriving at my destination, but this wasn't a failure. Along with all the fun I learned one very important lesson, to enjoy the experience no matter what the outcome!

In the spotlight

For athletes, especially successful ones, this is easy. An athlete gets to take the victory lap, or stand on the podium or lift the trophy. Not so for most musicians. In fact, most do all the heavy lifting without ever actually getting out of the starting gate.

The Inner Vision Tour was effectively my victory lap. Simply put, it is where I lived the lesson.

Let me digress for a second, if I may. On the subject of happiness, since the Inner Vision tour I have made a habit of observing people's happiness. Interestingly, I've found that the happiest people are the ones who are engaged in the moment. Even if they are doing a job they hate, it is better than doing nothing at all. Let yourself enjoy what you're doing today without losing sight of your goals, dreams and desires. Today is part of God's bigger plan for you and is just a stepping stone to your ultimate destination, as long as you keep your compass set.

The Inner Vision tour was a wild element I was able to weave into the serious pursuit of a business career. By then I was working for Edward Jones, travelling the United States extensively. With Jones being so widely represented across the country, I had been everywhere from Sebring, Florida to Norfolk, Virginia to Jennings and Lake Charles, Louisiana, to Anchorage, Alaska to Sonoma, California. Even tiny dots on the map like Hastings, Nebraska and Blackfoot, Idaho. Of course, I also made appearances on behalf of Edward Jones in all the big cities too, but you know those names.

Not to brag, but my wife Patti once read me a list of the 200 biggest cities in America, and I had been to everyone of them with Edward Jones, some numerous times. Turns out I had been to every state in the union, too. If there is an Edward Jones office in your community, I suspect I've probably been there and I'm sure your local financial advisor has heard me speak.

The support of Edward Jones had a lot to do with the success of the tour. I would come to town, connect with the Edward Jones Financial Advisor, do some radio-television-newspaper publicity and my speaking engagements. Some stops found me speaking at the local high school and numerous service club lunches. Other stops would see me speaking to an annual Chamber of Commerce dinner or other high profile audiences. Of course I spoke regularly at Edward Jones client events too. I was speaking approximately 200 times a year as an employee of Edward Jones to all manner of audiences, large and small, young and old, the up and coming and the well established. My role with Edward Jones was to help the company build positive brand recognition while working with individual financial advisors to develop and cultivate a successful corporate culture while heightening their visibility locally. It was tremendously rewarding work and created the connections that brought the Inner Vision tour back to so many of these communities.

As for the show itself, it was like my athletic career on stage. Most nights I'd use a wireless mic so I could run around. Honestly, I've never heard of another blind singer doing that before but I loved it. It wasn't scary for me at all. Remember, I'm the guy who once went fifty-miles-per-hour downhill on snow skis. I wasn't about to anchor myself to a piano or perch myself on a stool. This wasn't a collection of romantic ballads I was

Houston, Texas - mid 1980's

giving. No way, I wanted to give a high energy, rock-n-roll extravaganza.

We worked out a grid pattern on the stage using the equipment cords and a few pieces of tape. That told me where I was. That was the secret. Just because I couldn't see the stage didn't mean I couldn't feel it with my feet. If you want to do something bad enough, you find a way. Of course, just because we had all this strategy in place didn't mean everything always worked perfectly. When you take things to the edge, like I always seem to do, stuff happens.

One night during a show in Boise, Idaho, my guitar player, Sammie, was a victim of my exuberance, in the middle of his guitar solo. I got a little disoriented, maybe dizzy from all the running around, and I thought I was somewhere on the stage where I wasn't. I accidentally ran into Sammie, launching him, wireless guitar and all into the audience. Needless to say, Sammie was not impressed.

Speaking of Sammie, he was a victim numerous times during the tour. The one we all remember most happened after a concert one night, back at the hotel. We were riding the adrenaline rush, like most nights, and looking for distraction. On this particular evening we were staying at a hotel that happened to have horse shoe pits for the guests. We're talking a real horseshoe pit, sand pits, metal pegs and those classic heavy metal horse shoes. We decided to play a few games to wind down. When it was my turn, Sammie would take one of his metal horseshoes and tap the peg so I would know where I was tossing mine. One time, I heard the three taps, waited another second, and unloaded. I may have been too fast, or Sammie may have been slow on the draw, but my horse shoe flew right through his hair, an inch lower and it would have gone through his forehead. Thankfully, Sammie had classic rock musician hair, although I almost turned it into a buzz cut.

Most of the time, I was my own victim. I remember one night, I went bopping up to a speaker, tried to stand on it but being the ball of energy I was, I overshot and wound up doing a swan dive off the stage and into the crowd. People caught me in mid-dive, let me down and I kept on singing, pretending it was all part of the show. I think they believed it. I hope so anyway.

No discussion of the Inner Vision tour can be complete without telling you about my tour manager, Michael Theisen. Mike is a great guy and one of my dearest friends. He quit his job to become the manager of the Inner Vision tour and took care of every detail, every interview, every step, every mile, almost every note. He was great and I have never been able to thank him enough.

Along with all the work, Mike and I had some adventures too. I remember during our stop in Boise, Mike and I were walking down the street, back to our hotel after lunch and Mike said "Hey, there's our bus." Then, a second later, he shouted, "Oh, my God, it's on fire!"

Mike raced off after the bus. Fortunately, it had just come to a stoplight and Mike was able to alert the driver. Using the fire extinguisher from the front of the bus it took only a minute or two to put the flames out, but man, did it stink. Thank God for Mike's quick reaction, all our gear was stowed under the bus in the storage bays. Another minute or two and the Inner Vision tour may have gone up in smoke.

Mike was also responsible for my meeting with one of the giants of the music industry. We weren't the only music tour appearing in Boise as it turned out. Another group you may have heard of, Aerosmith, was in town as well. Mike had scored us some prime seats for the concert and took it upon himself to go for a walk while they were performing. When he didn't find any security, he just walked backstage. As he roamed the halls he eventually ran into a roadie, in the bowels of the building, who was there tuning one of Joe Perry's guitars. Mike gave this guy his best "dog and pony" show and by the time he was done, he had secured an invitation for me to come back stage and meet Steven Tyler. That was the beginning of my friendship with Steven.

Mike also, literally, saved my life one night, and almost lost his own doing it. We were playing an outdoor concert one night when a flash thunderstorm swept in on us. I'm talking a big, brutal, block out the sun, flood the streets cloudburst with thunder, lightning and these incredible high winds. It seemed to come out of nowhere but the second it hit, the band was gone. All musicians know that being on stage in a lightning storm is seriously dangerous, with all that electrical equipment. Problem was, they forgot about me. Michael raced up on stage, and literally pushed me to safety, just as a violent gust of wind pushed over this massively huge speaker tower. I felt the crash, but not as much as Mike. The tower glanced off his shoulder, leaving him battered and bruised but fortunately, still breathing.

Like I said, I owe Michael Theisen a lot. I still talk to Michael almost every day. He remains not only one of my closest friends, but also an intricate part of my career and my life.

Playing outdoors was always a "rush."

I treasured my time on stage. Meeting Huey Lewis and Steven Tyler and Steve Perry and Eddie Money, not to mention working with Elliot and Arnie, were total emotional highs and it's hard to describe the feeling of satisfaction that comes from completing a project like the Inner Vision album. I loved it all, but the ultimate, the pinnacle, the highest of all the highs came quite unexpectedly. It was on a trip back to Toronto, Canada's largest city and one of the largest media markets in North America. I was there to speak at a major corporate event and I was riding in the back of one of the company's courtesy limousines, heading for my hotel. I cranked the tunes on the stereo in the back, as was my nature in those days. I was just trying to relax after a long flight, but that didn't last long. I only wish there was a rewind button on live radio in those days because what I heard stunned me and excited me all in an instant. There was an announcer, on Q-107 no less, the country's premier rock station, introducing a song, by of all people, me! I wanted to call everybody I knew, open the sunroof and crank the music, tell the world that Craig MacFarlane was on the radio, SINGING!

It happened a few more times, travelling around my home province of Ontario. It was always exciting, but not like that first time. Hearing your music played on the radio in a market as massive as Toronto was the highest moment of my music career. It felt like approval, acceptance, recognition and most of all success, however fleeting.

I made many other friends in the music business too. It is a huge business, but it is a small community and I was, and suppose still am, proud to have a tiny place in it. One of my earliest friendships was the one I developed with Bryan Adams. I first met Bryan in 1983 when he was touring as the opening act for Journey. The tour stopped in Hartford, and with Gordie's influence, I not only got tickets but backstage passes.

Bryan and I stayed in touch for several years. I categorized the music of Inner Vision in the Bryan Adams vein. Music, like his, and I hope mine, is a wonderful way to express yourself. When the feeling is true and pure, and the words resonate with many, then it is the best way to express yourself.

Maybe Elton John, a favorite star I was not fortunate enough to meet, may have said it best in his hit Sad Songs:

> If someone else is suffering enough to write it down
> When every single word makes sense
> Then it's easier to have those songs around
> The kick inside is in the line that finally gets to you
> and it feels so good to hurt so bad
> And suffer just enough to sing the blues

20
Communication Is Everything

Looking back I would have to say that the single most important skill I have developed in my life, in terms of my success as an athlete, as a business consultant, as a keynote inspirational speaker, as a friend, as a father and as a husband is the ability to communicate.

In fact, I would go so far as to say that the single most important skill for anybody, in terms of their current and future success, is the ability to communicate. I say that not knowing if you work as a brick layer, a brain surgeon or anything else. I say that not knowing if you are blind, deaf, healthy, handicapped, old, young, tall or short. The statement simply applies. Period.

Let me explain what I mean by the skill of communication. Communication, in my experience, is your ability to be effectively understood. Please do not confuse that with your ability to be heard. That is something you already have, but what you have to ask yourself is whether or not the person hearing you is understanding your message. More importantly, are they receiving your message in terms and in a manner that they can comprehend and utilize effectively, on their own terms, at their own level?

If not, you are wasting your time.

This is what I mean. If you have read any of my stories in this book, then by now you know that I tend to be a focused, bottom-line kind of guy. I like to be around people, I prefer to work with others than to work alone, I like to laugh and joke but when there is a job that needs to be done, I like to get to the point and take care of business. When I am in my preferred environment, dealing with other people like me, with my values and my priorities, this is how I behave and how I communicate.

If you are similar to me in your natural behavior, you will probably think I am a great communicator, you'll get my message right away, understand me and together we will produce the result we want. Isn't that why we are talking in the first place?

The challenge is, as I have learned over the years, that not everybody is like me. Not everybody wants, needs, appreciates, understands, or can respond to a direct, straight from the hip, matter of fact style of communicating. You have to be able to adapt your style. Your message doesn't have to change, but the way you interact has to change if you want to be successful in dealing with other people.

You have probably heard the saying, "people don't care how much you know until they know how much you care." There is no better way to show someone how much you care than to connect with them on their terms.

Of course, you can't adapt how you connect to others unless you have a very good understanding of yourself first. Have you ever taken the time to really think about how you do things, how you communicate ideas, instructions and requests? What do you value in communication from others? How do you like to be treated? When you're treated this way are you more likely to respond favorably? Will you better understand what is expected of you or what is being told to you if it is told in a manner that you respect?

Don't you think the same is true of everybody else? Absolutely, it is. So please a make it a mission to develop a deep and sincere understanding of who you are. It will make you better in everything, particularly how you communicate.

Once you realize this, and start to understand your tendencies, you also start to become aware of the differences, and similarities, between you and everyone around you. You will start to notice that people speak at different paces, in different tones, that their focus and priorities within your message are different, that their pace and tone will change depending on how you engage them and what you are talking about. One person will focus on the people in your message, the next will want all the minor details, the next just major facts. This is where the skill of communication starts.

When you learn to recognize the differences and then adapt how (notice I didn't say what) yes, how you are connecting with others, you will notice that you become infinitely more effective.

Why is this? It is because everybody, including you and me, do things for their own reasons, not yours or mine. When you can communicate your ideas, thoughts, instructions, requests or demands so that the person you are dealing with can find their own reason to act on, appreciate or even care about what you are saying, the probability that both of you get a satisfactory result from your communication increases exponentially.

Become a great communicator. It is the key to a great life.

Remember, the professional "R" is about relationships. The single greatest key to successful relationships will be effective communication and the single greatest contributor to the failure of any relationship will be the breakdown of its communication.

Keep Your Eye on the Ball

By the time I was 23 most of my friends were playing golf. Never one to shy away from a new adventure, I decided to try my hand at the game as well.

I was living in The Woodlands, Texas, just outside of Houston.

Having never tried the game before, and obviously never having seen it, I knew, just like with skiing, I had to find myself a mentor. I reached out to The Woodlands Inn and Country Club and was connected with Mel Calendar, the club pro. We met at the club for what turned out to be a memorable first day on the links for me.

I hooked up with Mel at the driving range where he explained to me the do's and don'ts of hitting a golf ball. He painted those word pictures I needed to prepare myself for my first swing. He talked about how to hold the club properly, how to bend my knees just so, how to position my back and my head. After downhill and water skiing, visualizing a sport where I stayed in one place seemed easy enough and after about ten minutes, I

Keep your eye on the ball!

suggested that Mel do a practice swing, in slow motion, and I would feel how he was positioned. Remember the pattern, this would help me translate the visual images into physical motion. I have to give

Mel high marks for bravery, or maybe it was confidence. I realized just after we started this exercise that anyone looking out of the clubhouse at that moment would have to be raising an eyebrow, at least. It must have looked like I was "checking Mel out." Needless to say, I made it a quick study.

Then it was my turn. I took my stance as Mel had described it, with some "verbal" advice from him. Then, when I was comfortably balanced, Mel would physically put my club head in place behind the ball. The rest was up to me. My first two swings connected with nothing but air. The third rip connected with the ball, but somehow my shot went behind me. Mel laughed out loud saying, "I have never seen someone do that before. That was impressive."

The competitive juices were flowing now, not to mention an overwhelming sense of frustration. Remember how I told you that blind people don't like to look foolish? Guess how I felt at that moment? Well, my next swing just made that worse. I tried to crush the ball and that had me almost falling down. In fact, the divot went further than the ball. Mel stepped in. In a calm voice, not laughing anymore, he suggested it was time to relax. This was supposed to be fun. Don't try to kill the ball, let the club head do the work. I stepped back, got my mental vision back in order and, BINGO!. The next swing launched the ball 180 yards, straight down the middle. After a quick "high five" from Mel, I wanted more. A lot more.

I realized quickly, that if my golf game was going to achieve any level of respectability, I was going to have to rely heavily on muscle memory. The best way to do that was to hit a lot of golf balls, imprint the successful swings on my brain and, by extension, my muscles. In practice I would have Mel there to tell me the results of each shot. When I hit a good shot, I would step back and mentally recreate the shot in my mind, connecting the feeling of the swing with the weight shift and result, planting the process in my subconscious where it would hopefully recreate itself when I addressed the ball. I became addicted to the feeling. Like so many other golfers, most in fact, I discovered there is almost nothing that feels better, in the moment, than hitting an awesome golf shot.

Over the years I never became a really good golfer. Years ago when I was playing regularly, I did manage to shoot into the high 90s on a semi-regular basis and I was ecstatic with that. I never won any championships. That was never really my intent. I wasn't looking to earn my tour card on the PGA. I just wanted to have some fun, and I was successful at that.

It's a lot easier from the fairway.

My best game, by the way, was a 91, which I believe I achieved for two reasons. First, I became an effective putter. So much so that I was able to make up for a multitude of misadventures on the fairway. My real strength was long putts. I used to set up my putts by walking from the hole to the ball, getting a proper feel for the distance while feeling the break of the ground under my feet. Once I had the feel for the green firmly pictured in my mind, the second reason came into play. I would need my friend to line me up. After that, it was pure muscle memory. It worked with amazing consistency, often to the surprise of my golfing buddies.

Putting can salvage a multitude of errors.

The key here would ultimately come down to my partner. I was very dependent on whomever I was playing with. So, the more honestly they played the round, or the more skilled they

Thanks to one of my great partners, Mike Gillespie, this one dropped.

were in lining up a shot, the better I played. Of course, sometimes I appreciated a little lack of honesty.

I understand that golf can be a visually intimidating game. When you have one hundred yards of water to carry, or a valley full of trees in front of you, or a sand trap to clear in front of the green, it can be hard to get those images out of your mind. I just asked my partners not to tell me. No image, no problem.

As word of my golfing exploits spread, I began to receive invitations to participate in numerous celebrity golf tournaments on behalf of many charities. Most of these tournaments were four man scrambles so there was no pressure, as long as you had one good golfer in your group. You still wanted to make your best shot, but if you missed, you could laugh about it. It was unique for me to play without competing but I was maturing by now and enjoyed the fun, the light heartedness and of course, the camaraderie.

The most memorable of these charity events for me was my invitation to Pebble Beach in California, and not just because I was playing a world-class, undeniably beautiful golf course. Yes, the beauty and majesty of Pebble Beach was not lost, even on me. The sound of the ocean, off to your side, as you stroll along the fairway was magnificent. There are also the smells of the ocean air, mixed with the fragrance of the trees and flowers that gives it a special feel. There is the feel itself too. The fairways felt to me like I was walking on the carpet in my living room. You know, and can't help envisioning, an incredible picture of how wonderful the sight of this place must be.

There were other reasons, too. The ocean was intimidating. I'm still surprised I didn't drive my ball directly into it, like that irresistible force you hear about. There was another intimidating force, as well. My partner that day was Mickey Mantle. Of course, I'd met Mickey before, when we shared the stage together in St. Thomas and it was great to reconnect. Mickey, like so many of the other sports icons I've met, is really too nice a guy to be intimidating, especially after his first tee shot went 30 yards out of bounds. There was never a dull moment with Mickey around. He really was a character and just one of the guys.

The most memorable thing about that tournament had nothing to do with location or scenery or celebrity. It had to do with one particular hole, a par three. Par three's carry their own type of intimidation. You only, If you realistically hope to make par, have one shot to get on the green. Most of the time I am thankful if I land even remotely close to the green in regulation, and then scramble to make it back. Not so this time. They were running a "Hole in One" contest to win a car. This meant everyone's drive would be scrutinized. I took my turn and, almost unbelievably, hit a shot that ended up seven inches directly to the right of the hole. I found out at the banquet that evening, that nobody won the car, and my ball was the closest to the pin on that day. I was called up to the podium to receive the "closest to the pin" award and was asked, of course, how it felt. I replied, "Where the heck is the guy who lined me up?" The whole place exploded with laughter.

Charity events have been a wonderful way to play golf as a pastime. There are enough events every year to satisfy my desire to play the game. I meet so many executives and celebrities along the way that my career reaps benefits off the course as well. Don't they call that a Win-Win?

Being blind actually has its blessings when it comes to the game of golf. For example, I have a lot more opportunity to fit a round of golf into my schedule than most of my friends. When one of them invites me, or as often happens, challenges me to a game, I am always willing. My reply is usually, "I'd love to play against you. Let's tee off at midnight."

I also enjoy the benefit of not having to watch my shots after I hit them. More times than not that's a blessing, like during a recent match I played with my

Just another day on the beach.

son Dalton. I had just finished teeing off and Dalton said, "nice shot, Dad. You're on the green, close to the hole actually." Then he added, "too bad it's on the twelfth hole." We were playing the fourth at the time.

These days, hitting golf balls is something that happens for me at the driving range. It is purely for fun now and I find it a great way to relieve stress and tension. I didn't do great things as a golfer but I am satisfied to have brought a new meaning to the time-honored phrase, "Keep your eye on the ball."

The Big Stage

There comes a point in everyone's career where you have to find out if you can play in the big leagues. At the very least, the opportunity to test the upward levels of your ability will present itself, if you're looking for it, and you have to be ready to perform.

I don't know if it's fair to say I was performing in the minor leagues, but my work with The Hartford Whalers, performing at Cypress Gardens and my public appearances on behalf of Eagle USA Wetsuits had given me ample opportunity to hone my speaking skills. All this served to greatly develop my confidence level in front of large audiences as well. It had also attracted the attention of the people running the 1984 re-election campaign of Ronald Reagan and George Bush. They asked me to be part of the Reagan-Bush All-Star team, which was a group of athletes who traveled around the country speaking on behalf of the Republican ticket.

At first I thought I was being set up by one of my crazy buddies with the old fake White House call gag.

"Yeah, right!" I said when I answered the phone.

Lucky for me, the White House is used to this type of response. They convinced me I was actually talking to the Reagan-Bush people, which left me both excited and humbled at the same time. I'd never actually tried to define myself in terms of American politics at that time. I'd been in the country for less than three years, but when I stopped to think about it, I realized that most of my views were fairly conservative in many ways. I believe strongly in independence and self-reliance - typified by my refusal of my blind pension at age eighteen - and I thought the Republican philosophy was strongly along those lines.

I joined the Reagan-Bush All-Star team confident that my integrity and my message would not be compromised.

The next thing I knew, one month before I had even turned twenty-two, I was climbing the steps to the Philadelphia Art Museum - the ones Sylvester Stallone made famous in "Rocky" - with former heavyweight champs Joe Frazier and Floyd Patterson on either side of me as we kicked off the Reagan-Bush All Star tour. In the coming months I would make 231 appearances in thirty-nine states on behalf of Reagan-Bush. I travelled with New York Yankee storybook characters such as Whitey Ford, Mickey Mantle and Roger Maris. I roomed with Roger often on the road and discovered what an outstanding man he was although so often misunderstood because of his natural shyness. I am a baseball fanatic so getting to know the guy who held the single season home-run record at the time was a thrill.

With each stop on the tour, I began to develop a deeper understanding and appreciation for the people and spirit that makes America great. My work with the All Star team gave me the kind of visibility that led to my being asked - by President Reagan's office itself no less - to help do a leg of the Olympic Torch run through the streets of Washington, D.C.. This was near the beginning of the torch's journey across America to arrive in Los Angles for the Summer Games that July.

Guess who I got to accompany me on the torch run? Gordie Howe. As we cruised along the Jefferson Memorial Concourse, I'd hear people along our route going, "Who's that running with Gordie Howe?"

My White House connection brought another bolt of lightning out of the blue that year, and it came at a time when I needed it most. I had trained on one good leg and one weak leg for the Blind International Water Skiing Championships near Oslo, Norway. My performance in Norway was, to me especially, disappointing. I finished fourth. This would normally have me feeling frustrated and determined to avenge my failure to win but before I could really absorb the reality of not winning, I got a phone call.

It was from across the Atlantic. The White House was calling me again. This time I believed them. I think I was getting the hang of it. What I was not quite getting the hang of yet was being presented with almost inconceivable opportunities, at least to this simple kid from backwoods Canada.

The White House asked if I would speak at the Republican National Convention, as part of the evening agenda, in Prime Time. I was almost going to have to do it in a wetsuit because there was barely going to be time to dry off and change clothes. I'd have to be in Dallas in two days for the speech.

I never got higher on any of my ski jumps. I was ecstatic as I flew back to America. I was going to be on national television speaking on behalf of the President and Vice-President of the United States.

Several planes later, I was in the back seat of a limousine, rushing to Dallas Reunion Arena. Two blocks from the arena, the limo overheated and with steam billowing out from under the hood, we jumped out and hurried the last two blocks to the arena on foot. Looking pretty rumpled I was hustled in to the arena, where I was immediately escorted backstage. What a production. It was like being on the flight deck of the Enterprise with a literal sea of humanity attending to every conceivable detail.

I had to go through all the stages of preparation, just like everybody else, including hair and makeup. I remember the stylist asking, "How does that look?" when she finished my hair. I answered, "not bad, but I think hair twenty two on the left is a little out of place." Even Bob and Elizabeth Dole, who were sitting near me, laughed out loud.

This was prime-time, center stage. I wasn't the keynote speaker, not by a long shot, but this was an evening on national television and I was only four speeches removed from the main-event. My speech was prepared for me although I knew I'd be pretty familiar with the material. It was essentially the same message I'd been saying on the All-Star tour.

All this was intense, as I'm sure you can imagine, but try to imagine this! I'm standing there, fifteen minutes before Showtime and how do you think they have my speech prepared for me? In the worst possible way. It was on the teleprompter!

I laughed out loud and so did everyone else. Maybe they were hoping I'd regain my sight on prime-time television. That would have made the headlines!

Fortunately, I had a slate and stylus in my bag. I roughed out a few notes on some Braille paper. It was truly an ironic moment.

On the biggest stage of them all.

I was giving a speech about the administration's concern for the needs of the handicapped. Meanwhile, the blind guy's speech is on a teleprompter.

The laugh helped relax me. Next thing I knew, I was delivering my old familiar words to a jam-packed Dallas Reunion Arena crowd of 18,000 plus and to millions on television and radio. The reverberation of my voice and the sheer magnitude of this venue was awe-inspiring. I had officially arrived on the Big Stage.

The highlight of the evening for me came after the speech. After I finished my comments to a wonderful ovation (of course, everybody gets one on that stage,) I was warmly greeted, and congratulated, backstage by none other than the Gipper himself, President Ronald Reagan. With his arm around my shoulder, he and Vice President Bush both shook my hand and, with big smiles in their voices, thanked me for being part of the evening. That was a rush!

I ultimately, by the age of 30, had spoken at three Republican National Conventions, returning again in 1988 at the Superdome in New Orleans and in 1992 at the Astrodome in Houston. I don't know that the event could ever get any bigger but the venues actually did. These speeches remain a significant highlight in my speaking career.

On that evening in Dallas, my fate as a public speaker was sealed, at the tender age of twenty-two. This was a sub-four-minute mile, a bottom of the ninth game-winning home run. It had all come to me without asking. I had worked hard to be a good athlete and a good speaker and good things had come as a result.

I continue to enjoy a blessed career as a keynote speaker.

23

I like Myself Because...

I want you to get your watch, or something you can use to measure time. Now, go stand in front of a mirror, seriously, do it.

I have an assignment for you. I want you to talk for two minutes. I want you to talk while looking at yourself in that mirror and I want your body language to be positive and supportive while you talk. Your subject matter for the next two minutes is...I like myself because.

Ready, Go ahead.

Don't just talk for one minute, or thirty seconds. You need to tell that person in the mirror what you like about yourself for a full two minutes.

And remember, keep your body positive. Even I can hear somebody slouch and it disappoints me so it must be even more disappointing when you can see it.

Did you do it? Did you talk for the full two minutes? Was it difficult?

If you are honest with yourself, you are probably saying yes right now. I know, I found it very difficult, too, the first time. In fact, having seen (well heard) this exercise conducted in hundreds of workshops, classrooms and consulting sessions with executives, managers, sales reps and even students, I have yet to meet anybody who found it easy.

Why is that? There should not be a subject you are more familiar with than yourself. You've known yourself for quite a while now.

Why then do so many people, even those we consider the most successful, have such a challenge with this simple question?

It's because most of us have never taken the time to truly understand who we are and what makes us tick. Even worse, most of us seem to have very little understanding of our positive qualities or how those can affect our world. That is sad because success, true success, and happiness, in all aspects of your world really starts with this basic knowledge.

Let me give you just one example. Let's do the exercise again only this time I want you to envision yourself in my office, in a job interview. If you have made it that far then you know I've read your resume. I have checked out your references, am aware of your education, experience and qualifications. If you are in that meeting, we know you can do the job. Knowing that, when I ask you the question, "Why should I hire you to work for my company?" How are you going to answer me? What do you think I, or any other potential employer, wants to hear at that point?

You have two minutes. Pretend I just asked you the question and try to answer me. Go ahead and try, out loud.

Was it any easier the second time? Surprisingly, for most, it is still difficult.

Why does it matter? Let me tell you, in this case for starters.

If you have reached that stage where I am seriously considering hiring you to work in my company, my ultimate concern is going to be over how you affect the team that already works for me. Ultimately, it is the chemistry of that team and the culture of our office that determines our success. I need to know that you are going to have a positive impact on my team, or on the team you will be managing for me.

More importantly, I need to know that you understand how you will be a positive impact. So what do you think I wanted to hear? Still don't know? Then think about it this way.

Here's another real world example;

I want you to take a second and think about the best boss you ever worked for. More specifically, think about what it was that made this person the BEST.

What characteristics did they demonstrate, how did they act, what was it that you remember about them that brings them to mind right now? Go ahead and take a second or two and make a list.

I was first confronted with this question while sitting in a workshop with a group of twenty or more business people and managers. By the time we were done, not only had we each made our own list, but our trainer had assembled a class list of more than forty-five characteristics. I have seen this exercise performed countless times since, in classes comprised of all manner of participants, from senior executives to entry level factory workers. Interestingly, the list always turned out to be essentially the same. In fact, I have even seen classes of high school seniors do this exercise, just changing the focus from best boss to best teacher. Guess what. The list never changed.

If you actually took the time to do your own list, it would almost certainly includes some of these terms:

Patient	Thoughtful
Understanding	Creative
Disciplined	Direct, to
Honest	the point
Sincere	Compassionate
Caring	Open minded
Funny	Fair
Tough	Has my back
Organized	...

See, I told you, the list never changes and neither does the lesson it teaches. To understand that lesson, I want you to ask yourself one question. For every item on the list, ask yourself, is that item a skill or an attitude?

If you were honest with yourself, you have to admit that every item on this list, and I'm sure any items you may have that aren't listed above, is an attitude. Even if you want to suggest that something as abstract as Organized is a skill, I would counter that by arguing that it is, at best, a soft skill based on attitude. After all, if you don't want to be organized, you won't be, no matter how much organizational training you may have. But, when you consider the issue of skills that is a moot point at best. Consider this:

If this is the best boss you have ever worked for, then it is reasonable for me to believe that they have achieved some success. They have gained the necessary education, developed the ability and demonstrated that they can perform a specific task or deliver a specific result well enough to have earned the right to a more responsible position and the benefits that go with it. If that is the case, answer me this, why is it that nobody ever identifies a single, hard, specific skill that this person must have mastered in order to have reached their current level of success?

Why doesn't anybody ever say:

- He writes fabulous code

or

- He writes fabulous letters with great sentence structure

or

- He is an excellent mathematician

or

- He is a master machinist

or

- She could conjugate a verb like nobody's business

or

- She is a brilliant analyst

Why? Because if they hadn't connected with you effectively, on your terms, they never would have been able to teach you what they knew or lead you to produce what they required of you. That connection was manifested through their attitude, particularly the attitude that touched you the right way. Even more interesting, look at the range of attitudes. Some people liked a manager who was funny, others appreciated patience while still others needed discipline, or directness. People are different and the best managers invariably can connect with different people in different ways. Bottom line, the best bosses inspire you, for your reasons, they don't manipulate you for theirs!

The simple truth is that your best boss demonstrated what I consider to be the evolution of the Golden Rule, what I have often called "The Platinum Rule." The Platinum Rule states:

"Treat others as they like to be treated, not as you like to be treated"

And, by the way, if you want to know the best answer to my earlier question, why would I want you to work for my company, look back at your answers about your "Best Boss." That's the description of you I want to hear. Would others use the same characteristics to describe you? And how do those characteristics make you someone positive to have around?

You need to know the answer, for your own sake!

Which of those attitudes that made that person so effective as your boss are part of what make you good? How will you use those characteristics to maximize your skills and knowledge in a positive way, in cooperation with the rest of us, to produce superior results and sustain the positive culture of our company? Don't you think that you will be happier working under those conditions? Won't you be more likely to look forward to coming to work?

That is what will get you the job. Conversely, truth be known of me, and of most executives and managers, if I don't sense that you will be a positive impact, if I sense that you might be a little bit of a jerk, then I am going to turn over your resume and interview the next candidate, regardless of your "qualifications." Ultimately, if I don't find the right combination of attitude and qualifications, I will hire the right attitude and arrange training for the skills.

In fact, from what I have observed in twenty plus years of success coaching and corporate culture development, your skill, your knowledge, your absolute mastery of the technical actions and proprietary information of your business will get you all the way to level three on a scale of one to ten, in terms of your potential success. Beyond that it will be your ability to manifest that knowledge, skill and technique through others that determines the ultimate altitude you achieve. That will be the result of your attitudes and relationships.

Don't get me wrong. I'm not saying you don't need all the knowledge, skill, technique and information your business demands. If anything, if you want to maximize your potential, your knowledge, skill and technique need to be second to none. All I am saying is that the maximum rewards from all your training and experience will be delivered through the application of your attitudes and connections with the people you work with and for.

Do the work and get the knowledge. It is imperative, just not enough.

This is why understanding yourself is paramount to your success and happiness. Reality is that it applies throughout your life. Ask yourself what kind of impact you have on your friendships and your family. Are you an inspiration to them? Do you make them better by their association with you? How much better, how much happier, would your relationships, your home life, and you be, if you did?

Only you can do it!

24

I Didn't See it Coming

I've never talked about it and really don't know how to explain it. Talking is supposed to be his job so being asked to write a page, if I can make it that long, for this book, is a challenge for me.

I had a quiet, stable, comfortable job in September, 1994. I liked it that way. So when I was told that I was going to have some added responsibility for a couple of days, I was expecting more of an intrusion than anything else.

Wow, was I surprised, and pleasantly!

Meant for each other

Several Edward Jones offices in the region were hosting a Client Night, which was a big deal, and they were bringing in a keynote speaker from the company, Craig MacFarlane, to speak at the client dinner as well as several other functions. I would have the pleasure of chauffeuring and otherwise touring Craig around town.

I was aware of Craig, everyone in the company was, but I was still a little apprehensive. I'd never met a blind person in my life. Escorting a blind man from speech to speech, having him hang out in my office and still having to do my regular job. I always welcomed a new experience but this was different. I really didn't know what to anticipate.

Then Craig shows up. I met him the first time after his speech at the Client Night dinner. He was sitting beside me and just started talking to me. He was sweet, funny, curious and in all ways, absolutely adorable. I found myself, even on that first night, forgetting at moments that he was blind. He was just so genuine.

When he was in the office he was perceptive, animated and active, anything but boring. He talked to the clients, answered the phones, tried to make coffee, was just so completely not what I expected. Craig was not a burden or an intrusion at all. He would give impromptu concerts, or at least sing a few lines, and he seemed to know a thousand jokes, all of them appropriate to the situation. This was all overwhelming in a good way, but the most impressive thing about Craig was how he would look me directly in the eye when he spoke to me. My first indelible memory of Craig were those absolutely incredible blue eyes.

As it turned out, the three days Craig spent in Kalamazoo left an impression that I simply couldn't get out of my mind. His effervescent, almost laugh a minute, high energy, in charge style appealed to me. I remember actually feeling sad that he had to leave so soon.

I couldn't stop thinking about him after he left, but of course I didn't have to rely on my memory of him for long. In his usual style, Craig reached out to me. It was exciting to learn that he couldn't stop thinking about me either and soon we were in constant communication.

Craig captured my imagination. I started looking forward to his calls, then to his visits and not long after, my trips to Canada to spend more time with him. Those

Hawaii never felt so good!

trips were never long enough, so I changed my life and moved to Craig's home town. The rest, as they say, is history.

Our life together has been, and continues to be, wonderful, but Craig truly is the communicator in our relationship so I will leave all the descriptions to him.

I really just want to leave you with this one simple thought. That brilliant, captivating first impression Craig made on me in Kalamazoo so many years ago has never dimmed. He remains the light of my life, my white knight, my utterly dependable pillar of strength, an amazing father to our children, a responsible and loving husband and my best friend.

I will always be so grateful he came into my life.

PATTI MACFARLANE
2013

25
Life After Athletics

In early 1991, I started an incredible eighteen-year journey as an employee with the Edward Jones Company. I was invited to a lunch at the Four Seasons Hotel in Chicago. I was meeting with Jim Weddle, John Bachmann and John Beuerlein. These gentleman comprised the brain trust who so successfully kept Edward Jones at the forefront of the financial services industry. I was impressed that these three men, each highly successful in their own right, would come together to buy me lunch. In hindsight it turned out to be the single most positively impactful meeting of my life. I think it turned out pretty good for the company, too.

Jim, John and John were an effective team with incredible insight. They created a unique, leading edge position for me and offered me full-time employment. I quickly realized that Edward Jones was one of the great companies in America to work for. I was honored to accept their offer. What an opportunity!

That led to the morning of September, 12, 1994. Just another typical Monday, or so I thought.

Monday always started early for me. It was two a.m. when the alarm sounded in my room in Desbarats. As usual, I was heading out for another week on the road, fulfilling my duties as an International Goodwill Ambassador with the Edward Jones Company. In simple terms, that meant another week of constant motion, moving from speaking engagement to speaking engagement, from town to town, city to city, with numerous luncheons and dinners and media appearances as I worked with Edward Jones Financial Advisors across the United States and Canada and the United Kingdom.

That constant motion began by sharing an hour-long drive with Dad. This was our routine, but to make this memorable day just a little more special, September 12th is Dad's birthday. Dad was, as usual, driving me to the airport in Sault Ste. Marie. I'd be in the air with wheels up by five a.m., heading to my connection in Toronto. Today my connection would be taking me to St. Louis where I was scheduled to speak at twelve noon, sharp! It was a large event which, meant lots of hands to be shaken and pleasantries after I finished. This is something I always enjoy but which, on days like today, made me anxious sometimes too.

There was a limousine waiting for me downstairs. I was speaking again later that day, but not in St. Louis. I had to get back to the St. Louis airport and catch another flight. I was on my way to Kalamazoo, Michigan to speak at an Edward Jones Client night. As always, timing was tight, but I caught my flight, made the short hop over to Chicago, and after another quick plane change, my fourth flight of the day landed in Kalamazoo right on time. This was the kind of day I lived for. In constant motion, with

My dad and I enjoying the moment in his element.

Feeding wild deer with my dad is always a hands on experience.

the expectation, at every stop, to deliver at the highest level. After all, nobody brings you to town to be mediocre.

The room was full to overflowing that evening. My hosts had done a remarkable job assembling a packed house and it proved to be a fun night. The Q and A segment was particularly humorous, informative, entertaining and by the time I was finished I was feeling very satisfied with my day, and just a little tired too. It was finally time to relax and I did so while sharing a late bite to eat with my Edward Jones hosts. It turned out to be one of those great moments that "they" talk about. You know, the ones that happen when you're making other plans, when you least expect them, as "they" say.

During the meal I struck up a conversation with a lovely lady who was a Branch Office Administrator for an Edward Jones office near Kalamazoo. She was awesome, and so easy to talk to. As it turned out, she also was assigned to be my companion for the next two days as she accompanied me, driving me to all of my speaking engagements.

I am certain God was looking favorably on me that week. At that time in my career I almost never woke up in the same city two days in a row, but for reasons far beyond my control, I was actually scheduled to be in Kalamazoo for another two days. I couldn't remember when I had enjoyed a stopover so much. Patti and I laughed and kibitzed and conversed as if we had known each other forever, but all good things do, eventually come to an end.

This period of joy ended when Patti drove me to the airport on Wednesday afternoon. I had to speak Thursday morning in Los Angeles so there was no alternative, no excuse I could use to delay my departure. Patti and I gave each other a long, tight, goodbye hug. Her perfume was heaven to my nose and music to my soul. Those were things I could take with me that I wouldn't forget. I wanted to hold onto this moment forever. I entered the terminal, escorted by a Skycap who had been patiently waiting for Patti and I to release from our embrace. I'm sure he'd seen it a thousand times but for me that moment was one in a million.

I don't remember anything about that flight, not because all the flights start to blend together after awhile, but because all I could think about was her. Call it fate, call it destiny, call it magic, I don't know what happened between us, but I do know that Patti became the single most important person in my life. She filled the void in my heart and made me whole. She became my best friend, my soul mate, my wife, and the mother of our fabulous kids, Dalton, Derek, Ashley and Morgan. She is the love of my life and the single greatest reason I continue to strive as hard as I do.

When all those factors are present you have a dynamic situation and I have to tell you that life with Patti and the kids is nothing short of dynamic. In fact, dynamic best describes our lives together, right from the day we met.

Mendon, Michigan, is known for its high school state football championships and its vigorous farming community. It isn't exactly a thriving metropolis, but with a population of 870, it is more than twice the size of my home town. That's where Patti hails from, a quiet little community very much the same as I grew up in. I have often wondered if that is why we connected so easily and have such a relaxed and comfortable life together. Regardless, when we realized the strength of this unique bond between us Patti left Edward Jones and moved to Desbarats so that we could spend more time together. She fit right in, to both my life and the community.

The next few years were like a fairy tale.

We travelled together extensively from Honolulu, Hawaii to Austin, Texas to Denver, Colorado to Halifax, Nova Scotia to Orlando, Florida to Vancouver, British Columbia. And it didn't stop there, we were even in Germany, Austria, Killarney, Ireland and back, in a triumphant return, to Amsterdam. Even since the birth of our children, travel has remained a cornerstone of our lifestyle, not to mention a constant in mine.

Patti and I have enjoyed numerous international trips. There have definitely been too many highlights to mention although a few really stand out in our minds.

We loved our visit to Killarney, Ireland (what a gem of a town). The Ring of Kerry Tour was especially memorable even for a blind person. Patti described, in detail, the vibrant shades of green and how the countryside resembled nature's version of a magnificent patchwork quilt. The roads were narrow and full of twists and turns that weaved through the hills, connecting a wonderful network of little villages nestled between the hills and the sea. Utterly breathtaking!

In Amsterdam, the Van Gogh Museum was a pleasure to visit. Patti made the paintings seem so real with her vivid descriptions. The Anne Frank House, on the other hand, was simply surreal. As we climbed the stairs hidden behind the bookcase, it was hard to imagine how a family stayed hidden away from the Nazis for so long in such a small space. As you looked out of the window from their upstairs hideout, you were looking at the same tree that Anne referenced so many times in her diary. Her story is not only one of courage, but of an incredible will to survive.

Another great memory for Patti and I was taking the Sound of Music Tour from Salzburg, Austria. We visited numerous picturesque places where various scenes from the movie were filmed. We especially enjoyed Mirabell Palace where the song "Do-Re-Mi" was filmed. What an extensive variety of flowers! In Mondsee, we enjoyed eating lunch at an outdoor cafe amid a wide array of quaint shops. The highlight in this small town was visiting the famous church where the wedding of Maria and Baron Von Trapp was filmed. A trip to Salzburg wouldn't be complete without visiting the houses where Mozart was born and where he lived as an adult. What a fascinating glimpse into the life of such an iconic figure.

It goes without saying that, with our fondness of Disney, it was a great thrill to visit the Neuschwanstein Castle. This was the castle that Walt Disney World's Cinderella castle was modeled after. The castle is nestled on a rugged hill above the village of Hohenschwangau near Füssen in southwest Bavaria, Germany. We know firsthand it was quite a long and tedious hike up into the Alps to reach it. The cuckoo clock that hangs on our wall today is a friendly reminder of our awesome vacation to Germany.

When we were home in Desbarats we would stroll along the gravel roads on the outskirts of town where my parents lived. Fresh air would fill our lungs as we enjoyed the private time together. We would catch up on whatever happened while I had been away on my last business trip and Patti would paint word pictures of the scenery around us and we'd talk about our plans for the future. Sometimes we would be treated to aroma from a wood burning stove or the sight of (sound for me) a Mennonite family passing by in their horse-drawn carriage with the steel wheels clattering on the gravel. Patti was always amazed at how I would know they were coming before she did and I would be equally amazed at her descriptions, in detail, of the sights we passed.

We found lots of wonderful ways to spend time together, despite Desbarats being such a quaint place. Our mutual upbringings did make that easy as we appreciated so many of the same things. One of the best was to go swimming, either in one of the many spring fed

Dalton and Dad in the moment.

inland lakes in the area or sometimes in Lake Huron, which was also nearby. Even Northern Ontario can get hot and sticky in the middle of July but those spring-fed lakes never warmed up too much. It was refreshing, to say the least, invigorating would be more accurate many days, but always wonderful. Even today, we still enjoy Desbarats Lake on our visits back Canada. We always find time for a day or two of boating with my cousins Bonita and Robby Martin, and their kids Kyle, Colton and Hilary. Sometimes I even get my water skis on. Let

Cody Grant, Kyle Martin, Gavin Grant, me & Dalton on Diamond Lake.

the good times roll. Speaking of good times, I find it especially fun to get over to Diamond Lake and do a little "barefooting" with my good friend Gavin Grant. You can check this one out because Gavin's son, Cody, is a videographer and has posted some videos of my water skiing on my YouTube channel. I wish I could watch them. I hope you enjoy them.

04/07/2009

Craig, Mom, Dad and Ian, still going strong, April 2009

When we had a little more time in those early days, we often escaped Desbarats to Mackinac Island for weekend getaways. Located in Lake Huron, in the straits between Canada and Michigan, Mackinac Island is a major tourist attraction and favorite destination of Canadians and Americans from all over the continent. In fact, even the official summer residence of the Governor of Michigan is located on the Island. Patti and I used to love renting a tandem bicycle and touring the island, her steering and me providing propulsion from the rear. On one of our trips this led to Patti becoming the target of my irresistible persona as a prankster. We were enjoying yet another ride when Patti made the comment over her shoulder that she thought something might be wrong with our bike. She was, all of a sudden, finding it much more difficult to peddle. I responded that everything seemed fine to me, at which point she turned to look and found me sitting with my feet up on the handle bars, reading the tour guide. She laughed out loud, stopped peddling and gave me a playful slap. Another victim in the books.

We had our favorite things to do in Patti's hometown, too. We used to love canoeing down the St. Joseph River past the Langley Covered Bridge. It's a historically significant site as Langley is the longest remaining covered bridge in Michigan. It's a good thing we learned that I need to sit in the front of the boat or we might never have seen it at all. For some reason, when I sat in the back of the boat we just seemed to go in circles.

Of course, steering was never my strong suit and, fortunately, everybody knew it. That was probably in all our best interests, especially when visiting Patti's parents, Diane and Don Everson. When we weren't canoeing, we used to love to pile into my in-laws' 1918 Model A and 1929 Dodge. I may not have been allowed to drive, but I had great fun honking the horn as we toured the town. I love the sound of those old horns.

The Model A and the Dodge weren't the only antiques in Diane and Don's world. Don owns a very cool antique store called Serendipity in scenic downtown Mendon, backing onto the St Joseph River. Talk about sensory overload. When you learn by touch, this trip down memory lane into the worlds of our grand-parents and beyond, gave me a fascinating insight into our past that I could never have understood or appreciated through traditional means. For me, an antique store full of old and sometimes discarded items was an all new world of discovery. Speaking of appreciating the past, my father in-law, a fellow baseball fanatic, and I have often sat in his store listening to the Detroit Tigers on his assortment of antique tube radios. It is a different sound and sensation that painted special pictures and conjured my memories of growing up listening to Ernie Harwell, an experience not to be missed.

Now, don't get me wrong. We may have been the products of small-town upbringing, but we both loved getting to the city as well. For us, that meant Toronto, and in truth, they don't come much bigger. Toronto offered a tremendous array of entertainment options and we enjoyed most of them at one time or another, not to mention one of the most varied and extensive restaurant com-munities in the world.

Still, one of our most favorite things to do was to attend a Toronto Blue Jays game. As a retired athlete you know it had to be high on my list, but for me it was often about more than just the game. I had become quite good friends with Blue Jay's All-Star first baseman Carlos Delgado and on several occasions he would take us behind the scenes before a game.

Sitting in the dugout during batting practice was particularly special. It rekindled memories of the locker room before wrestling matches, which I will always cherish, but it was also just plain entertaining. The sound of the bat hitting the ball when you are up close like that is impressive and the sometimes choice words that came from players afterwards were hilarious, at least for a former athlete.

Roger Clemens   Carlos Delgado

Joe Carter   Cito Gaston

Of course, there is also the vastness of the SkyDome, which I could never really appreciate until Patti and Carlos took me on a tour. They walked me around the bases, allowed me to roam and feel how big the sliding area around each base was, they took me up on the pitcher's mound, which surprised me because I never knew how elevated it was, and they walked me to the outfield fence and around the warning track. The outfield seemed to go on forever. It really made me appreciate not only the strength it must take to hit a home run, but also the speed and skill an outfielder must possess to patrol such a vast area.

In moments like that it reminded me that the saying "seeing is believing" isn't the exclusive domain of the sighted world. I see through sound and touch and after having walked the distances, touched the bases, felt the infield dirt sift through my fingers and listened to the vastness as I roamed the stadium, the game came alive for me in a very meaningful way. I will always cherish those Blue Jay days. Before I had my tactile knowledge of the field and it's dimensions indelibly imprinted on my perceptions of baseball, I would always opt to book a room in the SkyDome Hotel. It is part of the outfield stands and had windows that open onto and overlook the field. I used to take in the aroma of the roasted peanuts and the popcorn and listen to the vendors and the fans and found the whole dynamic very entertaining. After being introduced to the game so up close and personal by Carlos, I found that I much preferred being down in the seats, near the infield, where I could hear everything and really experience the game. I went from a casual fan to a fanatic.

Dalton used to often join us on our excursions to Toronto. He played at an all-star level and travelled with the rep team for his age group from Sault Ste. Marie. Meeting the major leaguers he watched on television was exciting for him, but his real rush came when we attended Toronto Maple Leafs hockey games. Let's face it, he grew up in Canada, where hockey is virtually a religion and the Maple Leafs have forever been Canada's national team, loved and worshipped on a scale that I think exceeds the reach of even the New York Yankees, especially in Canada. Maple Leaf games were a little more special for us than most fans too because of my dear friend Paul Hendrick. Paul has been a broadcaster with the Maple Leaf organization for years and would always go out of his way when we came to town to get us phenomenal seats for the game and often access to the morning skate as well. For a kid who grew up playing hockey, like Dalton, it was a dream come true.

Hockey is such an intense game and for a blind fan the action really comes to life when you are there in person. I have to admit, though, that I am actually a Boston Bruins fan. I grew up in the era of Phil Esposito, who is from Sault Ste. Marie, and was rewriting the record book for scoring while Bobby Orr, from nearby Parry Sound, was simply establishing himself as the best defenseman who ever played the game. With both of them being virtually hometown boys and starring for the Bruins during my formative years, how could I cheer for anybody else? I have had the pleasure of getting to know them over the years and continue to have the utmost respect for them both.

Dalton may have played baseball, but he was a hockey player at heart. During the winter months our lives were governed by the hockey schedule with Patti and I all but living in hockey arenas throughout Northern Ontario, be it at a six a.m. practice before school to a tournament 500 miles away on the weekend. There is nothing like a forty-degree below zero morning heading to hockey practice. Thankfully, the ice rinks were all indoors.

Dalton can tie his own skates these days...

Any mention of Dalton's hockey career would be remiss without a special thank you to our close family friends, Terry and Eric Ableson, who's son Nathan was on Dalton's team. When our lives got especially hectic (and let's face it, with my travel schedule, that was a regular occurrence) Terry and Eric were always there to help with the travel logistics. So many times they got Dalton to his game while Patti picked me up at the airport, making it possible for us to catch up with Dalton just in time to cheer him on. There were so many other days that Patti and I left for the airport right after a game, while Terry and Eric waited and drove Dalton Home. I can't begin to count how many games he could have missed without the help of our dear friends.

Hockey still remains my all-time favorite sport. It must be the Canadian in me, and having a mentor like Gordie Howe doesn't hurt either. It's not always easy being a fan when your team never wins it all, so with my apologies to Chicago Cubs fans and Toronto Maple Leaf fans and all other long suffering fans, I have tell you that my passion for hockey has been reignited in recent times, with my beloved Bruins, after 39 years, finally winning it all, capturing the Stanley Cup again in 2011. I was on cloud 9 for so long after that victory and am still riding the wave. I hope I don't have to wait another 39 years.

Life became even more interesting, and rewarding, as our family began to grow.

Derek was born in Sault Ste. Marie, Ontario in 2001. Becoming a father again at the age of thirty-eight was definitely an experience in personal growth. For me that was learning to deal with the unexpected. For example, I have always prided myself on being a very "hands-on" dad. I've always been willing to get involved and do my share. I remember one occasion very clearly. Derek was about one and a half and I was giving him his bath when he presented me with a present he was very proud of. I calmly reached over and flushed it where it was supposed to go. When I think about, even today, I still chuckle. When it happened I couldn't help but laugh out loud.

Derek bonding with Dad.

The adventures continued as Ashley came along two years later and Morgan a few years after that. I've loved every minute of it and I have found out that fatherhood really has its moments, especially when you're totally blind.

Changing diapers, for example, was always an adventure. I admit, Patti did most of the heavy lifting when it came to diaper detail, but I was never afraid to respond when called in to duty. If Patti had errands to run or was busy with one of the other kids or another job around the house, I would do my best to hold up my end and help out. This did require that I develop some unique techniques of my own, one of which I'm sure the makers of Pampers wished more dads adopted. I didn't like to leave anything to chance so when the clean-up stage of the diaper change arrived, I would just take a big handful of baby wipes and create a wide swath that would ensure that every square millimeter of my patient's tiny backside was wiped clean. Maybe not standard operating procedure, but it worked for me. In fact, I had more or less perfected the technique by the time Morgan came along but no matter how effective it was, watching me always sent Ashley into fits of laughter. Entertaining and effective. Made me feel good.

There have been other moments too, like when Derek was eight years old and we were out in the yard playing baseball. I was actually throwing batting practice to him and his friend from next door when his friend's father came to join us. Derek's friend piped up right away saying, "Hey Dad, Craig is a better pitcher than you." Before he could protest, I told him to take a seat in the bullpen. We all laughed.

My experiences with the kids went both ways too, with them teaching me also. When I reminisce with Patti we continue to be impressed, to this day, with the kids' perception of the different ways we do things. For example, from the earliest days, when we would read books together, all of the kids would excitedly take my finger and touch it to the page as they "showed" me things. They never did this with Patti. They just seemed to understand my need for tactile learning and acted accordingly. I loved it when I had the opportunity to read to them from one of my Braille children's

These days Morgan reads to me.

books, but regardless of the book, they were always mindful of my uniqueness and remain so to this day.

The best laugh came totally unexpected. Patti and I were sitting in the living room one Sunday afternoon, not doing anything in particular, just relaxing. Morgan, who was six at the time, came in and asked if she could play a DVD. We said of course and she proceeded to plug my intro DVD in to play. It is a short introduction narrated by Bob Costas and is shown to audiences at the beginning of most of my speeches. Toward the end there are some pictures of me with some of the famous people I have had the pleasure to meet. At that point Morgan stopped the video and came over to Patti. She asked, "Mommy, who is that not so good looking woman on the TV with Daddy?" I couldn't get an image of the picture in my head at that second and then Patti responded, "That's not a woman honey, that's Steven Tyler, he's a friend of your Daddy."

I roared out loud. There was, of course, no way Morgan would know who Steven Tyler, lead singer of Aerosmith was, but it was hilarious all the same. I have so many memories like that and I sometimes call on them to sustain me during those long layovers between flights. I'm sure many people have walked by asking themselves, "I wonder what he is smiling about?" because they do always make me smile.

I'm glad Dalton doesn't live at home anymore.

By the middle of 2005 Patti and I were looking for a change of scenery, and a change of climate. We settled on Mount Dora, Florida, a beautiful and quaint town about 50 minutes north of Orlando. One great benefit of my career is that we can live anyplace that is within reasonable striking distance of an airport. Mount Dora was less than an hour's drive away from Orlando International and Florida appealed to our sensibilities at the time so we made the leap. It was the beginning of a love affair with Florida that continues to this day, even though we did eventually settle elsewhere.

As you can probably tell by now, I can honestly say that spending time with my family is my favorite thing to do in the entire world. We all need a place to go to recharge our batteries, kind of like hitting our personal reset button. That's what my wife and kids do for me.

Florida is often the focal point of our recharging experiences. As a family we love to take vacations, and over the years have taken so many, but our favorite vacation above all is to Disney World. Patti is a total Disney aficionado, some might even say a fanatic. We all love it, so at least once, if not twice, a year we indulge our mutual love of Disney by visiting Orlando. The kids, like Patti, can't seem to get enough and to be honest, neither can I.

It always seems to get our adrenaline flowing when we visit Disney. We all love the action filled rides such as Expedition Everest in Animal Kingdom or Space Mountain, and Big Thunder Mountain at the Magic Kingdom. One of the most exhilarating experiences is the Tower of Terror at Hollywood Studios. These rides are an incredible rush even without eyesight. Imagine doing this blindfolded! I cherish all of those memorable moments with my family and look forward to creating so many more.

Disney makes every walk in the park more interesting.

When we're not at Disney, the best place in the world for us to vacation is the beach. Are you seeing why Florida is our favorite escape? We spend ample time at our vacation house in Fort Myers, from which a multitude of beautiful beaches are just a short drive away.

The beaches of Sanibel Island have always been a favorite. For whatever reason, it is an incredibly therapeutic place for all of us. The sound of the water gently rolling up on the shore is music to my ears and a great source of nourishment to my soul and spirit. The smell of the salt water and the sun on my skin always leaves me thinking, "Does it get any better than this?"

Sanibel is great too because it gives me a chance to get involved in some family activities on an equal basis. Shelling is one of our favorites. I go searching with the kids and we find all sizes and shapes. I remember one recent visit where we were finding sand dollars that were up to eight or nine inches across. It was a marvelous time.

Building sand castles and decorating them with our shells or playing Frisbee are also favorite pastimes of ours, although I must admit I throw better than I catch. It's still great fun and the kids have become surprisingly good at hitting me with their throws so I don't have far to walk to pick up the Frisbee.

Often it is just getting back to nature that provides all the opportunity to recharge that we need. There is so much to appreciate and sometimes if you simply sit back and appreciate, you get rewarded. It has happened to us many times, like the time Ashley spotted dolphins jumping not far from shore. As we slowly walked toward them, they decided to put on a show. I could hear them jumping and splashing about. That coupled with the excitement of the kids provided a great experience.

The dolphins were not the only time that my kids surprised me by bringing me in touch with nature. When Morgan was six, this time back in Canada, at Bellevue Park in Sault Ste. Marie, she caught a full-grown seagull and excitedly ran over for me to feel it. I was amazed at how large this bird was and how soft it was to the touch. I still laugh when I try to imagine how Morgan got her hands on this wild creature. Of course, not to be outdone, on that same trip, Ashley caught a sparrow in my parents' backyard. She eagerly ran in the house and let me examine her catch of the day. It seems with our kids, it is an endless stream of hands-on experiences. They have brought me everything from frogs to toads to turtles to grasshoppers to worms and even the occasional snake. Never a dull moment to say the least.

Sometimes, when the kids are occupied, I let myself get lost in the moment, wondering how others find this boost to their inner strength. The beach, for me, is like throwing kindling on my internal fire. Even if it feels like it is on the verge of going out, a day at the beach brings me back. It's like immersing myself in my own private reflecting pool where I can be absorbed in my own thoughts. I swear I can feel the stress leaving my body and my spirit coming back to life.

If you don't have a place, somewhere to connect with yourself and reset your hard drive, so to speak, I strongly suggest you find one. If you don't know where to start, I suggest you try the beach.

One challenge I do have at the beach, especially when I'm lying in the sun soaking up some rays, is remembering to close my eyes. As strange as it may seem, the sun doesn't bother my eyes at all but seeing a motionless man lying on his back looking directly into the sun with his eyes wide open can spook some people. Go figure.

I always come back from Florida invigorated, with a renewed focus and a great sense of purpose. I am ready to jump right back into work, to make a difference and continue to deliver an inspired effort. To me it's a choice. I go on vacation to get recharged so I can be this way on my return. It's the purpose of the trip. I simply don't understand those people, and we all know some, who come back from vacation and mope around for a week or two lamenting the fact that they are back instead of looking forward to their next great adventure. That mindset is just a counterproductive waste of time that can do nothing but delay a return to the vacation experience they are so sad they're missing.

If you are lucky enough to take a vacation, relish it and appreciate it. Otherwise, why go in the first place. It's your choice.

Of course, coming back from Florida doesn't mean that life slows down while we wait to vacation again. As a family we remain very active, the games just change. In the wintertime you will frequently find all of us out sledding at Mulberry Hill in the park near our home, or making snowmen and snow forts of all shapes and sizes in our backyard. The occasional snowball fight happens too, just to keep things interesting. In the spring and summer the trampoline is a favorite pastime for all of us, as is bike riding, for the kids anyway, but I'm still right there as much as possible.

One of my favorite things in the summer is to pitch batting practice to Derek. Before each pitch I always ask if he is ready. His answer allows me to hear precisely where he is so I can gauge distance and factor in the height of his bat. When Derek was small, I took a number of line drives to the face, leading Patti to suggest that I really was crazy. I didn't think so, but like everything else athletic, you have to learn and grow if you want a good experience. What I learned was to always wear my glove and raise it in front of my face as soon as I released the pitch. I haven't taken a direct hit since.

Derek always said I can't catch very well.

We have a few special games that we have developed over the years that we thought would make the conditions fair for all of us. One of these is a game we call Ogre. It is actually "hide and seek" but we play it in the basement of the house, with all the lights out.

(Get the picture?) I can always find Patti by the smell of her perfume, even if she has climbed up on top of a dresser. Now she claims I have an unfair advantage.

We play a version of Ogre in the pool too. It seems that I am almost always "it" and I have to catch the kids as they swim about. They like to swim under water to avoid being heard but, invariably I hear them gasp when they come up for air. Then it is a race to see if I can reach them before they descend again. It is great, and frantic, fun.

We lived almost a year in Florida. We loved it but decided to move before Derek started kindergarten. Florida is a paradise and we wanted to hold on to it in that sense, but felt maybe paradise wasn't the best place to raise a family. I also thought that establishing ourselves more centrally might ease my travel schedule by reducing the number of really long flights. (That was wishful thinking but when you fly more than 100,000 air miles a year, it makes little difference.)

I had always been impressed with Indianapolis, having spent many months there with Mario Andretti and his family. I had the privilege, several times, of watching the Indianapolis 500 from the Andretti suite on turn two of the Indianapolis Motor Speedway. Mario was really a dear friend.

We decided to seriously investigate Indy as a place to put down roots, a place for our kids to grow up and go to school, a place for the long term.

My first move was to give my friend Mario a call. I asked his advice on the best neighborhood in the Indianapolis area for a family with two young kids and another on the way to settle down. He didn't hesitate at all. He recommended Zionsville, Indiana. I think I laughed out loud and replied "that sounds like a bad disease!"

With Ashley on bring Dad to pre-school day.

I'm not laughing now. We took Mario's advice and discovered an absolutely super town. Zionsville features a quaint downtown with a cobblestone main street, walking and biking trails galore and, arguably, the best education in the state, certainly excellent by any standard. It combines Midwest values with a more laid-back lifestyle. When I return home from my road trips it's an ideal place to regroup and catch my breath. We couldn't be happier.

The biking trails provide a wonderful opportunity that Derek and I take advantage of whenever possible. In the spirit of father/son bonding, a concept I totally support, Derek and I like to go for longs walks, just to stay caught up with each other. We usually walk to Starbuck's, where I thoroughly enjoy stopping to share a treat with Derek while I enjoy my Mocha Frappuccino.

Zionsville also treats us to some special experiences that Florida just can't offer. As northern kids, Patti and I both grew up enjoying all four seasons, and still do. Her favorite season is the fall, with all its color and brilliance, a visual extravaganza to be sure, but for me, the greatest rush comes in the spring. Listening to the snow melt, hearing the drops of water from the roof, feeling the grass renewing under my feet as I walk around my yard, the breeze getting warmer each day, sitting on the garden swing and absorbing all the scents and smells as the flowers start to bloom and the trees come back to life, especially the lilacs. The sounds aren't lost on me either. It is delightful to listen to all the different birds announcing their arrival back in the trees of our yard. That, for me, is the extravaganza. I especially like going to the garden center with Patti to pick out the plants and flowers that we will put in the garden

Morgan helping with landscaping.

when the thaw is complete. It may be sensory overload, but I love it.

I have been blessed with wonderful and supportive employers throughout my career. This has allowed me to intertwine my business obligations with my personal passions in a highly satisfying and, I hope, effective experience that has been ongoing now for more than 20 years.

One of those passions has always been working with younger generations. In fact, in my own charity, 20/20 Inner Vision Foundation, our mission statement or objective, if you will, is "To Increase High School Graduation Rates in America." To that end, I have, during the course of my travels, spoken at more than 2,700 schools to date. I have spoken to schools in every state in the United States, including Alaska and Hawaii, as well as in every province in Canada.

I have received numerous acknowledgments and accolades over the years for my work with the youth of our society, from mayors to governors to presidents, but one shines above all. It wasn't just an accolade, it was an honor that I will always remember.

It came in the fall of 2006 when I was invited by my friend, Cardinal Pio Laghi, to visit Vatican City for a meeting with Pope Benedict XVI. I was overwhelmed. My only regret is that Patti was not going to be able to accompany me. Morgan was still just a baby at that time and, above and beyond all my passions and ambitions, my first commitment is to family. Patti agreed. As much as she wanted to come with me, it was best that she stay home with the kids. You know you've found your soul mate when you are on the same page like that.

Of course, you can't take a trip like that alone. It is a once in a lifetime experience and I wanted someone to share it with, someone to describe everything to me, someone I knew who would appreciate the experience as much as I would. I asked my lifetime friend, Michael Theisen, to accompany me. He jumped at the chance and his contribution made it all that much more memorable.

Rome is an awe-inspiring city, so vibrant and so steeped in history. Walking through the coliseum, with Michael painting word pictures for me, left me in amazement. When I touched the columns and felt the rough cobblestones under my feet it gave me great appreciation for those who constructed them so many centuries ago. Michael's descriptions were so vibrant that I can still recall visions of just how beautiful that city must be.

As part of my invitation to the Sistine Chapel, Michael and I were escorted into the Chapel through a door not used by the public, and to our amazement, once inside we discovered that we were the only ones in that section of the Chapel. Imagine, we felt like we had the Sistine Chapel all to ourselves! We toured ourselves around, taking in all the paintings, statues and architecture. I was already feeling privileged.

Then, the Cardinal drove us to the Pope's private gardens for a leisurely stroll. The sense of honor and privilege continued to grow as we were informed that it is a rare occasion when anyone is permitted to walk there. It was so tranquil that you couldn't help but feel at peace.

My conversation with the Pope was just as, if not more, memorable. He was very informed, not just about my efforts, but about the specifics of my life and my work. I was so impressed, flattered actually, that he knew anything about me. After all, here was one of the most powerful men in the world and he had taken the time to learn the specifics of my commitment to the next generation. How humbling! He grasped my hand tightly between both of his and encouraged me, while looking directly into my soul, to keep reaching out to, and inspiring, young people. After all, they are the future. He showed me the patience of Job, so genuine, so engaged, so sincere, so unrushed, so real! I left our meeting truly inspired as he not only complimented my efforts, but endorsed them whole heartedly.

I'm not Catholic, but I think if I had spent one more day in and around Vatican City, I may well have become one. What an awesome, inspiring, milestone moment, for anyone. I'm so grateful it was me.

Another benefit of having such supportive employers has been the opportunity for Patti to stay home and raise our children. This has provided great "peace of mind" for me as I am on the road so much. It has also been great for the kids as one or both of us have always been there for them. Patti is a fantastic mother and being able to support her desire to give one hundred percent of her attention to our children is very satisfying to me. After all, kids do spell love T-I-M-E. They get all of hers and, because of her, all of mine when I am home. It has been a wonderful arrangement for all of us. We are all very happy and blessed.

It was great having Michael with me on the Vatican trip, especially that one as it was so memorable. In reality, however, probably 99 percent of the time, I travel alone. That can have its moments too.

Patience is by far the most critical asset I need where travel is concerned. For me, travel is mostly about "hurry up and wait" but that takes on a whole different meaning when you are blind and alone and in some mammoth, impersonal airport terminal. The typical routine for me is to be dropped off at curbside, then be escorted by one or more skycaps to my gate, and be left to wait for departure. That's it. I could be there for 30 minutes or three hours. There is generally nobody close by, except total strangers, until it's time to board the plane. It's just me, in my seat, waiting.

Not so long ago I was making a connection in Toronto and there was a seven-hour delay. That's a bad scenario even for a sighted person, but at least YOU can walk around, YOU can read a newspaper or magazine, YOU can find a television in a lounge, or YOU can even just people watch. Not me. Thank God for my cell phone and few Braille notes in my carryon bag. At least, on that occasion, I could punch out a few more thoughts for this manuscript. Someone from Passenger Assistance just walked me to my gate, made sure I was comfortable, and left me, FOR FIVE HOURS! Seriously, I was completely alone. Sure I could get up and stretch my legs only to sit back in the same seat. The impersonality of a major airport gives a blind person no reference with which to navigate. There is literally nothing dependable to use in order to find my way around. All I could do was stand up and sit down. I didn't hear any footsteps, no voices, no vacuum cleaners, no janitor's carts rolling by, the occasional public address static in the distance, but no contact with humanity of any kind, nothing! I was picturing my flight leaving from the bowels of Pearson International, not a pretty picture by the way. I seriously doubt if I had yelled fire at the top of lungs that anyone would have heard me. So, I sat there, getting hungrier by the hour, praying that a call of nature didn't catch up to me before some signs of life returned. Of course, you can't just sit there like a stump. I made the time productive, catching up on all those messages we never seem to have time for, but I must admit I found relief, in more ways than one, when someone finally showed up...

That's what I mean by patience. Now, I admit, five hours is a little extreme, but when you fly to as many small towns and make as many connections as I have to, three-hour layovers are actually a common part of my life. Have you ever tried to sit still for three hours? You really have to anticipate and plan ahead as much as possible, for things like food, a drink or just the use of a rest room because once they walk you to your seat, you're stuck. There may be plenty of helpful people at airports, but they are busy too. They can't always be there just because I need something. Trust me, I'm not looking for sympathy or saying poor me, but welcome to my world when it comes to travelling.

More than ninety-nine percent of the time that I am on the road, I'm by myself. I rarely work alone so I do have contact with those colleagues who brought me to town, but that invariably ends when the speeches are over. As much as my work is social in nature, it involves very little social life. I eat most of my dinners alone. In fact, I'd be willing to bet I've eaten more room service than anyone you've ever met. What's my alternative? I'd rather listen to Fox News or ESPN in my room than sit alone in some restaurant at a table set for two.

It has often been said that loneliness for a blind person is the worst prison you could have. I have no doubt about the reality of that and I won't let it happen to me. My saving grace is that I am always so busy coordinating the logistics of my travel arrangements or following up on speaking inquiries that I am rarely idle long enough to feel lonely. I handle all my own affairs. It keeps me engaged and I have found that most people appreciate that there is no middleman when it comes to booking me. I get to know the people I deal with on a more personal level and develop deeper relationships with them. This personal connection keeps my life very interesting. No two days are ever the same. When the phone rings I never know who it will be on the other end inviting me to speak or to what part of the world I am being invited.

In 2009, I stepped out of my role at Edward Jones after eighteen plus wonderful years. I had witnessed some amazing growth as the company went from 1,600 offices to over 11,000 offices, spread across the United States and Canada. They were certainly at the forefront of the industry when I joined the company, and a major player when I left, all for the right reasons. The biggest reason being their people and their commitment to deeply serving the individual investor.

We all grow. I reached a point in my life where I thought that in order to achieve my full potential. I would have to take some risks and broaden my horizons. It was scary, especially those first few months without that old familiar routine and without the financial backbone of a major corporation. I had so much pent-up emotion inside that with time, effort and energy I made the transition and, I think, even made that scariness work for me.

Proper strategy was the critical component. If you're going to take a leap of faith on that level, you have to have a plan and the faith to follow it through. You have to know that you are going to fail some of the time and you can't be afraid of that or you'll never make it. I set my sights on my goal and then relied on my wisdom, knowledge and experience, coupled with patient and persistent action, to ramp up my speaking career. I suppose you could say that I took a dose of my own advice, but when you don't have a boss there is only one person you can blame if you don't succeed.

Despite all the pent-up emotion and ambition and vision and goals, the key to the transition was ACTION. Ask yourself, how many people do you know who have great ambitions but they never get there, or even remotely close. They may have a great plan, seems like they always do, but nothing ever happens for them. They never take action. Any action is better than no action. Even if you don't have total success, at least you're moving, you're gaining experience, you're learning something, and that can be put to use to improve your next action, but if you don't take action, you have nothing. Things don't just happen. You have to make them happen. You can follow your heart, but don't expect it to lead you. You'll still have to think for yourself. Make your plan, set your short-term, concrete goals, get fixed on your long-term vision AND THEN DO SOMETHING. The journey of a thousand miles begins with a single step, but you have to take the step.

I'm pleased that Dalton has learned this lesson. His hockey career never took him to the NHL but that hasn't held him back on the road to a successful business life. He has taken the first several steps following his ambitions to be successful in the investment world and the results are showing.

Sometimes taking action requires a little creativity, too. With a schedule like mine just creating time for business meetings, especially when I'm home, can be quite the challenge. My favorite solution for this was a routine that my partner Mark Harris and I worked up when he came to live Indianapolis in 2008 to run the Career Dynamics Initiative for 20/20 Inner Vision foundation. By the way, that was a great pilot project that connected graduating students with the local business community. I'm sure you'll be hearing about it elsewhere so I won't go into it here.

As for Mark and I, it seemed that he was always busy when I was in town and by the time his day was through I was always busy with family matters. You know the routine. Finally, one day, we found the solution, or more accurately stumbled on to it. I called and invited Mark over for lunch one Saturday. He accepted, but told me he had to stop at the local MARSH supermarket on the way over. I suggested he pick me up first because Patti needed a few things, too. That was our first shopping trip, but over the next year we repeated the routine at least once, if not twice, a week. With me holding the bar of the shopping cart and Mark pulling the cart from up front we toured that store while talking about business matters. As I memorized where everything was in the store, I became very good at picking up extra items too, especially those that appealed to my sweet tooth. It became an anticipated event, both for us and the store. The manager of the store, Steve Carroll, made a point of greeting us each week with a handshake and a hearty welcome. His staff got to know us by name, too, and often suggested they were going to call the local TV station and have a story done about us. The TV cameras never arrived, but Steve still shakes my hand every time I'm in his store.

I hope you get a sense that my life, after athletics, has remained a fully engaged and rewarding experience. I trust, also, that you can see how the lessons I learned in my athletic career translated into the wonderful life I live now. Even more, I hope that you can apply the same principles in your life and be even happier.

Reflections

They say that we all have perfect memories. The challenge we face is with our recall. Writing this book, reliving my life in the creation

Indianapolis 2013

of these pages, has confirmed that for me. I have amazed myself with how much I have done, how many people I have met, how many special moments I've been part of. The medals, the championships and the trophies are all quantified, easy to count, easy to recall. To some extent they are just cold, impersonal history.

It is the people side of life that ultimately matters. The contacts, the relationships and the events hold the real inspirational juice for me. Countless people, at countless events, have left an indelible impression on my life, from the

disadvantaged to the ordinary to the extraordinary. I couldn't even begin to talk about all of them, but I don't want to gloss over them either. Here is a list, certainly not complete, and not in any particular order, but representative of the unforgettable people I've encountered along my life's highway. Some of them you already know, all of them I wish you could have met:

- Pope Benedict the 16th - A tremendous highlight. I was invited by Cardinal Pio Laghi to an audience with Pope

Benedict in 2006. Cardinal Laghi had seen me speak on numerous occasions during his time serving as Papal Nuncio in the United States. Meeting Pope Benedict was a most impressive experience. This extremely busy and powerful man had taken the time to learn about my work with youth and made me feel that he was personally interested in me. He held my hand in both of his and I could just sense that he was looking me directly in the eye. He was gracious, relaxed, accommodating and supportive. I was even invited to sit in the front row of St. Peter's Basilica for Pope Benedicts special Wednesday Mass. What an inspiring experience!

- Ronald Reagan – 40th President of the United States. 1984 was my year of Ronald Reagan. It began with an invitation from the Office of the President to carry the Olympic torch, in Washington D.C., for a leg of its journey to the 1984 Los Angeles Olympics. I was then asked to join the Reagan-Bush All Star team and spoke over 231 times in 39 states as part of the tour. Over the course of the year I met President Reagan, himself, several times, including more several lengthy one-on-one conversations in the oval office. He was funny, engaging and tremendously perceptive. It was at his invitation that I spoke at my first Republican National Convention that year, in Dallas. He treated me wonderfully.

- George H. W. Bush – 41st President of the United States. The Reagan–Bush year was significant in many ways, not the least of which was the beginning of my life long relationship with George H.W. Bush. I met the 41st President of the United States while he was still Vice President, when he would drop in on the tour at many of our appearances. President Bush had a way of making me feel like I was making a special contribution through my work with the All-Star team, but I'm sure he had that rapport with everybody. None the less, we became close and he continued to take a personal interest in me even after the election campaign was over. In fact, President Bush and I became so close that in 1985 he and his wife Barbara actually "crashed" my poolside 23rd birthday party at the Houstonian Club and he stayed long enough that we were able to share a piece of birthday cake together. No doubt one of the most unique memories of any president anyone can share. This kind of connection continued. I enjoyed many wonderful visits with the President, often in the Oval Office. We would have wonderful, deep conversations, always interspersed with humor, because he is such a personable man. I have been to his summer home in Kennebunkport and to his office in Houston many times. Over the years I have sat with him often, petting his dog, while I absorbed the benefit of his wisdom. Just after he won the 1988 Presidential election, he was kind enough to record a short tribute to me which is still part of the introduction video shown before everyone of my speeches. We never did lose contact. In fact, just a few years ago, while having breakfast with Patti on a Saturday morning, I received a phone call from the President's long time Executive Assistant, Linda Casey. The President was in his limousine, on his way to the Houston Open Tennis Tournament and had asked Linda to call me. He didn't have any other reason than to catch up as we hadn't spoken in while. Just a "Hi Craig, how you doing?" The President called me to ask how I was. What a wonderful, thoughtful man. We have even been in contact during the writing of this book, but I guess his Foreword gave that away. I am more than lucky, I am definitely blessed to have him in my life.

- Mario Andretti - Childhood hero who became a friend and took me in like one of his family, year after year, not only at the Indy 500, but numerous other races as well. One of the most humble, approachable, down to earth celebrities I have gotten to know.

- Mickey Mantle - I travelled to one of my first keynote speeches at the tender age of 20, in the U.S. Virgin Islands, on a flight with Mickey Mantle, who I was going to be sharing the stage with. When we landed, a flight attendant was walking me off. Mickey yelled out from behind, "don't forget me, I'm blind too." Based on how much he drank on that flight, he wasn't kidding. It wasn't my only encounter with Mickey, but it certainly left an impression, which he built on over time.

• Roger Maris – Much like Mickey, Roger Maris left an impression on me too, although quite different. Roger was my roommate for much of the Reagan Bush All Star Team Tour. We had so many deep, prolonged conversations that would stretch late into the night. I was impressed by his humble, unpretentious view of life and wisdom he shared with me. It is so sad that he was so misunderstood by the media in 1961. He was a very intelligent, special, genuine but shy man who just wanted to be the best he could be.

• Bob Costas – The voice of NBC Sports and narrator of a documentary on my life. From the time I met Bob in the late 80's at Yankee spring training, he remains a friend that I have great respect for.

• Gordie Howe – Mr. Hockey. Mentor, father figure, dear friend! If lives have cornerstones, Gordie would be one of mine. He brought me to America and launched my career. Enough said!

• Steven Tyler – I don't have to tell you who this man is. What I do want to tell you about Steven is that he is incredibly perceptive. Every time we met, which was often, he would make the effort to reach out to me on my terms. I felt a special connection with Steven. He was animated and personable, yet when engaged in conversation, incredibly focused, like he only had time for me. If he treated every one like he treated me, it's no wonder his iconic status has endured, and spread far beyond the boundaries of rock'n'roll.

• Steve Perry – Huey Lewis wasn't the only big time recording artist laying down tracks at Fantasy Studios while I was recording my first album. Steve Perry, Neil Schon, Ross Valory and the rest of Journey, were in the studio right beside me. As a matter of fact, Ross played bass on my album, while Eddie Money did some background vocals for me. Steve, however, took a personal interest in me. We chatted at length during breaks in our recording sessions. When we weren't chatting I would hang out in Steve's control room. To tell you the truth, he has the single most impressive voice I've ever heard, not just on his recordings, but in the studio and on stage as well. I was always so impressed that despite such awesome talent, the man had no pretense about him at all. He was simply my friend.

- Bryan Adams - A Canadian compatriot who was rising to stardom in the United States at the same time I was establishing my foot hold south of the 49th. I got to know Bryan so well that one year he personally sent me a Christmas card. The note inside read, "you better appreciate this, I picked it just for you." I think he picked the roughest feeling Christmas card ever produced.

- Bob & Tom - During my visits to Indianapolis, at the invitation of Mario Andretti, I often appeared as a guest on the nationally syndicated Bob and Tom radio show. Without a doubt these were the funniest interviews I may have ever done. These guys really are hilarious and definitely cutting edge. On one occasion, when we went water skiing together, I actually wound up driving the boat. Their humor is genuine and straight from the heart. They are simply fun to be around and to listen to.

- Paul Newman - I met Paul through Mario Andretti when Mario was driving for the Newman-Haas racing team. Often times during inclement weather at the track I found myself taking shelter with Paul in the team bus. We had some amazing, one on one conversations about life, success, ambition and all manner of subjects. His honest, genuine, unpretentious nature and straight forward style endeared him to me, as much as the wisdom he shared. He treated me like a friend whenever he encountered me and that was special.

- Tim Allen - One of the most memorable characters I have ever met. Tim is funny, crazy and energized. My stomach always hurt from laughing after spending a few hours with him.

- Tony Robbins – I got to know Tony on a personal level when he invited me to be a featured speaker in Hawaii at one of his major events. I spoke on the Tony Robbins stage several more times and hope I soaked up some residue from my personal connection with him. He does walk his talk and makes everyone around him better.
- Dog, The Bounty Hunter – When I first met Dog, he was a bailiff in Hawaii. During that first speaking appearance for Tony, Dog was assigned as my right hand man and made whatever I needed real. I can tell you, from experience, that what you see of Dog on TV is the real deal. He is a very cool guy.
- Walter Cronkite – Earlier in my career, at a large international corporate conference, I had the honor of sharing the stage with Walter Cronkite. My time with Walter was short, but his genuine, down to earth demeanor, left a lifelong impression on my psyche. It's not surprising he rose to iconic status in the world of broadcasting.
- Norman Vincent Peale – If Walter was an icon, then Dr. Peale was a legend. I worked with Dr. Peale on more than one occasion and often joked with him that I was his warm up act, but truth be told, he taught me the difference between motivating and inspiring.
- Rev. Robert H. Schuller – Genuine, soft spoken and charismatic, my encounters with Rev. Schuller, including an appearance on the Hour of Power early in my career, taught me intrinsic lessons that I am sure still come through in my message today.
- John Bachmann – Former Managing Partner of Edward Jones and visionary who hired me and created my role as an ambassador with the company, effectively perpetuating my travel schedule for the next 18 plus years. I'm sure the airlines are still grateful for his decision, I certainly am.
- Jim Weddle – Managing Partner of Edward Jones. I spent my first eleven years at Edward Jones benefiting from the wisdom, experience and leadership I received as I reported

directly to Jim. His influence was significant, with gusts to impactful. He guided the early days of my career before retiring to the role of my mentor when he assumed more responsibility as the leader of Edward Jones. I was certainly one of the beneficiaries of his cutting edge, revolutionary vision.

- Lee Iacocca - In my early twenties, Mr. Iacocca had an incredible belief in me and my message. I frequently found myself speaking at Chrysler events. He provided me with major injections of confidence, time after time, as my speaking career was ramping up.

- David Glass - Former Chairman of Wal-Mart and Owner of the Kansas City Royals. Another fan and influential mentor who taught me the value I could bring to an organization and its culture. He employed my services as a speaker on numerous occasions, in a multitude of fashions. The highlight was speaking to over 21,000 people at Dallas Reunion Arena as part of an annual Wal-Mart convention. In fact I still have a video of Mr. Glass talking about me. Imagine that.

- Bob Steggert - Global VP of Claims, Marriott International. I've come to know Bob incredibly well over the past several years. Our paths have crossed at numerous speaking engagements as I travel back and forth across the country, not to mention in many Marriott hotels. I have always been impressed with the prompt quickness with which Bob manages his communication, always responding, and usually within hours, if not minutes. He has recommended me numerous times as a speaker and I value his support.

- Bob Crandall and American Airlines - Former President and Chairman of American Airlines. My passion for giving back, especially to students, has never waned from that first time I gave my championship trophy to that disabled boy. It has been an integral part of all my travels, so much so that I have spoken at almost 3,000 high schools over the course of my career.

Bob Crandall was the first big corporate executive who truly understood the value of my speaking at high schools. He took a personal interest in my passion early in my career. He made sure I was able to address students who would not otherwise have had the chance to hear my message by providing complimentary airfare on American when no other passage was available. He helped build the vision that ultimately became 20/20 Inner Vision Foundation. For that I am eternally grateful.

- Jim Croson – President of 20/20 Inner Vision Foundation and one of the most successful men within my inner circle of friends. Along with being a mentor and confidant, Jim Croson was also the financial catalyst who made 20/20 Inner Vision Foundation possible. He is, without a doubt, the most generous man I ever met. He has made it possible for me to help countless young people through his personal contributions to the foundation. His influence has had a profound effect on me and the direction of my life. He is much more than just another friend. He is, in my mind and in my heart, family!

- Ken Ransom – My water ski coach. Ken was the person in my life who most personified the phrase "lived life to the fullest." I think it would be fair to say that Ken, who hailed from Great Britain, lived five years for every one he was alive. He had a special way of keeping life light and making things enjoyable, even during the most serious or challenging moments. I lived with Ken, and his wife Trish, while I was training for the World Blind Water Ski Championships. Ken was the spark plug, the catalyst, the pillar I could lean on throughout my training and I give him all the credit for my victory in Norway. He was a special presence in my life. It makes me sad that Ken was taken from this world far too early.

- Paul Hendrick – Reporter and Host on Toronto Maple Leafs television broadcasts and Leafs TV. Paul is a dear friend of mine who I can always call for some advice or just to chat. He narrated my first introduction video and always seemed able to get Dalton, Patti and I great seats to Leaf games, which isn't easy. The Leafs have been sold out for virtually every game since 1931. Paul is a good friend who I don't talk to often enough.

- George Steinbrenner - Owner of the New York Yankees. One evening, in the late 1980's, when I was living in the Tampa area, I found myself sharing the stage with a larger than life character named George Steinbrenner. I struck up a conversation with George over the course of the night. The banter developed into a friendly dialogue that lead to my being invited to his office in Tampa the following week. I connected with "The Boss" several more times including a special night as his personal guest at Yankee Stadium. George was powerful in many respects. I will always be struck by his passion for baseball and his undeniable desire to win.

- Howard Cosell - Legendary sports broadcaster. I came to know Howard very well in the mid 80's through my friend-ship with Andy Robostelli. Howard was a character to say the least. When we would eat together you could hear his unmistakable voice everywhere. He was not bashful and was incredibly opinionated. In fact, even his comment about me is vintage Howard. "I've covered the sports beat for nearly 40 years of my life and worked with all the great ones at close hand. Jackie Roosevelt Robinson, Muhammad Ali, John Unitas, Johnny McEnroe... you name them. But I must tell you the most remarkable athlete I have ever seen - ever known - is Craig MacFarlane. When I asked him how he did it, he responded simply, I did it my way."

- Wayne Gretzky - I got to know Wayne when we were still teenagers. I spent some serious, quality time with Wayne during his Edmonton Oilers days, along with Paul Coffey, Mark Messier and Glen Anderson. From the long, late night, personal conversations on his parents front porch in Brantford, to the NHL Entry Draft in Montreal, to the NHL All Star Slow Pitch Tournament in Niagara Falls, to sitting as Honorary Chair of the Wayne Gretzky Celebrity Tennis Tournament, to numerous arenas throughout the National

Hockey League, my association with Wayne grew well beyond that of colleague. Wayne treated me as a personal friend.

- Paul Coffey – In the 1980's Paul was one of my favorite professional athletes to hang out with. Whether it was on the All Star Slow Pitch tour every summer, or at Edmonton Oilers' hockey games. Even at the Canada Cup in the mid 90's Paul always extended amazing hospitality to me. We are still great friends.

- Bobby Orr – The hero of my childhood and possibly the greatest defenseman to ever play in the National Hockey League. Became a good friend and along with his parents, served as role models in the early stages of my career. A great guy who always had time to take my phone calls.

- Walter Payton – Member of NFL Hall of Fame. During 1988 I found myself spending a great deal of time in Chicago working with the National Society to Prevent Blindness. During this project I spent a lot of time working with Walter Payton. Walter would often go out of his way to pick me up for dinner just because he cared. He was an awesome man with a heart of gold and certainly deserved his nickname "Sweetness."

- Evander Holyfield – Heavy Weight Boxing Champion of the World. Evander's manager, Shelly Finkel, invited me to several heavy weight championship bouts in Las Vegas. In fact, I was there the night that Mike Tyson bit a chunk out of Evander's ear, remember that one. I didn't just meet Evander at his fights but I got to know him so well that he invited me to his house, no make that MANSION, in Atlanta. I even have a video of him teaching me how to hit a punching bag. When he hit that punching bag there was an undeniable sound of pure strength and power, but that was nothing compared to the sound of him working the speed bag. I've never heard anything as awesome as that.

- Andy Robestelli – New York Giant Football Hall of Famer. In the mid 80's I stayed with Andy in Stamford, Connecticut. He owned a large, leading edge, full service travel business.

Andy was instrumental in shaping my speaking career along with my message.

- Edward Jones Investment Company - An incredible and rewarding journey, covering more than eighteen years of my professional career, all of which was made possible thanks to the insight, vision and commitment of three extraordinary men - Jim Weddle, John Bachmann and John Beuerlein. One of the greatest companies in the world to work for, Edward Jones empowered me to play a meaningful role every day in so many lives and reap many personal rewards as a result. I also established countless contacts, many of whom have developed into close, personal friendships. The most enduring and special of those, of course, being my wife Patti.

- MFS Investment Management - I would be remiss if I didn't mention two of my greatest champions, Jim Jessee and Jim Adams of MFS, one of the world's leading edge mutual fund management companies. No one has had a greater impact on my independent professional life than these gentlemen. It has been my pleasure to travel nationwide, speaking on behalf of MFS more than thirty-five times a year for three consecutive years and still going strong. It truly is a highlight in my life to have my message associated with a company that sets and maintains the benchmark of excellence in the mutual fund industry. If you're not familiar with MFS, you should check them out. It could pay great dividends in your future.

- The family of Marriott Hotels - I can't forget to express my gratitude to Marriott Hotels and all their brands. As independent as I try to be, when I travel I do need to put my trust in someone to provide a safe and comfortable place to stay. I have spent at least one hundred nights a year with Marriott throughout my career. They have taken fabulous care of me.

- Delta Airlines - I have made my way from hotel to hotel through the excellent services of Delta. I have flown with them over 100,000 air miles a year for more than twenty years and their treatment of me has always been impeccable.

- Sun Life Financial Canada - Another financial behemoth that has welcomed my message and utilized my services as a speaker. I admire The Sun Life corporate culture and I've enjoyed working and getting to know their executive team, starting of course with President Kevin Dougherty. I look forward to the relationship continuing.

There are so many others that I've met who have, in one way or another, left a positive impression on me that has benefited my life. People like Joe Theismann, Roger Staubach, Floyd Patterson, Joe Frazier, Phil Esposito, Ron Francis, Don Cherry, Mark Messier, Joe Thornton, Coach Lou Holtz of Notre Dame, Red Berenson from the University of Michigan, Jeff Jackson of Notre Dame, Dennis Erickson of the University of Miami, June Jones from the University of Hawaii and Barry Alvarez from the University of Wisconsin.

There have been so many people come into my life, some for short stays, some forever. I have met so many employees in countless locations across the United States and Canada over the course of my speaking career. I have certainly spoken in as many or more places than any speaker I am aware of. I have spoken in every state in the union and every province in Canada, all of them on multiple occasions. It doesn't stop there. My speaking career has brought me to such wonderful places as New Zealand, London, Paris, Munich, Berlin, Dublin, Amsterdam, Zurich, Madrid, Rome, Stockholm, Copenhagen, Helsinki, Oslo, St. Thomas, St. Johns, St. Lucia, St. Kitts and Nevis, Barbados, Grand Cayman and Bermuda. The big events, and there have been plenty of those, are always memorable but my work at the community level has meant that the vast majority of my speaking engagements have been with the small and medium sized companies that truly form the backbone of our society.

I cherish these more intimate opportunities to speak because they are more personal. They take place in the home town of the company and, invariably, there is opportunity to take questions and personalize my answers, to meet and mingle with both the management and employees, to make connections and, in some cases develop friendships. I like to say that a company brings me in to connect with its people while management reaps the benefits. These connections, these personal conversations, this feedback is what keeps me inspired. It's why I love my job.

I can't gloss over the big events though. I admit that I thrive on the bread and butter nature of my day to day work. It keeps me going, keeps me stable and grounded and inspired. The big events are different. They are the occasional seats at the big banquet and come with emotional highs that have to be experienced to be understood. They are like starting in the Superbowl or singing a show stopping solo on the Broadway stage. The big events are my sensorially overloaded, adrenaline packed reward for doing my job to the best of my ability, day in and day out. I have been rewarded many times, speaking on behalf of many large, often huge, corporations, associations and universities. Some of those highlights that jump to mind include:

- Wal-Mart
- Amway International
- Lions International
- Rotary International
- Canadian National Grocers Association
- Coaches Lou Holtz and Jeff Jackson of the Notre Dame University Fighting Irish
- Dennis Erikson and the University of Miami Hurricanes
- Barry Alvarez and the University of Wisconsin
- June Jones and the University of Hawaii
- Whirlpool
- General Motors
- Ford
- Chrysler numerous times on behalf of Lee Iacocca
- Eli Lilly
- Pfizer
- Disney
- Microsoft
- Sun Life
- Republican National Convention (3 times)

- Associated Builders and Contractors
- IBM
- Energizer
- Royal Bank of Canada
- Edward Jones Investments
- Coca Cola
- 3M Corporation
- Fidelity Investments
- Merrill Lynch
- Morgan Stanley
- Canadian Imperial Bank of Commerce
- National Sportswriters and Sportscasters Association
- A. T. & T.

If we haven't had the chance to meet yet, I sincerely look forward to shaking your hand at your organization's next conference or convention.

27
The Way I See It

There are so many stories I want to share with you, but not all of them deserve their own chapter. Some just deserve a paragraph. Here are some odds and sods, some examples and observations that came to mind as I have been writing.

Recently I received a rather "interesting" phone call. It definitely left me wondering. It was from State Farm Insurance. They asked for me specifically and then proceeded to congratulate me on my excellent driving record over the past 25 years. They were so impressed that I'd never had an accident claim or ticket. He sounded very excited to be offering me a big discount if I would transfer my insurance to them. I couldn't resist so I played along, asking questions about how they did their research. After making him squirm for a couple minutes, I informed him that I didn't have much faith in State Farm if they were seriously going to offer such a policy to me over the phone. He literally got offended, almost angry in fact. Then I dropped the hammer, "Sir, I have been totally blind since I was two years old." That brought dead silence. So I continued, "if your due diligence will allow you to insure someone like me and let me drive, then I want to know when your drivers are on the road. I'll stay home." Needless to say, we didn't transfer our insurance to State Farm.

I appreciate every effort made to help visually impaired people cope in public. One of the ways many try is through the placement of Braille for assistance. I do wish they would pay just a little more attention to detail. For example, one time while riding in an elevator in a very swanky hotel, my host pointed out to me that there was Braille on the buttons of the control panel. He put my hand on the panel and asked if I could read it. I hesitated for a second, then said, "I can but it would be easier if it wasn't upside down!"

Maybe the Braille thing is being taken a bit too far. I still cannot comprehend why they put Braille on drive through ATM's. Of course, maybe Braille on American money wouldn't be such a bad thing. Truth is, when I'm in the United States I can't tell the difference in my bills. I can organize my money, with the help of Patti and the kids, to know what I am dealing with, but when it comes to change, I just can't tell. All American bills feel the same. The coins are no problem, it's the American bills that are the nightmare. At least Canada marks their bills so blind people can tell the difference. In Europe the bills tend to be different sizes so you can tell there too.

In the modern era of mobile, instantaneous communication, I have wondered if the time hasn't come to advance Braille to a new level. On more than one occasion I have received a call from a friend who will open our conversation with the comment, "I sent you a couple text messages yesterday, never heard back from..." followed by a long pause and usually some kind of sheepish laugh, then a comment like, "sorry, I forgot you can't read those anyway." They always clue in right away, but sometimes I find it a little frustrating to be left out, wishing that once in a while I could receive a text. I know I could get a fancy phone that would read text messages to me, but that is not always convenient either. Like most of you, I don't need everyone around me hearing my text messages. Some kind of mobile Braille text software would be a great invention, in my opinion.

Then there is the issue of the fancy phones, themselves. Everyone tells me I should get an "iPhone" or an Android, but I ask, "Why bother?" The screens on those things are perfectly smooth. No tactile clues whatsoever and useless to me. I still use my old flip phone, and will until some modern device proves more useful.

You know I am big proponent of developing good relationships. This is why I favor shopping at local, owner operated merchants in my adopted home town of Zionsville whenever I can. I appreciate the camaraderie and always find that a better shopping experience is my reward. One such merchant is Bill Kern, owner of Kern Brother's Shoes in Boone Village. I buy virtually all my family's shoes from Bill. Just before the 2012 presidential election, I visited Bill to buy a new pair of dress shoes. Bill got all excited, telling me he had just received the perfect pair of shoes for me. He took me across the store and handed me a pair of hip waders, laughing as he said, "These are what we call Obama Boots." I couldn't help but laugh too. Regardless of your politics, you will simply never develop that level of rapport without putting the relationship first.

I'd like to take a moment to acknowledge Keith Ritchie, manager of the West Carmel branch of Fifth/Third Bank, on Michigan Road in Carmel, Indiana. His branch is a standout example of Professional P.R.I.D.E. as I have talked about in this book. They perform, finding ways to deliver even under the most challenging circumstances. When they tell you something, you can trust them, you can rest assured that they will do what they say, when they said they would do it and it will be ready when you need it. No excuses, ever. Why do I mention this? Because experiencing great service, on this level, from anybody, happens so rarely that it simply can't be ignored.

By the way, have you ever wondered how you get great customers? Try delivering great customer service!

I am not much of a fan of long car rides, or overly long flights. Let's face it, if the person beside me can't carry on a good conversation then it can get very boring, very quickly, especially considering how much I am able to enjoy great scenery. There have been a few long trips though where silence has been much appreciated. I remember one time, boarding a plane for a 7 hour flight from Chicago to Hawaii. Just after I got in my seat, this very chatty woman settled in beside me and began to tell me all the problems of her day, so far. She was escalating toward the problems in her marriage and with her kids when she paused for a moment, and just out courtesy I think, said, "by the way, what do you do for a living?" I responded, "For the past ten years I've sold life insurance." I didn't hear another word out of her the rest of the trip.

Success to me is about living a happy life. Certainly, success suggests a certain level of accomplishment and acquisition and status, but those are almost irrelevant. Success to me is more about the progressive realization of worthwhile goals while remaining grounded and appreciative of what you have now. Balance is the key, in my opinion, to a successful life. I have met, and am friends with, some incredibly wealthy people who will admit to me that they are not happy. They are successful in a conventional sense, but are not enjoying their lives. In some cases they have pushed so hard to acquire money or assets or status or power that they have sacrificed their marriage, their connection to their kids, their integrity or worse, their health. The price they paid for their alleged success was very high. I have many more friends who, like most of us, struggle day to day with bills and house payments and traffic and ... but if you spend an hour with them you can't help but notice that they are happy and enjoying their lives. Who is more successful?

Success in any respect, regardless of how you define it, takes effort. From what I've observed the majority of people never reach their full potential, never become successful, never accomplish anything worthwhile let alone realize their personal dreams or ambitions for one very simple reason. They never try. It can almost always be attributed to a simple lack of effort. They live their lives going through the motions, doing the minimum somebody else set for them instead of deciding what they should be doing to achieve their goal and then giving their all. If they would just try, step back,

Horseback riding has always helped keep me balanced.

learn, adapt and try again, they would be closer to their goal. I could say a lot more about the steps of achieving a goal, but the steps really don't matter until you decide to try. I understand that getting started isn't easy. If it was, more people would. Isn't it really all so simple, when you think about it? If you don't make an effort, nothing is going to happen.

I like to shoot baskets, partially because it is fun, and partially because it is a very effective way that I applied the principles of trying. I had to learn the technique, which involves having someone

stand under the basket and count to five. This allows me to judge the distance and direction. Then, knowing that the height of the basket never changes, I can judge the loft, and distance, necessary to drop the ball through the hoop, right above the voice. Sounds simple but I also had to try, over and over and over. I can't begin to count how many free throws I've attempted or how many have bounced back to hit me on top of my head, bounced up and hit my chin, or worse, my nose. I didn't care. I knew I had to take the shots to refine my skill, but it worked. Today I can sink 6 or 7 out of 10 free throws because I didn't give up. What could you do if you didn't give up?

I walked into the kitchen for breakfast one morning and was greeted by Patti with the comment, "You forgot to turn the basement light off last night." Turn it off, heck, I didn't even know it was on. No complaint or defense from me though. I am always flattered when Patti forgets I'm blind.

Keep trying, you only fail when you give up.

In the mid eighties, during my recovery from my injuries at Cypress Gardens and my transition to Eagle USA Wetsuits, a friend's tragedy taught me a great lesson about the trappings of success. While I was healing, Ricky McCormick opened up his home to me. On one occasion, we returned home from an out of town trip to find that part of Ricky's house had burned down. That was a tragedy for Ricky and initially felt like one for me too. Several of my medals and trophies were in Ricky's house and I lost them all. All that hardware was gone. I was heartbroken, for an instant. Then I realized, I wasn't burnt, I wasn't bleeding, I was fine. I still had the experience and the lessons I'd learned and my life was still better for having pursued those trophies, whether I had them to display, or not. From that day forward, I always had my reason, my "why," for pursuing any goal, but never again was it about the hardware.

Patti and I have such well established routines that forgetting I'm blind is almost Patti's natural state of mind. For example, whenever we are out together, when Patti parks, I simply get out my side and go around to the back of our SUV. Patti will just come around, once the kids are dealt with, take my elbow and we carry on. Recently she was out shopping with her mother, and much to her mother's surprise, the two of them had a near head on collision when Patti came around the back of the SUV and turned left instead of right. Without hesitation, she had simply gone to where I would be, and tried to lead her mother by the arm.

One of our primary reasons for settling in Zionsville was the reputation of its education system. It has been all it was reported to be, with one tremendous added bonus, in the person of Tracy Vermillion. Tracy is the school secretary at Pleasant View Elementary School, but in reality she is so much more. She is one of those extraordinary people who makes everybody around them better. She is a memorable, animated, effective, efficient, delightful, impactful person who you look forward to seeing every day. If more schools had just one person like her, all our kids would be much better off. She always greets you by name with a smile in her voice and a positive message. She is the heart and soul of the school and I'm glad that my children were touched by her personality. She is a special part of our town.

I am a big supporter of everyone who makes an effort to support themselves. I believe it shows great character to work for a living rather than take the charity of government. At the same time, I do think that employers should take some responsibility to ensure that the requirements of the job match the capabilities of their employees, for the benefit of both the employee and the customer. Let me give you an example. When I travel, as much as I strive to be independent, I do require the help of Passenger Assistance in many airports. Changing planes in Denver one time a young man was sent by Passenger Assistance to help me. The challenge was that this young man could speak practically no English whatsoever. I found it nearly impossible to be understood, and to make matters worse, I also needed to grab a bite to eat on this stopover as there would be no chance to eat for the rest of the day. We did manage to find the food court, but he was completely unable to describe any of my meal choices. I was eventually saved by a fellow passenger from my incoming flight who came to my rescue, described my options and actually bought my lunch, which was so nice. I can only imagine how embarrassing it must have been for this young man that a total stranger had to step up and do his job. It didn't end there either. He took me to the wrong gate. Does his employer really consider it fair to anybody to put this man in this job? Really?

Why are staircases longer for blind people? Invariably, when I am walking with someone and we approach a staircase, they will tell me, "we're going up ten steps." In every case, it will turn out that I will have to raise my foot eleven times to climb that staircase although my companion will swear they counted ten steps. Same thing descending stairs. If I'm told we are going down ten steps, I know to expect that I will step down eleven times. I have no idea what a staircase looks like, so I can't explain the difference in perception or understanding that is going on, but I do know I learned this lesson the hard way. I don't know how many top steps I tripped over or how many bottom steps I almost fell off before I made this adjustment. I'm sure I must have looked hilarious on stairs until I figured this out. I'm glad I learned this when I was very young.

Let me give a shout out to all the taxi drivers, service workers and fellow passengers who have helped me over the years. Taxi drivers are always getting a bad rap, but I have found them, every single one of them, to be helpful considerate and honest. I have never been taken for an unnecessary tour and never been taken advantage of in all my years of travel. Even when it comes to something like making change, they have always got it right. And the most unexpected sources have come through for me too, often unsolicited. I have been escorted by Delta Pilots and Flight Attendants who have found me in need of help or abandoned in a big, impersonal airport. One time even a janitor, who I interrupted with a question, stopped his work to escort me to a connecting flight one evening in Detroit. I just wanted to mention that the vast majority of people are good and kind and helpful. Thank you all.

Have airline seats gotten narrower or has the general public gotten bigger? Just wondering.

Hotel keys can be incredibly frustrating. Every time I check in, which as you know is often, I am handed a rectangular piece of plastic which is perfectly smooth in all respects. There is no way, by touch, to differentiate the top or bottom, front or back, yet they expect me to put it in the slot a specific way or I can't enter my room. I try to keep a small roll of tape with me so I can mark my hotel keys, and in some cases I have had to make a notch in the key so I would know how to use it. I just mention this as another example of a seemingly simple matter that gets complicated when you can't see.

Being totally blind does create more than its share of opportunities for me to embarrass myself. For example, even with my allegedly super sensitive hearing, it is surprising how often I find it all but impossible to figure out if I am speaking with a man or a woman. I know many people have experienced this over the telephone, but with me the possibility is always present, in person and on the phone. I've embarrassed myself more than once, sometimes in hilarious fashion. The most comical episode happened in full view of my family during one of our numerous vacations. Ashley and Morgan needed a battery changed in one of their toys. I called down to the front desk of our hotel to see if there was anybody who could bring us a screwdriver. Within a few minutes someone arrived at our door and graciously offered to change the batteries for us. Within minutes the job was finished. As our white knight from the hotel was about to leave I suggested, very sincerely, that one of the girls should thank this nice lady for fixing their toy. Ashley meekly blurted out a thank you. I closed the room door and as I turned back Ashley said, "Daddy, that woman had a beard." Patti couldn't control herself anymore. She burst out in laughter and the kids did likewise. Turns out our helper from the hotel was a burley, two hundred pound custodian who just happened to be about my height. In my defense, put yourself in my shoes. Sometimes, with no visual clues for reference, like our custodian's beard, it's impossible by voice alone to tell the genders apart.

Speaking of hotels, there are always two things that I need help with every time I check into a new hotel room. The first thing I always ask the staff who have escorted me to my room is how to operate the thermostat. Not only does it seem that it is never in the same place, meaning I can't use my logic to figure out where it is, but it never operates the same way twice. Without the proper instructions, I am as likely to freeze myself as roast myself. The other question I always have is in the bathroom. I need to separate the shampoo, conditioner and hand lotion. I've learned to put the shampoo and conditioner in the shower right away and my personal style is to flip open the conditioner so I know the difference. Before I made this part of my routine, I found myself putting hand lotion in my hair far too often.

If there is one thing that is more frustrating than people who can't count stairs, it is the unbelievable number of people who routinely confuse left and right. It can even be embarrassing. Imagine, when I'm walking with someone, I will usually be on their left side, occasionally touching their elbow for guidance. Then they'll say, we're going to turn right up ahead. We get to the corner, I turn right, they turn left, and bang, we run right into each other. It happens a lot more than you would expect. More than I would have anyway.

Hotels offer other adventures for me that the normal world doesn't think about too, like going to the gym. Not only do I need an escort, but once I get there I need instruction in how to use the treadmill itself. Even then it is a challenge. It seems that hotel treadmills take so much abuse that they always put a sheet of smooth plastic over the buttons to protect them. Great if you can see, but it eliminates any sense of touch. It is just smooth, no way to tell the functions apart, except to memorize the approximate locations of the buttons with the help of the hotel staff. And there is the issue of the staff as well. Although always nice and helpful they are, like the rest of us, always busy. This presents a challenge to me as I not only need them to escort me to the treadmill, but also need them to come and get me. My issues have come when the staff forgets to come back. I now take my cell phone to the gym with me so I can call if nobody shows. This is another lesson learned after running myself into exhaustion a couple times, waiting for someone to come and get me. After all, I never intended to run a marathon.

Televisions in hotels are a challenge too. Modern televisions in hotels give no audio clues as to what they are doing when you turn them on. I used to hear a click and could listen for the hum to know if the Television had actually turned on. I always need a lesson on how to use the remote control and the numbers of my favorite channels. Most of the time I will leave Fox News playing in the background. When I have a little free time on the road, I don't mind catching some Bill O'Reilly or Sean Hannity, or Megyn Kelly and if it's a slow news day, I'll flip over to ESPN. In the mornings, I always catch "Fox & Friends," first thing, to make sure I'm informed for the day. Brian Kilmeade, Steve Doocy and Elisabeth Hasselbeck frequently share room service with me as I enjoy breakfast in my hotel room. Gretchen, you'll be missed in this time slot.

If you haven't figured it out yet, I am a total news junkie. I rarely settle for only the news I can gather from the television. I enjoy opinion and debate on current issues. I'm a big fan of Rush Limbaugh and Glenn Beck and listen to them as often as possible.

In my day to day work, I find that most people I coach, train or simply chat with after speaking engagements are so busy, wrapped up in the minutiae of earning a living, that they never make any real money. It all comes back to knowing "why." In everything you do, always ask yourself if the action you are about to take will advance you closer to your goal, closer to making your big picture real? If it doesn't, delegate it, postpone or even consider not doing it at all. Stay focused on the activities that directly impact your big picture and you'll experience more success sooner than you could have imagined. Why chase pennies when you can chase dollars?

If you are not happy with the how you spend your days chasing those dollars, why do you keep chasing them that way? If you're not happy in your daily pursuits, the odds of you ever earning any real dollars is very limited anyway. If your work feels too much like a job, it's time to change the work. It's time to make a plan. I know you can't just make changes instantly, but with thought, organization and Inner Vision you can realize your dreams while enjoying your day to day work as well. Align your job with your passions and you will be happier with the results you see. In other words, if you don't like the view, move to a different window.

On the subject of dollars, sometimes you can collect them very quickly, when everything lines up perfectly. For me, it happened on one of my many speaking engagements in Las Vegas. I was waiting in the wings, which in this case meant standing outside one of those huge hotel ballrooms, waiting for my introduction DVD to finish. Being the restless type I am, I decided to try my hand at a dollar slot machine nearby. I pulled the handle and all of a sudden, bells started to ring, just as the gentleman showed up to escort me to the stage. He couldn't believe it. I had hit the jackpot and a waterfall of tokens were tumbling out of the slot machine. I couldn't wait, the DVD had ended and I had to be on stage, that moment. I entered the ballroom and followed my host to the podium. A couple moments later, before I had even finished my opening remarks, two gentlemen entered carrying several of the casinos plastic token buckets. One of them came up to me at the podium and whispered in my ear. I then returned my attention to my audience, which erupted in laughter when I apologized for my late entry, explaining that I had just won $2,500 at the slot machine outside the ballroom door.

Does anything bring a family together better than the addition of a new pet? We just added Coconut, a delightful, blue-eyed, white ragdoll kitten. Life at the MacFarlane house was already wonderful, but there is definitely a spirit of renewal and a contagious atmosphere of happiness in our house since Coconut arrived.

Coconut

I think a major contributing reason to why we can't stay focused and chase dollars is because most of us have no way to clear the "noise" out of our minds and relax with some clarity. I used to find that clarity through competition, but these days I am much more inclined to sit down at my piano, in the den, and jam a little. Some days I may give the house a concert, just singing for the pure pleasure of it. Other days I will follow the creative juices and try to compose a song or two, succeeding as often as not. Writing songs is a great way to express my inner most feelings. Sometimes I just let the music flow through me, taking my tension away through the notes my fingers tickle. It can turn into a truly inspiring event as well. My kids are all into music and have been known to join me on occasion in truly energized jam sessions. Whether it is Derek with his tuba, Ashley with her alto sax, Morgan on vocals, or any combination of all three. I love creating music with my kids. It works brilliantly for me. I suggest you find a release that works as well for you, and go there regularly.

Jamming with Ashley always makes my day.

One particularly special time that I often get to spend at the piano is playing for Ashley when she wants to serenade me with the latest song she has learned. I love listening to her sing and she does treat me to many impromptu, spontaneous concerts. Playing along with her just adds another, uplifting element to an already wonderful experience.

My biggest pet peeve in this world is people who say they will get back to you and never do. You create resentment and possibly worse, anger. You risk irreparable damage to your credibility, over potentially vast numbers of people in today's era of social media. Remember the Professional "I". If you say you're going to do something, DO IT!

One benefit that I have found invariably results from adhering to the principles of P.R.I.D.E. is that your customers will experience exceptional service. You, in return, will receive exceptional customer loyalty and business from sources you never anticipated. It works kind of like this. There is a commercial painter in Fort Myers, Florida, named Ryan Hammond who I have used on several occasions. He has under promised and over delivered with such integrity of word and action that I have found myself recommending him to everyone I know who owns a house or building. I guess you could say I am even recommending him here. Does your behavior earn that kind of respect and loyalty? It should. It is so rare that any business delivers great customer service. When you do, you immediately rise above your competition.

The 10 questions I am asked most often that I haven't already answered:

What do you see?

Describing what I "see" would be like asking you to describe the taste of pure water. I don't see light or dark, black or white. Rather, I see absolutely nothing. My kids will always tell me that I must see black, but you have to remember, I don't know what black is, so I can't tell you if that is what I see. There is nothing distinguishable. I literally see nothing at all.

Do you dream in color?

I don't know. In your terms I really do not know what color is. My dreams are very realistic to the way I imagine what things must look like, but they may have no base in actual reality at all. My life experience is totally auditory and tactile, as opposed to your visual experience. For all I know, what my imagination creates as blue, for example, might not even exist in reality. I think probably not. After all, it's not like you fall asleep and you start seeing again.

Do you have a favorite city?

Not really, they all look the same to me. Of course cities usually have their own unique ambiance. There are different sounds and smells and foods but I'm the kind of person who is happy wherever I am. I love learning about new places, people and cultures, but cities to me are the memories of the people I associate with them. I do look forward to New York because of the inexhaustible variety of sounds and smells that play to my senses like a symphony. There is no place like it, even for me.

Who picks out your clothes?

I have some good friends that I would never trust to take me clothes shopping. Before I was married, I was much less secure about my appearance because all I had were my friends. I have always been a prankster and my friends rarely missed an opportunity to repay my mischievousness. I can't say that I blame them either.

Thankfully I'm told my wife has good taste when it comes to selecting my suits and accessories. I go forth these days with complete confidence, knowing my clothes always look good.

Would you have accomplished as much if you hadn't gone blind?

It's impossible to speculate, I'll never know what I could have done, but that doesn't matter, blindness is the hand I was dealt. I can say this. Blindness has always inspired me to put my best foot forward, in part from a fear of failure and, in part, to prove to myself that blindness wouldn't stand in the way of me living and leading a normal life. I may have pushed myself harder, but who knows how hard I may pushed if I could see.

Where did you get your strength?

I would have to say that my strength comes primarily from my faith. I grew up in a strong Christian family where we reaffirmed our faith on a daily basis. This fueled the deep belief I have always had in my ability to be whoever I wanted to be. Faith has often been defined as a belief in things unseen and in my case, that couldn't be more accurate. I developed my inner strength over time by learning to reset my internal compass, sometimes hour to hour, sometimes once a day but always whenever I needed it. The great benefit is that I no longer have bad days. I set my focus every morning and recalibrate throughout the day. As I said earlier, it's not what happens to you, it is how you react and one of the ways I always react is to reset my focus. My persistent positive attitude comes from my powerful inner vision.

Do you know how you look?

I don't, at least not in your terms, but I do give thanks every day that I don't have to look in the mirror when I wake up in the morning. I have always taken PRIDE in my appearance, from paying attention to the clothes I wear to staying physically fit, to keeping my hair neat and stylish. In real terms I'll never know because appearance is visual and I have no reference to run with. I'm really at your mercy.

How has technology helped you?

It is truly amazing how technology has empowered blind people. As a group, we have more independence today than at any time in history and the potential it has opened up is tremendous.

Think about it. Today almost everything can talk to you, so everything you can see, I can hear. From my watch to my computer to my phones to my home security system to elevators to GPS navigators to Braille readers to our car to the thermometer I use to take my kids temperature with, I have the ability to use the same technology as you. The playing field is leveling and it is great.

Have your other senses heightened?

It's not like you lose your sight one day and the good lord jacks up your hearing 50% the next day. My senses of hearing and touch are so acute because I pay so much more attention to them than most of you ever will. I rely on them, I need them and consequently, over time have developed the capacity to use them much more effectively than someone who doesn't rely on them. My hearing, in a mechanical sense, is no different than yours. The difference lies in the reality that 90% of your world comes to you through your eyes while 90%, or more, of my world comes to me through my ears. Ironically, someone will notice I'm blind and will start talking louder to me. I have to remind them that I'm blind, not deaf. Turning up the volume that way to me is like setting off a strobe light in the eyes of a sighted person. With that kind of experience, doesn't it just make sense that my hearing would seem heightened?

How do you know what someone looks like when you meet them?

I don't, and I believe that is one of my great advantages. I can't judge, or pre-judge, someone based on their appearance so I have to pay attention to their inner beauty. I "see" people from the inside out and have no doubt, after meeting thousands of people a year, that the world would be a better place if sighted people could put on blinders and not be so judgmental of others until they get to know each other.

At the end of the day, all of this has brought me to one experience that is the ultimate culmination and downright best experience any man could ask for and I am blessed to go through it on a regular basis. It begins when the taxi drops me off in my driveway. I open the garage using the electronic key pad and follow the oh so familiar steps that lead me to the inside door. I will turn the knob, enter the house and almost immediately, in every case, coming from the kitchen or the family room or the den, one of my girls yells out, "Daddy's home!" With that Derek, Ashley and Morgan will come running, hitting me with full body hugs as I step into the hallway. I always seem to have one kid in my arms and the other two wrapped around me within seconds of coming home. Patti will invariably be there too, with a smile in her voice, and yet another wonderful hug as we reunite. This is what I live for and what I miss most when I'm on the road. My family sustains me and rejuvenates me. They are why I take the red eye as often as I can. I like to get home as soon as possible. They make the early mornings, late nights and long flights worthwhile. That's what it is all about.

I'm so proud of Dalton too. Even though he doesn't live at home anymore I am in contact with him every day. He travels with me on occasion too. He is blazing a trail of tremendous results these days, launching into his new career as a Financial Advisor with Edward Jones. I look forward to our daily conversations and relish the relationship we have.

Home Sweet Home

I am grateful for the life I live. I continue to speak, to an ever widening range of audiences, sharing the stage with more and more influential people. Recently, in fact, I was on the same program as Arnold Schwarzenegger, The Terminator, himself. A great opportunity and learning experience. No two days are ever the same, which is great because, as you know, they all look alike to me.

As you close the final page of this book, please accept my heart-felt thanks for taking a few moments from your life to spend with me. I trust you feel like you have gotten to know me a little better. Even more so, I sincerely hope you found it worthy of your time, effort and energy to read my story. If it was, please share it with one your friends.

I sincerely hope that you have been able to re-ignite your small internal flame and that you will be able to raise the bar higher in all phases and aspects of your life than you ever thought you could. It all begins with a smile on your face and profound belief in yourself. The bottom line is that if I can do it, So Can You!

Should our paths ever cross as we continue our respective journeys along life's highway, please reach out and shake my hand. I would be honored to meet you.

Let me leave you with one final thought to ponder...

"The art of living is more like wrestling than dancing."

MARCUS AURELIUS ANTONINUS
Roman Emperor, A.D. 161-180

Connect with Craig MacFarlane

Craig MacFarlane is constantly being approached by corporations and associations, large and small, television networks, local TV stations, radio stations, podcasts, universities, colleges and high schools, executives and sports teams who wish to hear more of and benefit further from the insight and experience of this remarkable man.

   If you would like to make contact with and book Craig MacFarlane as your next Keynote Inspirational Speaker, Trainer, Coach or to order additional copies of Craig's books, Craig has made it easy for you:

You can call him at 727-442-4400.
You can e-mail him at craig@cmpride.com
You can keep up to date on everything about Craig at
www.cmpride.com
Be sure to check out his contact page and:
Follow Craig on Twitter
Like him on FaceBook
Watch him on YouTube
Connect with him on Linkedin
and
Subscribe to his Blog
(and be sure to tell your friends)